Mining Coal and
Undermining Gender

Mining Coal and Undermining Gender

Rhythms of Work and Family in the American West

JESSICA SMITH ROLSTON

Rutgers University Press

New Brunswick, New Jersey, and London

Library of Congress Cataloging-in-Publication Data

Rolston, Jessica Smith, 1980–
Mining coal and undermining gender : rhythms of work and family in the
American West / Jessica Smith Rolston.
pages cm
Includes bibliographical references and index.
ISBN 978–0–8135–6368–8 (hardcover : alk. paper) — ISBN 978–0–8135–6367–1
(pbk. : alk. paper) — ISBN 978–0–8135–6369–5 (e-book)
1. Women coal miners—Wyoming. 2. Coal mines and mining—Social aspects—Wyoming. 3.
Sex role. 4. Work and family. I. Title.

HD6073.M62U676 2014
331.4'82233409787—dc2   2013021945

A British Cataloging-in-Publication record for this book is available from the British Library.

Visit our website: http://rutgerspress.rutgers.edu

Manufactured in the United States of America

For my parents, Mike and Juanita

Contents

Preface and Acknowledgments

In many ways, this book's roots stretch back to 2000, when I spent my first summer home from college working at a coal mine south of my hometown in northeastern Wyoming. My father had spent most of his working life as a mechanic at a different mine owned by the same company, and the "summer student" program in the Powder River Basin was a rite of passage for all of us who had grown up with parents working in the mines. I did not originally relish the thought of spending the summer washing down the heavy machinery in the processing plant with what I imagined to be a crew full of macho old guys. To my delight, my coworkers turned out to be hilarious company and thoughtful mentors, as we spent days and nights sharing conversations, jokes, and meals. Getting to know so many women who enjoyed their work in the mines also surprised me and inspired me to want to know more. The experience seemed like fieldwork to me, having taken Introduction to Cultural Anthropology that spring at Macalester College. I was learning not just a new vocabulary of mine terms (for those unfamiliar with such terms, see the glossary) but styled ways of speaking that traversed the tricky territory of negotiating a fair division of labor on the crew, of giving directions without offending someone else's expertise, and of telling jokes that could comment on longer histories of social relations. In 2003 and 2005 I returned for another two summers at a different mine, driving haul trucks in circles from the shovels and loaders to the crushers and dumps.

I always assumed that I would eventually write about my experience, but I did not intend for the mines to become my dissertation research as a graduate student at the University of Michigan. My plan was to return to Cuba, where I had spent a semester studying women taxi drivers in the tourist industry. But reading anthropological research about the industry in different time periods and parts of the world in Stuart Kirsch's Mining Ethnographies seminar convinced me to change topics. On page 225 in my copy of Michael Taussig's *The Devil and Commodity Fetishism* I wrote, "11 pm, 2/11/04, Jessi has a breakthrough." The margins of the page are full of furiously scribbled notes connecting Taussig's argument about the materiality of the Tío—the devilish spirit of the Bolivian tin mines who can take on commodity form—with the embodiment of labor in the Wyoming mines. I had been considering changing my dissertation research all semester, but struggled to mesh my academic interest and personal experiences in the mining industry. Ethnographic details about miners' family lives, their labor, and even lunch buckets seemed familiar based on my experiences as a mine employee and the daughter of one. At the same time, very different historical and cultural contexts made them feel strange, and the academic jargon I was still learning created additional distance between the ethnographies and myself. This analytic circling, moving closer and stepping back, would come to define my research as a native ethnographer. Engaging in fieldwork with friends and family invited intimacy, but placing their experiences in wider historical trajectories and academic conversations required drawing back and denaturalizing the categories and concepts that I took for granted as someone who grew up in Gillette.

It is my hope that this book respects the trust many different people put in me to do this research and share parts of it with a broader audience. The mining industry is often painted in broad brushstrokes, to use the words of one manager, appearing in the news and popular culture in cases of environmental ruin and human tragedy. I share those frustrations. In fact, one of the reasons I switched research topics was to show the positive elements of the industry that I felt were missing from both the academic and popular portrayals of the industry. Miners' and company officials' sense of being misunderstood is the basis of their skepticism toward journalists and others looking for a good story, so I do not doubt that it was my status as a hometown girl and daughter of a mine employee that helped people open their doors to me. I have done my best to represent their experiences as fairly and accurately as possible, though I can think of exceptions for every one of the general patterns I sketch out in the following pages.

But at the same time as I share the frustration about the negative portrayals of mining, it would be equally disingenuous to ignore the bodily and social stresses borne by people who have dedicated their lives to the industry. Miners and managers themselves critique certain aspects of the industry's operation and pour their own energy into improving them, even if they are not able to change the larger systems that structure their work. I therefore view the book as a contribution to those efforts to recognize and build on the industry's already existing accomplishments in the Powder River Basin (hereafter basin).

Finding that balance as gracefully as possible required the generosity of both my home and academic communities.

In Gillette I am indebted to the three crews who adopted me as a coworker, the four crews who took me on as an anthropologist, and the company personnel who gave me permission to conduct on-site research—an incredible and rare gift in the industry. I am grateful to the miners, family members, and other residents who took the time to visit with me off-site, and I hope that the book attests to the profound respect I hold for you and your work. I do not doubt that you will find yourselves in the following pages despite the pseudonyms. I wish I could have included many more of your stories and insights that would further attest to your humor, warmth, and goodwill. I thank Robert Henning at the Campbell County Rockpile Museum for the opportunity to share my work publicly in conjunction with an exhibit about women miners. The support from women miners who found their lives reflected in the stories even though they hadn't participated in the research helped me to finally allow the book manuscript to leave my hands. Longtime friendships continue to inspire and inform this research. A special thank you goes to Erin Roosa Cohen, Christine Marvin, Amanda Miller, John Bayles, and Peter Gartrell for countless conversations. The book is partially an homage to an older Gillette, since the situation in 2013 is very different from the one framing the research, as I explain in the conclusion.

Stuart Kirsch never fails to be a generous mentor. Working with such a witty, perceptive, and ethical anthropologist convinced me to change topics more than did any theoretical puzzle posed by the industry. Thank you for helping me transform a heartfelt interest in the industry into an organized research agenda. The influence of others at the University of Michigan—especially Gillian Feeley-Harnik, Tom Fricke, Alaina Lemon, Barbra Meek, and Abigail Stewart—lingers throughout the pages that follow. I thank Janet Finn, Dorothy Hodgson, Dinah Rajak, Elizabeth Emma Ferry, Sara Dickey, Stephen Sweet, and Sarah Damaske for feedback at critical moments. I have been blessed with wonderful friends who are also amazing anthropologists: Kelly Fayard, Sherina Feliciano-Santos, Bridget Guarasci, Jess Robbins, Mikaela Rogozen-Soltar, Xochitl Ruiz, Kirstin Swagman, Cecilia Tomori, and Emily Wentzell. I would not have survived graduate school without Laurie Marx. Thanks are also due to Marlie Wasserman for having faith in the book, to John Raymond for thoughtfully and meticulously editing it, and to the anonymous reviewers for helping to strengthen its arguments. The shortcomings are my own.

It was a dream come true to finish the book as a faculty member in the Division of Liberal Arts and International Studies at the Colorado School of Mines. I am extraordinarily lucky to enjoy the support of good friends and colleagues, especially during the hard first year as a new faculty member and a new mom. Juan Lucena and Liz Cox generously helped ease both of those transitions, and Elizabeth Davis offered crucial flexibility in course scheduling. My first stop back west at the University of Colorado at Boulder was enriched by Kira Hall, Donna Goldstein, and Dennis McGilvray. I continue to be inspired by Patty Limerick, whose wit and balanced approach to extractive industries is welcome in the otherwise polarized debates about them. I thank her and the Center of the American West book club members for their thoughtful feedback on the manuscript. Thanks are also due to Su Il Kim for a great year at Pikes Peak Community College.

Financial support for the original research came from the National Science Foundation (Dissertation Improvement Grant #0612829), the Beinecke Scholarship Program, the PEO Foundation and the University of Michigan's Department of Anthropology, Rackham Graduate School, and the Alfred P. Sloan Center for the Ethnography of Everyday Life, especially its director Tom Fricke. A National Endowment for the Humanities Fellowship provided the crucial time to write. Any views, findings, conclusions, or recommendations expressed in this publication do not necessarily represent those of the National Endowment for the Humanities or the other institutions acknowledged here. Sections of chapter 2 originally appeared in a chapter, "Workplace Egalitarianism in Nonunion Mines: Lessons from Wyoming's Powder River Basin," written for Paul Durrenberger and Karaleah Reichart's *The Anthropology of Labor Unions* (Boulder: University Press of Colorado, 2010), and I gratefully acknowledge the University Press of Colorado for permission to repurpose them here. Other ethnographic examples from chapter 2 are reproduced by permission of the Society for Applied Anthropology from my article "Risky Business: Neoliberalism and Workplace Safety in Wyoming Coal Mines," *Human Organization* 69, no. 4: 331–342.

The book in its final form was born a year after our daughter, Lena Mae. My husband Mike's unwavering support makes it possible for me to be both a professor and a mom. I love you both and am blessed to share in your lives. We could not have done it without Rachel, who loved Lena while we were working. Mike and I continue to find inspiration and support from our families. I dedicate this book to my parents, Mike and Juanita, who made it possible for my sister Katie and me to pursue careers that are meaningful to us. Thank you for working so many nights in the mine, Dad, and in the hospital, Mom.

Part I

Orientation

1

Putting Kinship to Work

"Gender is not the most important part of my day," Mary said to me during one of the shifts I spent with her at an enormous surface coal mine in northeastern Wyoming's Powder River Basin, a region that is the largest coal producer in the United States.[1] Mary had just completed her second decade of work at a mine that is one of the largest in the basin and the entire country. Surface miners like Mary spend their shifts operating heavy machinery to remove the top layer of overburden (the layer of rock and dirt above a coal seam), extract and transport the coal, and then replace the overburden during reclamation. On the particular day of our conversation, she was operating a giant electric shovel whose bucket could hold a few of the massive pickup trucks that were parked outside of every house and overcrowded apartment building in the area. From her perch on a worn seat in the cab, she maneuvered the shovel using joysticks at the end of the armrests and foot pedals on the floor. I was sitting behind her in a hard plastic chair usually reserved for trainees or supervisors, scribbling notes as we swayed back and forth with each pass from the dirt face to the trucks.[2] Our conversation began at the beginning of the shift, before the sun rose, with her asking about my experience in mining. We talked about my father, a mine mechanic approaching his twentieth anniversary with a different company, and the summers my former high school classmates and I spent at the mines driving trucks and washing down machinery while on break from college. For our part, this annual rite of passage provided sizeable savings accounts, photos of us with imposing equipment, and a visceral appreciation for the work our parents had done to send us to school in the first place. Our summer employment presented mine employees with a rare opportunity to introduce their children to both the mines and their coworkers, who eagerly initiated the new recruits into long-running histories of practical jokes and the art of making the shift clock tick by swiftly.

Shifting our conversation to why I was voluntarily lacing up my steel-toe boots to report for shifts without the incentive of a paycheck, I explained that the summers working on production crews had inspired the research project I was conducting as a graduate student in anthropology. I had just mentioned my interest in studying gender when Mary downplayed its importance for her everyday life. She continued, "There are lots of other interesting things that people should care about." One of the first lessons mine trainees learn is the importance of finessing and abstracting directions in order to suggest a course of action to a coworker without directly telling them what to do, so I deduced that the "people" she referenced in her statement were actually the future readers of my research, and me. I asked Mary what those more important things might include. She deftly positioned the shovel bucket over the bed of the haul truck she was loading and then tripped the cable to release the bottom of the bucket. Watching the dirt and rocks cascade into the bed, she said, "Like *human* needs. How to be a human out here, not how to be a woman out here."

Mary then winked at me, picked up the handheld radio, and told the haul truck driver who was approaching us in the shovel that I was impressed by his "fine driving abilities." They had been exchanging jokes on the radio over the course of the day. He guffawed and said thanks, but he already knew that I was an expert in "the behavioral sciences, which we can shorten to B.S." The pun on the English expletive simultaneously poked fun at my college education and his own driving abilities, since it insinuated that he was not a good driver since I was not qualified to evaluate him. I grabbed the radio and told him that I was under the impression that the mine was the only place where people became experts in that field. He laughed as he pulled away and said I might be learning something after all. Mary chuckled to herself as she scooped the next bucket and waited for the next driver to make her approach.

The Powder River Basin stands out as an exception to an industry typically viewed as exceptionally masculine, if not openly hostile to women. Women like Mary represent a significant portion of the workforce that make the region the largest producer of coal in the United States. According to the federal Energy Information Administration, in 2011 just over a dozen surface mines on the Wyoming side of the basin and two in Montana churned out over 462 million tons of coal, surpassing the 454 million tons produced that year by all mines in all states east of the Mississippi. Coal from the Powder River Basin is burned in more than two hundred power plants in thirty-five states, including the states of the Appalachian region. Although mining is largely considered the epitome of masculine industries, production crews in the basin average 20 percent women. Both men and women miners in the Powder River Basin are over 90 percent White (European-American), reflecting the racial composition of Gillette and the surrounding communities.[3] These crews operate and repair some of the largest heavy equipment in the world, such as three-story haul trucks whose wheels stretch twelve feet tall. Rank in the pit correlates with the hierarchy of machines used to expose and extract the coal, and women operate the most prestigious loading machines, alongside men. They also direct entire crews as frontline supervisors. Women play an even larger role in engineering and administrative activities in the office, where they are well represented in the upper echelons of management. During my research, a well-liked and well-respected woman led one of the largest companies as its president before taking a promotion as the chief executive for the parent firm's entire southwestern region. The women I came to know during my research all expressed a deep satisfaction with their work and their workplace relationships, though they were not unlike other employees in pointing to aspects of their jobs they would change if they could.

Understanding the overall successful integration of women into the Wyoming mines requires moving away from prominent stereotypes about the industry to examine the everyday lives of the miners and their families, including the cultural frames they use to make sense of the challenges and joys they encounter along the way. When Mary said that gender was not the most important part of her day, she did not mean that gender never mattered. In fact, later that afternoon she spoke poignantly about some of the cultural and practical factors that discouraged some women from taking jobs as shovel operators. For instance, the shovels do not have their own toilet facilities and are stationary, which means that their operators cannot easily access the port-a-potties located around the pit close to areas frequented by truck drivers. If they do not wish to use the mine radio to announce their need to be picked up and transported to a bathroom—and slow down the pace of production in the process of doing so—they must creatively do their business off the side of the grated metal catwalk or inside the shovel's engine room. Those maneuvers are more difficult for women than men. Furthermore, shovel operators are the leaders of the pit and give instructions to the trucks they load, and the few macho guys (discussed in greater detail in chapter 5) balked when taking directions from women (see also Rolston 2010a).

In our conversation, however, Mary pushed me to consider gender difference not as an ever-present feature of the workplace but as a social process that comes to matter in particular moments and places. In fact, she and most of her coworkers had dedicated their working lives to diminishing the salience of gender in the mines so that they could work on equal footing with men. Although they were keenly aware that they were not entirely successful in meeting the goal of total gender neutrality, they were rightfully proud of what they had accomplished. They urged me to not forget those efforts when I wrote about them and their work, as they were also keenly aware that popular representations of the industry were steeped in perceptions of abusive attitudes toward women. Mary, for instance, spoke at length about the frustration she felt when trying to explain her work to people who assumed, because they had no personal experience with the industry, that she was "an oppressed person, toiling underground all day, and getting harassed by guys." Adding to her troubles was the 2005 film *North Country*, which had recently brought national attention to the sexual harassment women miners in Minnesota's Iron Range faced in the 1980s. Many of the women miners I came to know had experienced harassment and hostility in previous jobs as bar tenders, waitresses, or construction workers, but very few had been harassed at the mines. Knowing the subject of the film, very few women in the basin saw it because they were concerned that the film would unduly reinforce stereotypes about macho male miners. For those who did see the film, like Mary, it confirmed their fears. While not denying that incidents such as those documented in the film occurred in other regions and eras of the industry, she was troubled that it would reinforce mining's already bad reputation since people did not distinguish among regions, types of mining, or even specific companies.

Mary had also confronted popular opinions about mining when she found herself the subject of a Canadian television documentary about women equipment operators. The producers lavished praise on her technical prowess in operating the "Cadillac of dozers" and gleefully showed her riding her large and loud Harley-Davidson motorcycle on the highways that wound through the grassy hills on the outskirts of Gillette, the largest town in the basin with approximately thirty thousand residents. Yet she ultimately found the attention silly since she "was just doing the same things that everybody else out here does." So did her coworker Jenny, who was happy that the final cut included her statement that she enjoyed joking around with the guys on her crew and had never experienced sexual harassment. But she also remembered, "The producer wanted to film some short commercials [advertising the documentary], so he asked me to climb up on the blade and put all of my long hair up under my hard hat. Then I was supposed to climb down, take it off, and shake out my hair. I felt so stupid! That's not the way things are here." The producer was trying to capitalize on the viewers' expectation that the operator descending from the blade would be a man and surprise them with a markedly sexy and feminine woman. This framing was inappropriate at best and offensive at worst, as the basin's men and women believe that their biggest achievement is turning gender into what they call a "nonissue" in their everyday relationships, challenges, and achievements.

A story told by Patty, a thirty-year veteran of the industry, illustrates the discomfort many women feel when gender difference is explicitly introduced into the fabric of social life at the mines, even when done with good intentions. I had rented an office in downtown Gillette to conduct private interviews, and she appeared in the doorway wearing blue jeans, work boots, and a heavy winter jacket emblazoned with her first name along with the name and logo of the company for whom she had worked for the previous three decades. She had come from the company office, where she worked in management after starting as a general laborer nearly three decades earlier. As we settled in to our coffee and conversation, she recalled a story from her first years in the mines. A beloved mine manager asked her and two other women truck drivers to see him at the office. When they arrived, he could barely contain his excitement. He announced that the local newspaper was doing an article on women in the coal mines, and he thought it would be fun to have all of the women at the mine pose for a picture. "I must have said something stupid out loud, like 'that's the dumbest thing I've ever heard,'" she said, "because he said that he thought we'd be excited and wanted to know why we weren't." Patty remembered telling him, "You know, for every step forward we try and take, it's things like this, where you want our picture splayed in the paper because we're women in mining. We're just trying to say we're no better than anybody else, and that takes us two steps backward." The manager took her words to heart. The photographer ended up being late for the shoot, and the manager informed him that they had decided not to participate after talking to the women on-site. Patty summed up the incident by saying, "It was just one of those things. I don't have to fight for a chance, but on the other hand, don't make a big deal out of the fact that I'm out there doing it also." It is telling that she said this incident was the only time in her thirty-year career that she ever "got vocal about women in the workforce" because for the most part it was a "nonissue." Rather than being an all-pervasive feature of her relationships and work at the mine, Patty argued that gender difference had to be brought into play by particular statements or actions.

In fact, Mary, Jenny, Patty, and their coworkers guided many of our conversations to the moments in which gender difference faded into the background, which they sensed were missing from popular understandings of the industry. For the rest of the afternoon I spent with Mary on the shovel, for instance, she unwound the long histories of practical jokes that she and her crew had played on each other over the previous decades. Through these jokes, miners cultivated similar dispositions as they came to know, trust, and care for one another as a family. Like almost all miners in the basin, Mary views her coworkers as family, and these close workplace ties help address the "human issues" she found more troubling than the gender ones: ensuring the safety of the entire crew, finding meaning in monotonous tasks, and crafting relationships that safeguard everyone's respect and dignity. People who view their coworkers as family treat each other like the unique persons they are, rather than as numbers or replaceable cogs in a machine. As miners such as Mary helped me interpret workplace events and debates from their point of view, they drew my attention to the similarities as well as differences that emerged as men and women cultivated, transformed, and evaluated those work-family relationships.

This ethnography therefore makes two major arguments. The first is that kinship, specifically what I call workplace relatedness, animates social relationships in the Powder River Basin coal mines. By extending the new anthropological kinship studies into an industrial workplace, I show that miners construct relatedness with one another not simply by working together in the same place but by sharing the uniquely demanding temporal regime of rotating shiftwork. Over a twenty-eight-day cycle, crews work a series of alternating twelve-hour dayshifts and nightshifts, which conflict with the rhythms of home life but create intense camaraderie among coworkers. All miners recognize the crew families, though they place varying degrees of importance on those ties, as explained below. When used by miners, talk of crew families signals egalitarian relationships based in shared respect for hard work. It points to the interdependence that underlines specific job tasks and ties each person's well-being to the actions of their coworkers.[4] Miners use the generic term "family" to refer to these relationships, likely because the otherwise egalitarian terms brother or sister would evoke the labor unions they voted against and draw attention to gender difference. Exceptions are made for mentoring relationships, in which younger or less experienced workers refer to their guides as being "like a father" or "like a mother."[5] When used by management, the same kinship talk can take on more hierarchical tones depending on the purpose to which it is directed. The crew families do not replace the relatives that miners, like other Americans, recognize through blood and marriage. But the time-based notion of kinship developed in the workplace does translate back into their families at home. According to miners, their spouses, and their children alike, shiftwork imperils kin-ties because the miner does not share the daily rhythms of the home, frequently missing morning breakfasts and evening bedtime stories, as well as many of the more momentous rituals of holiday celebrations and school award ceremonies. Analyzing the emphasis on time for these families deepens understandings of Euro-American folk theories of kinship beyond the belief in shared biogenetic substances.

The second argument builds on the first. The ethnographic materials demonstrate that in the process of crafting workplace relatedness, miners both construct and undo gender difference. By tracing the ways in which gender differences are reduced as well as reproduced, the book happily builds on a growing trajectory of feminist scholarship that argues for increased attention to "undoing gender" in order to understand and dismantle inequalities between men and women (Deutsch 2007; Lorber 2005; Risman 1998, 2009). These scholars argue that a singular focus on the construction and reproduction of gender difference—while valuable for identifying and rectifying some forms of discrimination—nonetheless obscures our understanding of how such differences can be challenged and sometimes made irrelevant. Instead of assuming the sociocultural salience of gender difference on the basis of differently sexed bodies—the tautological error identified by multiple generations of feminist theorists—I investigate where, when, how, and for whom gender difference comes to matter or fades away.

The turn to studying the ways in which gender is undone builds on a foundational, if overlooked (Carsten 2004: 69) insight of feminist anthropology: the cultural construction of gender difference rests on the "suppression of natural similarities" (Rubin 1975: 180). Studies of North American and European kinship practices attest to the power of gender binaries, with the exception of works by ethnographers who work with lesbian, gay, bisexual, and transgender families (e.g., Carrington 2002; Lewin 2009; Weston 1991). This pattern can be attributed to a tenacious equation of gender and sexuality in social theory that leads to the assumption that alternative practices in one arena presume the same in the other (de Lauretis 1987; McElhinny 2003). In fact, kinship studies may be prone to reproducing dominant notions of binary masculinity and femininity due to entrenched Euro-American cultural links between kinship and heterosexuality (Butler 2002; Rubin 1975; Weston 1991).

Keeping an eye to both the doing and undoing of gender is necessary to understand the Wyoming workplace families. With few exceptions, women and men who are the most satisfied with their jobs and workplace relationships are those who are the most tightly integrated into the crew families and consciously work to minimize perceptions of gender difference. These women and men make up the majority of crews. Chapter 6 traces this orientation to their common adherence to an agricultural work ethic, built out of many miners' experiences growing up on or nearby ranches and farms, which minimizes (but does not completely erase) gender difference.

Miners who do not privilege that specific form of work ethic find themselves on the fringe of the crew families, without being excluded completely. Chapter 5 shows that these departures from their coworkers' expectations for workplace behavior are read in gendered terms: "macho" men who work "too hard" and lack empathy for others; "ladies" whose loyalty to stereotypical notions of femininity makes it difficult for them to comply with the requirements of their jobs; and "sissies" and "bitches" who exemplify the worst features attributed to exaggerated stereotypes of the opposite sex—prissiness and competitiveness in men and women, respectively. On the other hand, the men and women who form the foundation of the crew families take on the labels of "softies" and "tomboys." While gendered, these terms notably signal distance from stereotypical notions of masculinity and femininity alike: women identified as tomboys eschew the conventionally feminine distaste for dirt and muscle in their love of the outdoors and willingness to give their all in a muddy, dusty, and greasy work environment; men identified as softies set aside cultural expectations for male emotional distance, competitiveness, and invincible swagger to make themselves vulnerable and treat their coworkers with conspicuous care. This mutual accommodation suggests that the successfully integrated women miners are not simply adapting to masculine norms disguised in the language of gender blindness.[6] The crew families' expectations for workplace behaviors and relationships are to a certain extent gender neutral, though they are imperfectly realized in practice.

The processes through which miners craft and unravel workplace relatedness with one another are therefore simultaneously contestations over constructing and undoing gender difference. Understanding those processes provides a crucial perspective on the negotiation of workplace power, since what is at stake is job security: belonging to the crew families provides dense horizontal support networks, whereas distancing oneself from these networks either aligns miners vertically with management or isolates them as independent agents. In this case, men as well as women experience alienation that endangers their desire and ability to maintain well-paying jobs. Yet women who fall outside the norms for workplace kin may be more vulnerable since one of the last ideological strongholds of gender difference in the basin—and one of the main targets of contestation by women miners and their allies—is the cultural association between masculinity and technology (Rolston 2010a). What is unique about the Powder River Basin mines is that this alienation happens not because men and women *fail* to conform to the ideals of macho masculinity, as research in other regions and sectors of the mining industry has found, but precisely because workers alienated from workplace families *do* embody exaggerated forms of masculinity or femininity. The core group of workers in the crew families value and try to create workplace dispositions and relationships that diminish gender difference, even if it cannot be erased entirely.

Mining Gender Politics

This book builds on a key insight of studies of gender and mining: the industry is not a naturally or inherently masculine one. Women actually dominate artisanal and small-scale mining in the developing world (Lahiri-Dutt 2011a; Lahiri-Dutt and Macintyre 2006).[7] Women also worked in mines in Europe and the United States until Victorian-era bourgeois reformers made tremendous efforts to change public opinion and pass laws banning women miners from working in underground coal mines (Hilden 1991; John 1980).[8] In the preindustrial United States women worked alongside their male kin to extract coal for their households, and historical documents reveal that female slaves were forced to work in a Virginia coal mine (Moore 1996; Tallichet 2006: 5). As the mines industrialized at the beginning of the twentieth century, seventeen states including Wyoming passed laws banning women's work underground, even though oral histories reveal that many women ignored these prohibitions.

On top of legislation, cultural cosmologies establish mining as the proper activity of men. Within a series of symbolic oppositions that have "both historical depth and cultural breadth," orebodies (a well-defined mass of ore-bearing rock) and mine spaces are understood as female in contrast with the laboring bodies of masculine miners (Ferry 2011: 295; see also Ferry 2005; Finn 1998; Nash 1993). In the United States in the early 1980s, Richard Trumka, president of the United Mine Workers of America, made the case for integrating women into the industry by criticizing the gendering of coal, telling a 1983 union conference in West Virginia, "The coal you mine has no gender. It's not female coal or male coal. It's just coal" (Tallichet 2006: 106). The Wyoming case is an exception to a larger pattern, since miners there do not describe the coal as female, attribute feminine qualities to it, or use the feminine pronoun to refer to it.[9] As analyzed in chapter 5, this symbolic opposition may appear in the workplace when they sometimes refer to equipment in what may be feminine terms: the word 'er, which could be a shortened version of her, as in "Bring 'er to the shop."

The distinctly gendered spheres of mine and community, work and home, and masculinity and femininity may be incredibly durable because they appear natural when people embody and reinscribe them in their everyday practice. Elizabeth Ferry (2005, 2011) elegantly pairs June Nash's ([1979] 1993) analysis of the gendered symbolism of a Bolivian tin mining community with Pierre Bourdieu's (1977) theory of practice to argue that everyday activities construct the domains of mine and home as "parallel though distinct" (Ferry 2005: 100). The mine and the silver vein (the Veta Madre, literally, mother lode) are construed as feminine and womb-like, enclosing the masculinized work of the male miners. In contrast, the everyday actions of the miners' female kin produce the inside of the home as a space of feminine labor that is enclosed by the masculine structure of the house, since men are responsible for using the money that returns to the community in the sale of silver to build homes. The house and mine therefore provide models for gendered social life (Ferry 2005: 101).

In mining communities the distinction between the masculine sphere of work and the feminine sphere of home and family is a cultural and historical construction whose force can make them seem impervious. Historians, anthropologists, and sociologists show that even if these spheres appear culturally distinct, they are nonetheless interdependent.[10] In particular, J. K. Gibson-Graham's research with wives of Australian miners shows that while dominant discourses may posit gender divisions as natural or seemingly impervious to change, such arrangements are rarely replicated perfectly in everyday life.

Research should therefore attend to both dimensions, in order to "represent the social space as a space of gender diversity and overlap, while acknowledging the existence and even the dominance of mutually exclusive gender in the discursive realm" (Gibson-Graham 2006: 218). This book builds on Gibson-Graham's insight by acknowledging the force of binary gender ideologies—such as those animating popular conceptions of mining as naturally masculine or women as naturally safer equipment operators—without losing sight of their creative and sometimes contradictory embodiment in actual practice.

Women Miners

The first way I capture these contradictions is by focusing on women miners. The book builds on the existing literature about women miners by offering the first major study of their integration into a nonunionzed surface mine in the American West. The unique ethnographic context sheds light on the regional, technological, and institutional factors that contour possibilities for women's participation in the industry as production workers.

One main hypothesis of the existing research is that industrialization is a prime contributor to the masculinization of minework (e.g., Lahiri-Dutt 2011b: 14; Mercier and Gier 2006: 5).[11] Sociologist Suzanne Tallichet's study of an underground Appalachian mine, for example, finds that "the twin forces of advancing technology and bureaucratic organization have made work and gender roles increasingly interdependent, so that the work itself strongly encourages conformity to masculine-identified norms" (2006: 39). Miners and company officials frequently use the technology argument to justify the exclusion of women from mines and particular jobs, explaining away mechanically gifted women as exceptions to a more general rule (Tallichet 2006: 40; see also Rolston 2010a).[12] Yet women miners do master the technology needed for their jobs when given training opportunities, in surface as well as underground operations (Keck and Powell 2000; Lahiri-Dutt 2006, 2011b; Lahiri-Dutt and Macintyre 2006: 6; Lahiri-Dutt and Robinson 2008; Smith 2008, 2009).

Complicating the theory that industrialization masculinizes mining is the simultaneous assertion by miners that women do not succeed in the industry because they lack the physical strength required by the work (e.g., Lahiri-Dutt 2011b: 2, 14). Ethnographic research challenges the cliché that women lack the strength to be miners, demonstrating that women can engage in the physical labor deemed appropriate only for men. In fact, Barbara Kingsolver's nonfiction work on an Arizona mine strike includes tales of a woman who was physically stronger than other men in her shop in an Arizona copper mine (1989: 74), and Tallichet reports that women miners in Appalachia proved they could do the dirtiest, most physically demanding labor assigned to them (2006: 76). Though technological advances actually lessen the need for heavy manual labor historically associated with masculine work (Keck and Powell

2000; Lahiri-Dutt and Macintyre 2006: 6), the cultural association between masculinity and technology probably lessens the extent to which increased mechanization could facilitate women's participation in the industry.

The Powder River Basin shows that industrialization does not necessarily masculinize minework. Miners there actually point to the technological requirements of the jobs as enabling women to work in particular areas of the mines. Women are especially successful in the pit, they say, because driving haul trucks and other equipment does not require brute strength the way that working in the shop does. Women mechanics deconstruct the argument a step further by showing that men also use technology and assistance instead of pure muscle to do their jobs. Additionally, they argue that trade-offs actually make it easier for them to do particular jobs considered demanding. The mechanic Barb, for instance, wishes that tools were made lighter for women like her to handle, but she argues that she can get into tight spots such as the area around the belt on a haul truck. "It only takes me twenty minutes because there's so much room in there it's like a football field," she reported, "but it takes guys who can't reach it a lot longer." She can also fit between a tire rim and a frame on a rubber tire dozer, whereas many men cannot, and her comparatively thinner and longer fingers can get into places that theirs cannot reach. Miners like Barb and the women Tallichet interviewed (2006: 33, 64–68) thus challenge local arguments that women cannot handle mining because it is either too physically demanding or technologically complicated.

The contradictions among the scholarly and popular theories about the role of technology in the masculinization of minework may emerge from the tensions among the different forms of masculinity that animate the industry. Sociologist Rebecca Scott (2010) argues that in Appalachia the figures of the family man, tough guy, and modern man emphasized the cultural significance of financial support for families, bravery and physical strength, and technological prowess, respectively. These elements of masculinity can contradict one another. With the advent of mountaintop removal mining, which celebrates the risk and excitement of the technological domination over nature, the family man and tough guy are losing ground to the modern man, though they remain culturally significant (Scott 2010: 70–72).

In this book I build on research showing that arguments about technical skill and brute strength are both ideological justifications for excluding women from minework: if women's participation in the industry decreases along with industrialization it is due to cultural notions of gender and work rather than actual ability. To understand the cultural construction of minework as masculine, it is essential to examine the institutional policies, social structures, and workplace practices that build up norms for workplace performance and interactions.

In North America, shiftwork makes mine employment challenging for women who maintain primary responsibility for childcare (Keck and Powell 2001: 210; Tallichet 2006: 97; see also Lahiri-Dutt and Robinson 2008: 133 for Indonesian surface mines). Strict seniority systems impede women's advance in Appalachian underground mines, and unions have had mixed effectiveness in representing issues specific to women rather than the general workforce (Scott 2010: 66; Tallichet 2006: 103–133; see also Kingsolver 1989 for surface mining). Men in Appalachian mines viewed women as less technically competent and discouraged them from taking advantage of formal training opportunities (Tallichet 2006: 6). Even formal training preserves male dominance when opportunities to be trained originate in informal interactions among men (Tallichet 2006: 78–102). Finally, sexual harassment also impedes women's integration into the industry. Joking practices in unionized mines in Appalachia, Arizona, and Canada turn women into sexual objects and naturalize mining as a masculine endeavor (Keck and Powell 2000; Kingsolver 1989: 21, 73–89; Tallichet 2006; Yount 1991, 2005).

The Wyoming women miners share some of these challenges. As I have shown in previous studies, they hold a greater burden for everyday family care, making sustained shiftwork difficult (Smith 2008 and chapter 4), and they have to prove their technical competence on-site (Rolston 2010a and chapter 6). They do not, however, face the same endemic sexual harassment as do their counterparts in other sectors of the industry. Understanding why draws attention to the salience of regional gender ideologies in workplace relationships.

Tallichet explicitly argues that regional gender ideologies shaped the integration of women into the Appalachian mine she studied. Tracing the "hyper-traditional" Appalachian gender system back to the region's history of colonial exploitation (2006: 37), she argues that the "work families" developed by crews may provide mutual support for miners, but they also reflect the patriarchal ones found in the home: women miners were "expected to perform tasks that mirrored the work they traditionally performed in their homes in support of and in service to men" (2006: 75). The same attention to regional gender ideologies is not found in sociologist Kristen Yount's work on harassment, though she does note the location of the mines in rural communities with sex-segregated homes and workplaces (2005: 86). Kingsolver's (1989) journalistic account of women miners in Arizona suggests that women's participation in a major strike transformed traditional gender ideologies. One woman said, "We have started to realize they're not any better than we are. In fact, today I told my husband, 'Why don't you wash the dishes? Why is it that I have to wash your towels, your sheets, change your bed? You're not able to do these simple things? Nobody waits on me!'" (Kingsolver 1989: 103). Those traditional gender ideologies may have informed the harassment some women miners experienced in the Arizona mines.

Although the Wyoming women miners are not immune from harassment, in chapter 6 I show that strikingly different regional gender ideologies shape the ways in which people interpret and practice everyday workplace behavior. Rather than cordoning off men and women in separate spheres of work and home, the local agricultural work ethic enjoins men and women alike to contribute to collective, physically demanding, outdoor labor. When miners craft feelings of relatedness with one another through shared labor, it prompts them to interpret bawdy humor from both men and women as a key means of crafting trust and kin-ties in their crew families. In contrast, when sexual innuendo comes from men and women occupying marginal positions in the crew families, miners are more likely to label the behavior harassment and therefore instigate a formal disciplinary process. Why? People on the margins of the crew families usually ended up in that position as a result of having violated the work ethic upheld by crews, and the disciplinary process is one strategy for formally sanctioning a longer history of antisocial behavior.

Men Miners

The first way in which the book questions the contested space between binary gender ideologies and everyday practice is by examining the everyday lives of women miners. The second is by deconstructing the masculinity of men miners. The legendary macho masculinity attributed to miners permeates popular films, books, and academic texts about the industry.[13] The lure of miners might rest with their status as both victim and hero. "Life itself is endangered, their enemy is the elements, their tragedy derives from forces greater than they, forces of nature and vengeful acts of God . . . miners are the Clark Gables, the Reds of class struggle" (Campbell 1984: 97). This potent masculinity can be denigrated as much as it is lauded, however, since miners are made to appear as "walking contradictions of wisdom and ignorance, humility and bravado" (Finn 1998: 112). This contradiction is especially clear in accounts of male miners' relationships with women, as men appear sadistic and infantile in descriptions of their harassment of women coworkers (e.g., Bingham and Gansler 2002; Vaught and Smith 1980). Even a well-respected anthropologist casually extrapolates an evening in a bar with bawdy Zambian copper workers to represent "only a specific instance of an only all-too-familiar global pattern of working-class male sexism" (Ferguson 1999: 188).

In analyzing the give-and-take of gender dynamics, I investigate how particular forms of masculinity become meaningful, dominant, or irrelevant in a particular ethnographic context. It shows that in the course of their everyday lives, men as well as women miners consciously and unconsciously move their social interactions and senses of self outside of strict gender dichotomies. The pages that follow share the experiences of men who listen to audio books of Danielle Steele novels while operating some of the world's "biggest and baddest" heavy machinery, men who have a reputation for being cantankerous shovel operators at work but are patient and meticulous gardeners at home, and men who enjoy cold beers and the occasional off-color joke but are also the first to support women's advancement in the pit and their own daughters' independence. These ethnographic vignettes are not meant to gloss over troubling instances in which miners shore up their power by aligning themselves with stereotypically masculine ways of being—which I also critique—but are intended to flesh out the actual complexities that men and women navigate over the course of a heated debate or an entire career.

One of the strategies I employed to capture the moments in which masculinity is undone was to spend time with male miners both off and on the worksite. Paying attention to men raising their children or leading a church youth group draws attention to less heavily masculinized thoughts and practices about mentoring, for example, that can also be found in the workplace if one looks carefully. Although dominant notions of masculinity may be more impervious to change (Connell and Messerschmidt 2005), the flourishing field of masculinity studies shows that they are not static, monolithic, or all-encompassing. This analysis confirms that because there is nothing inherently gendered about particular forms of labor, particular tasks and entire occupations take on gendered associations at the intersection of everyday life and structural forces (Britton 2000; Risman 1998; Salzinger 2003). Denaturalizing the masculinity of mine labor in this way affirms that the cultural link between masculinity and mining is not inevitable or natural; it is specific to particular times and places and emerges through contested laws, reform programs, and the daily practices of men and women.

Successfully Integrating Women into Unlikely Workplaces

The largest contribution this book makes to studies of women miners is analyzing a case in which a large number of women integrated themselves into one sector of the mining industry with comparatively few ideological, structural, and interpersonal conflicts. Previous research offers a few examples of women—especially single mothers and self-described pranksters—who were eventually welcomed into originally hostile workplaces (Tallichet 2006: 4–5, 29–33, 132; Yount 1991). But these researchers are skeptical about their strategies to integrate themselves into the workplace. These studies find that the camaraderie and occasionally bawdy humor women enjoy with their coworkers perpetuates masculine dominance and intensified harassment (Yount 1991: 416–417) and is symptomatic of a double consciousness in which women identify with their oppressors at their own peril (Tallichet 2006).

The Wyoming case does not give rise to the same skepticism. There are three explanations for the significant qualitative differences between the women's experiences in the Wyoming mines and the ones previously under study. The existing research comprises studies from very different underground and surface mines across the United States that nonetheless share two characteristics. First, women miners represented a small percentage of the workforce. The statistical highpoint of the "women's mine" studied by Tallichet was 12 percent (2006: 29). The percentage of women coal miners nationally has hovered between 5 and 6 percent from 1986 to 2010 (Tallichet 2006: 88).[14] Conversely, the Powder River Basin mines average between 20 and 25 percent women in production, both in general and at the four specific mines I studied. Greater numbers may facilitate greater support networks and recognition (Kanter 1977), though my study confirms Tallichet's (2006: 149) earlier finding of tensions among women miners. In Wyoming these issues included some specific to women (such as the politics of bathroom breaks, described in chapter 6) as well as those shared with men (such as potentially dehumanizing treatment by coworkers). Second, the mines forming the backbone of the existing literature were already in operation when women went to work for them. In the case of the Appalachian mines in particular, the integration happened forcibly as a result of successful lawsuits against the companies.[15] The Wyoming mines are distinct in that they all included women in production from the first day they opened their doors in the late 1970s and early 1980s. The women there did not have to change or adapt to an already existing masculine work culture, but worked with men to create workplace relationships they all valued. This creation of workplace culture points to the third possible explanation. The cultural figures, to use Scott's term, that animate minework are less gendered in Wyoming: being a good miner does not require the same demonstration of specifically masculine breadwinning and toughness. Yet the association of technological mastery with masculinity remains a lingering source of frustration for women miners there.

The integration of women into the Powder River Basin mining industry presents both hope and concern for the perennial question of women's equitable participation in the paid workforce. These issues are becoming ever more urgent as employment in the United States and around the world becomes increasingly precarious in the wake of the Great Recession. Of particular concern is the lingering occupational segregation that systematically disadvantages women and perpetuates the gender wage gap (Gauchat, Kelly, and Wallace 2012). Great numbers of women made inroads into historically masculine fields in the 1970s and 1980s, but further progress has stalled since the 1990s. Research consistently finds that the more women dominate an occupation, the lower average earnings tend to be. This problem is especially grave for women without college degrees, leading the author of a report by the Institute for Women's Policy Research to warn, "In the least-skilled jobs, working in a female rather than male dominated occupation may make the difference between wages close to poverty and wages that can support a family" (Hegewisch et al. 2010: 13). One strategy for women to increase their overall earnings, therefore, is to enter male-dominated fields. Although these efforts have been encouraged for women of all educational backgrounds, they have been particularly urgent in breaking down the fortress-like "pink collar ghetto" in which many women with high school diplomas find themselves stuck (Mastracci 2004).

At first blush a Wyoming coal mine may seem like an inauspicious place for an experiment in desegregating gendered workforces, since mining is not simply one historically masculinized occupation among many, but the archetype for them. But the historical and cultural context undoubtedly shaped personal ideas and institutional policies surrounding women and mine labor. All of the mines except two were opened in the final years of the 1970s or later. By then the women's liberation movement was in full swing with its demands for equal political, economic, and social rights and opportunities. Title IX guaranteeing equal access to educational programs and sports had been made law, and the Equal Rights Amendment had been passed by Congress even if it was not ultimately ratified by the states. Debates about employment played a major role in the women's movement. As middle-class women entered the paid workforce in unprecedented numbers—after all, working-class women have nearly always worked outside the home to support their families—they confronted and attempted to dismantle the harassment, uneven pay scales, and glass ceilings they encountered. Appalachian women fighting to get and keep coal mining jobs became a cause célèbre, and their efforts to combat sexual harassment were chronicled in the popular media and the academy alike.[16]

It is no coincidence that at the same time as the country was captivated by the struggles of the Appalachian women, the new mines in northeastern Wyoming welcomed large numbers of women employees on-site. As the mines were being planned, permitted, and opened during the 1970s, coal company executives echoed a deep-seated cultural truism about the West by stating that they viewed the industry's expansion into the Rocky Mountain region as an opportunity to make a fresh start. Losing a public relations battle over the treatment of Appalachian women prompted corporate personnel in Wyoming not only to hire women but also to ensure that they were treated fairly throughout their employment. Some also hoped that the presence of women would shore up a more positive image of the industry since popular wisdom holds that women in general are safe, caring, and environmentally responsible. Others were simply happy to hire "anyone who was willing and had a pulse," since the local labor shortage slowed the speed with which the mines could open and begin combating the protracted national energy crisis of the 1970s.

The women who originally went to work in the mines did not consider themselves feminists or personally link their pathbreaking experiences to the larger movement (even if the movement did at least partially facilitate their ventures into the industry). Women's lib, they explained to me when looking back on their lives, was something for liberal, college-educated people who lived on the coast. They espoused a rhetoric of gender egalitarianism born out of hard labor on the family ranch or farm, not consciousness-raising groups near the university. Some of the lore surrounding the region's plucky women homesteaders and ranchers has more to do with myth than everyday life, like so many treasured western tales and characters. But this first cohort of women miners, as well as the younger one now taking their place, brought this image of women's strength and their own experiences of rural life to work with them along with their tools, hard hats, and steel-toed boots.[17] As chapter 6 describes, beliefs about the gender neutrality of frontier labor continue to resonate on the minesite and provide one arena in which differences between men and women are debated and often diminished.

Though not without its hiccups and missteps, the integration of women into the mines has been successful overall. The average crew in the basin consists of just under a quarter women. Wages for hourly production workers are solely based on a quantifiable scale of skills. For example, pit technicians make progressively more money per hour based on the number of machines they are certified to operate. A few women encounter trouble in securing equal access to training, as described in chapter 6 and analyzed in a separate context by Tallichet (2006), but women miners in general express satisfaction with their opportunities to advance. A shovel operator like Mary who also operates dozers, haul trucks, and blades makes the same exact hourly wage as a male coworker who also operates shovels, dozers, haul trucks, and blades. These wages are sizeable. The miners here may represent the last of the blue-collar aristocracy, making between $65,000 and $100,000 a year without the benefit of a college education. When combined with generous insurance plans and retirement programs, these wages attract many workers, especially those with families to support.

Contrary to popular views of the industry as a bastion of unbridled misogyny, the women miners do not have to sacrifice their own personal well-being to enjoy equal pay for equal work. Sexual discrimination and harassment are extremely rare, though not entirely absent. In our conversations, people had to reach back decades to offer an example from their friends, crews, or the gossip mill. In fact, during twenty-two months of formal research in the area and nine months of my own employment there, only one incident materialized in which a crew turned in one of their coworkers for harassment. Chapter 6 explores the seeming paradox of low reports of harassment in the mines. The ethnographic materials suggest that reports of sexual harassment are never simply about gender, but represent larger contestations about appropriate forms of workplace relationships and blue-collar work ethics.

This book's approach to studying the construction and undoing of gender in the same analytic frames builds on research about women who work in nontraditional occupations in the United States. This literature demonstrates that such women find themselves stuck in a double bind: act in socially acceptable feminine ways but give up being treated as equal, or gain acceptance by adopting masculine practices but risk being reprimanded for crossing gender boundaries (see Valian 1998 for a summary). Studies find that women can employ symbolic markers of masculinity in their efforts to adapt and blend in to the workplace, or, in other words, "perform gender so that gender will be ignored" (McElhinny 1995: 220; Weston 1990: 143–145). At the same time, other research raises the possibility that this work can encourage exaggerated expressions of femininity as men create boundaries between themselves and their women coworkers (see C. Williams 1989 for the foundational case of women members of the U.S. Marine Corps). Sociologists document these seemingly contradictory dynamics in different areas of the mining industry as well as within particular mines themselves. For example, Tallichet and Yount both show that men in underground coal mines emphasize the femininity of their women coworkers in order to maintain their interpersonal dominance as well as the cultural association of mining with masculinity. On the other hand, they also note that women miners who are happiest with their work and most accepted by their coworkers adopt linguistic markers (such as cursing and telling off-color jokes) and practices (such as playing practical jokes) associated with men.[18]

Closely analyzing interviews and observations of everyday life reveals that these strategies are not mutually exclusive; women in historically masculinized fields may align with masculine and feminine norms on a moment-by-moment, turn-by-turn basis, according to what is at stake in each context (Bergvall 1996: 192; Landström 2007; McElhinny 1995). Linguistic anthropologist Bonnie McElhinny (1995) in particular advances this literature by showing that the women police officers in Pittsburgh that she studied do not simply adopt masculine forms of speech or interaction, but actively challenge the hegemonic masculinity associated with the police. They position themselves as competent police officers by exhibiting characteristics associated with objectivity rather than brute force, and in so doing redefine the image of police work. Specifically, they challenge the working-class masculinity associated with policing and replace it with the masculinity associated with the middle class.

In this book I extend the literature on women in nontraditional occupations by documenting and theorizing the moments and social configurations within which men and women are able to unmoor their interactions from either masculine or feminine norms to align themselves with more gender-neutral expectations for workers. In the process, men and women alike redefine the local image of coal miners. Like McElhinny's police officers, they decouple it from norms of working-class masculinity by positioning themselves as skilled professionals who operate and fix some of the most technologically sophisticated equipment in the world. But they also partially distance their understanding of coal miners from masculinity in general by centering their expectations for coworkers' behavior around a work ethic that is at least partially gender neutral, as described in chapter 6. Being a "good miner" in the Wyoming coal mines is less about macho bravado, strength, courage, and rugged individualism and more about being professional, competent, safe, and careful with coworkers' emotional and physical well-being. Some men find it easier to fit those expectations, since women's technical expertise has to be proven socially in a way that men's does not, but there are also ways in which some women find it easier than many men to fit the role of the good miner, since the competitive pressure felt by some men leads them to step on other people's dignity. This redefinition is crucial for facilitating women's entry into historically masculine fields, since cultural schemas of gender and occupations shape who will be viewed as competent workers and whose behavior will be censured (McElhinny 1995; Valian 1998). In Wyoming, the successful integration of women into mining stems from them not simply adopting masculine personas but from working with their male coworkers to construct expectations for good miners and coworkers that are not based in strictly masculine or feminine qualities.

The Mines

The Powder River Basin mines are surface operations located between ten and sixty miles outside of Gillette. This separation between living and working spaces is common in the industry, since the immobility of the resources being extracted means that companies cannot simply mine where they choose, but where the minerals are located and can be reached. Mining economies are often, but not always, predicated on the physical separation of the mine and its workers from family members and larger communities (e.g., Ferguson 1999, 2005, 2006; Gibson-Graham 2006; Rajak 2011). This separation takes its most dramatic form in Fly-In, Fly-Out operations, in which employees are flown in for a stretch of work, sleep and eat at the mine compound, and then are flown back to their homes and families for a stretch of days off (Cheshire 2010; Ferguson 2005).[19] Even in towns or camps in which the mine and other community spaces such as homes, businesses, and public gathering places are located in close proximity to one another, nonemployees such as family members are almost always barred from entering the mine itself. In the Powder River Basin, the spatial distinction between the mines and communities grounds the sense of empathy and relatedness shared by crewmembers.

The shiftwork schedule also creates feelings of empathy among coworkers. The most common schedule is designed for four crews and consists of twenty-eight-day cycles of twelve-hour shifts: four nights on, three days off, three days on, one day off, three nights on, three days off, four days on, seven days off. The schedule then starts over at the beginning.[20] Each group of shifts, such as the three days in a row, is called a block. The stretch of three day shifts and three night shifts punctuated by one day of reprieve is infamous enough to earn its own name: hell week. Miners also accumulate multiple personal vacation days, depending on their seniority, to use at their discretion throughout the year.

Explanations for the use of a rotating schedule vary. Keeping the machinery running twenty-four hours a day, seven days a week, requires workers to be onsite around the clock, but it does not necessarily require workers to rotate through different shifts. Other mines and other industries assign workers to one regular schedule, such that they always work nights, days, or swings rather than switching between them. Most managers and some miners in the basin said that the mines did not use a straight schedule because they doubted that anyone would willingly always work nights, thus making it impossible to find enough people to work on that crew. A few more critical theories percolated in the workforce, including speculation by a few very critical miners that the schedule was designed to "wear people out" so that they would not keep their jobs long enough to claim retirement benefits. Although the schedule engenders both social and bodily stresses, as analyzed in chapter 3, it is crucial to note that most miners defend it for the significant days off they enjoy every month and for the overtime pay that is built into their regular schedule.

Extracting, processing, and shipping millions of tons of coal a year requires the close coordination of many different people working in many different areas of the mine. One of the most salient distinctions exists between people who spend their days in the office—managers, engineers, and the administrative staff—and the production workers in the shop, the plant, and the pit. This distinction is made immediately visible by the clothes worn while at work. The office staff tends to wear jeans and polos or button-up shirts, while most company policies encourage the technicians (hourly workers) to wear company-issued coveralls on top of their jeans, T-shirts, or flannel shirts while on the clock. The office staff generally works "straight days," meaning that they go to work in the early morning four or five times a week at the same time each day, rather than being subject to the rotating shiftwork schedule. The main salaried employees who do rotate are crew supervisors, who act as intermediaries between the workers and the office staff, coordinating the miners' activities to achieve the official goals while simultaneously modifying management protocols whose inefficiencies are revealed by the miners' practical knowledge.

The actual extraction of the coal happens in the pit, which can extend up to two hundred feet deep at the largest mines without ever being technically underground (for more about the equipment and mining processes mentioned

FIG. 1 An aerial view of an active pit. The dragline in the upper left of the picture is exposing the coal seam by moving overburden from the right to the spoil piles on the left. The shovel at the bottom right is loading coal into the haul truck, which will transport it to the processing plant. Photo courtesy David R. Frazier.

in this section, see the glossary). One equipment operator described his job to his son by saying, "I'm not some mole underground. I get to look at the big, blue sky all day."

The pits are dug out and then filled back in with dirt by miners operating large pieces of heavy equipment. First, scraper operators remove and specially store the delicate topsoil. After the overburden, the dirt and rock layer covering the coal seam, has been drilled and blasted, miners operating draglines, shovels, and haul trucks move it to a pit that has just been emptied of coal and is ready to be reclaimed. A dragline is an extremely large piece of equipment operated by only two people: an "oiler" or maintenance technician, and the operator who uses a set of controls to maneuver a large bucket that picks up, moves, and then drops overburden into an already excavated pit, which comprises the first phase of reclamation, the final step in the mining process in which the land is restored to similar contours and its previous use. One of the largest draglines in the basin weighs sixty-seven hundred tons and took three years to assemble at a cost of fifty million dollars. Its 133-square yard bucket is supported by a 120-yard boom. Shovels are also used to remove overburden, but they rely on haul trucks to move the material they dig. In this type of operation, the shovel operator digs the overburden and empties it into the bed of a large haul truck, which can often hold up to three hundred tons of material. The truck driver then hauls it to a dump, where the overburden is placed directly into old pits or stored until needed for reclamation.

Once the coal in a large horizontal seam is exposed and blasted, shovel or loader operators extract it in a process similar to removing overburden. The main difference is that the truck driver hauls his or her load of coal to the plant, tipping the truck bed to allow the coal to fall into a series of machines that break it down into manageable chunks for later burning by power plants. After the coal has been crushed into smaller chunks, it drops onto conveyor belts that carry it to the silos for storage. Train tracks run through the bottom of these silos, and plant technicians load trains by pushing a button to open up the chutes through which the coal falls down into the slowly moving train cars below. When people working in the plant are not loading trains, they are responsible for minimizing the collection of dust in the buildings and for keeping the maze of machines that process the coal in good working order. If dust is allowed to collect in any of the buildings, it could spark a fire, and a machine in poor working condition could cause damage to other machinery or people in its vicinity.

The process of preparing, extracting, and transporting overburden and coal in the pit relies on a variety of support equipment. Large dozer operators prepare the pits, shape the dump, build roads, and push down coal and dirt to put it within the reach of smaller loading equipment. Operators running blades

FIG. 2 A train waiting outside the silos. Photo courtesy Peter Gartrell.

clean up coal spills and smooth out the roads to minimize damage to equipment caused by potholes and to give their coworkers a smoother ride. Scraper operators transport the most fragile layers of topsoil, but they also put down rock on icy winter or slick mine roads. Especially in the hot summers, these roads can become extremely dusty and dangerous, so water truck drivers spray water on them to help keep down the dust. Some mines also rely on backhoe operators to form the first highwalls of a new pit.

Equipment operators are responsible for monitoring the condition of their machinery, but maintaining all of this equipment in good working order necessitates the expertise of a large number of mechanics who perform on-the-spot troubleshooting and regular preventative maintenance. Depending on the specific circumstances, mechanics fix equipment in the shop or in the pit. Though some plant crews have their own dedicated mechanics, those from the shop also work in the plant buildings, performing repairs and maintenance on the equipment and conveyors used to process, store, and load the coal. The shop is also the home base for people who staff the warehouse, disbursing and keeping track of inventory.

The great variety of people who have a legitimate reason to be in the shop—such as office administrators collecting supplies from the warehouse, operators dropping off their equipment, or plant technicians picking up tools—make it an excellent place for face-to-face visiting with coworkers. Those types of interactions are more difficult in the pit, since it requires stopping and either shutting down or disembarking from the large, noisy machinery. To converse with one another without having to use the mine radio, operators take advantage of the downtime before and after the start of their shift as well as during lunch breaks, equipment malfunctions, and bus rides to and from the pit.[21] This relative isolation is reflected in the ethnographic material, which includes social interactions but relies heavily on interviews with operators in their equipment.

Research Methods and the Case for Native Ethnography

Kinship ties sparked my original interest in mining and continue to frame my engagement with the industry. Perils and possibilities alike emerge from my unique position in the research as someone who grew up in Gillette as the daughter of a mine mechanic but ultimately left the state for college and graduate school; as someone who drove haul trucks at the mines for a summer job long before deciding to become a social scientist; and as someone who defends the industry from unreasonable criticism but also holds an intellectual kinship with scholars who demand increased responsibility and accountability from it.

Working through these tensions prompts me to make a case for the continued relevance of the term native ethnography, used by anthropologists to signal the unique merits and challenges of conducting research in their "home" communities, though the definition of those homes is rightly contested. Some criticism of the term is merited, as emphasizing points of identification between the anthropologist and the people with whom they conduct research runs the risk of glossing over salient differences between them, and the discipline's larger history suggests that further use of the category may ghettoize anthropologists from minority backgrounds into conducting research only with "their" people.[22] Although these criticisms are apt, in a more limited usage the category also brings together many of the challenges faced by ethnographers who work in their own communities, not simply in their countries of origin or residence. The term draws attention to their efforts to manage the intimacies afforded by longstanding personal ties with research participants and to critique the discipline's representational tropes and colonial legacy. As such, the following sections introduce my strategies for attending to the differences that crosscut the strands of identification among my research participants and myself, and for working with research participants to critique existing representations of mining communities.

Working at a Coal Mine

The first time I stepped foot onto a coal mine in the Powder River Basin I was in elementary school. The mine where my father had recently begun working as a heavy equipment mechanic was hosting a family day, and my parents took my sister and me to see where my dad worked. I remember being awed by the giant machines and earth-shaking dynamite blast. Just over ten years later, I returned to the mines along with many of my former high school classmates as a temporary summer employee. Having recently taken my first course in anthropology at college, I was fascinated by my new job working in the plant. My crew taught me how to wash down the machinery and load coal trains that stretched over a mile long, but they also taught me how to play the best practical jokes and be a good sport when I found myself the target of one. Three years later I returned as a recent college graduate about to begin a doctoral program in anthropology. As I spent the summer driving a 290-ton Caterpillar haul truck in the pit, I could not help but think ethnographically about the mine and the social relations in which I was participating. Finally, two years later, I returned to the same mine to "drive truck" and begin formulating a larger dissertation fieldwork project about gender, kinship, and labor. The people who took me under their wings during those three initial summers profoundly shaped the questions that would eventually make up the backbone of my research project. In total, I spent ten months working in production at the mines as a summer student employee.

From 2004 to 2012, I conducted an additional twenty-two months of ethnographic research in Gillette, including a focused twelve-month stay from

FIG. 3 The author in front of the haul truck she drove while employed as a summer student at one of the mines.

2006 to 2007. The year of fieldwork included on-site research at four mines spanning the range of mine sizes in the basin. The first was one of the largest, employing approximately a thousand people and producing about ninety million tons of coal per year. The second was one of the smallest, employing around two hundred people and producing less than twenty million tons a year. The other two fell in the middle. Family friends and acquaintances facilitated my access to these sites by introducing me to management personnel who could in turn introduce my project and me to the people in a position to grant permission for research. My own positioning as a former Gillette resident and mine employee whose father worked for one of the mines figured prominently during our meetings. These personal connections facilitated rapport and trust with the mine officials, most of whom were otherwise wary of granting site access or interviews to nonemployees due to negative portrayals of the industry in the news media.

At three of the mines I rotated with one crew. When they went in for night or day shifts, I did as well. While on-site, I transcribed conversations on the mine radio, since it is the primary form of spoken communication in the pit, given that workers spend the majority of the shifts sitting in the cabs of heavy equipment. I also spent shifts with people as they went about their everyday work. Most often, I spent an entire twelve-hour shift riding around with one person in their piece of equipment, scribbling notes about their life histories, families, and opinions of the industry as we bumped along the haul roads. On my crew's days off, I interviewed that company's office workers and continued my work with other community members. At the fourth mine where I did not rotate with a production crew, I focused my time in the office with engineers and administrative personnel. In total, I conducted multiple in-depth interviews with sixty women and thirty-five men and enjoyed informal conversations with countless more, on-site as well as in the town's coffeeshops, bars, and restaurants.

This in-depth on-site research is relatively rare in ethnographies of mining, in which research tends to be conducted in the surrounding communities because companies often restrict on-site access to their administrative offices and short tours of the actual mines (Ferguson 1999; Ferry 2005; Nash 1993; Welker 2009).[23] Conversely, I was able to actively participate in workplace social relationships at the same time as I observed them. This perspective offered me the chance to compare miners' descriptions of their everyday working lives with observations of them unfolding in real time. Being there also helped to ground the issues we discussed in interviews. For instance, we could talk about workplace safety while driving under a towering highwall (the unexcavated overburden or coal that forms the walls of pits) or witnessing a temporary worker back up to a shaky berm (a ridge of earthen material that serves as a guard to keep vehicles and equipment within the confines of a road or raised working area) with too much force.[24]

At the mines where I engaged in on-site participant-observation, I met people for the first time through my research, which presented a fruitful counterpoint to the research I was simultaneously conducting with family, friends, and former coworkers. My first interactions with miners usually involved clarification of my project that was then passed along among the workforce. One case is telling. After spending the morning with the water truck operator, we stopped for fuel. As the mechanic running the fuel truck began making small talk with me about my family and my project, the operator told him, "Yeah, she's even coming in for night shifts!" The mechanic's eyebrows shot up and he asked, "Night shifts? Why in the hell would you want to do that?" I told him that I was there to get the whole perspective of what it was like to work there, and that I knew that the mine was an entirely different place at night. He cracked a smile and said, "Well, I suppose you've got a point there." Our conversation then turned to my prior work history and the day's gossip. After the truck was fueled, he gave me a gruff pat on the back and said, "You're all right, kid." The mechanic's original surprise that I would work night shifts with the crew revealed his association of me with office people who only work days, and my choice to also work nights partially realigned me with the technicians. This temporal syncing also influenced their view of my project as an attempt to understand their perspective rather than an evaluation from above.

During my first shifts with a crew, most people treated me like a trainee, which made sense given that training is the only other situation in which two people ride in equipment together and that I had expressed a desire to learn about their work and their lives. Crewmembers often made jokes to and about me, especially by asking if I was ready to operate the equipment by myself. When the person I was riding with made a mistake, their coworkers made fun of them by asking if I was the one behind the wheel, thereby equating their performance with that of a novice. As time went on, many of the miners with whom I developed the closest relationships began treating me like a coworker or even a coconspirator. A woman who worked in drilling and blasting gave me stakes to help her mark out the next drilling pattern and helped me learn how to operate the drill. A man who drove truck shared all of his tricks for avoiding their supervisor while maintaining the look of a busy, diligent employee. Some dispatch operators eventually showed me the games they played on the Internet during slow times.

Being positioned as a trainee or coconspirator shaped my relationships with people differently than when kinship ties framed our relationship. In conversations with both my former coworkers and family friends, my parents' presence was palpable even if they were not present in the room. My interlocutors often referenced them while telling stories, and I think that they often shared information or opinions with me that they wanted my parents to know. And while full of good-natured teasing and lively debates, my daughterly interactions with family friends and coworkers my parents' age tended to be steered by those in the parenting role. Authority rested with them according to local ideas about parent-child relationships, though I sometimes challenged them, just as their own children would have done (see also Finn 1998: 22). The deference characteristic of these relationships was rarely found in those where I first met people as an anthropologist doing research. My initial positioning at the mines created expectations that I would be the one asking questions, even though our conversations became more balanced the more time I spent with new acquaintances.[25]

These two different entry points illustrate one of the greatest—and most unique—methodological challenges of conducting research in the community in which one grew up: managing the "intimacies that may never have been divulged to an outsider" (Finn 1998: 22; see also Dudley 2000: xiii). As Finn, who conducted research in her hometown community of Butte, Montana, writes, "Friendship, kinship and scholarship make odd bedfellows. . . . As I tell here the stories of the mining community, I am fully implicated in the tensions of trust and betrayal. I have a mandate to tell some stories and guard others" (1998: 22). In this book I follow a similar strategy for managing these tensions and obligations. Engaging in ethnographic research with people with whom I had enjoyed close relationships before becoming an anthropologist—family friends who had watched me grow up, friends who had gone through school with me, and coworkers who had spent countless hours working with me—presented a more immediate intimacy and rapport than did my interactions with people I met for the first time during my research. Negotiating these interactions took careful framing on both our parts. I learned to identify cues—a subtle change in tone or register, a shift in body language or an explicit commentary—indicating that a conversation had crossed the line from friendly catching up to potential ethnographic material and back again.

The unique care it took to manage relationships with longtime acquaintances points to a key difference between the intimacies managed by native ethnographers and their peers. It is common for anthropologists over years of fieldwork to become close with the people among whom they conduct research, often to the point of being considered a member of the community or even kin. But while these intimacies may emerge for ethnographers after years of work with a community, they appear on day one for native ethnographers. Whereas most anthropologists work to create rapport and turn research contacts into close acquaintances, native ethnographers turn friends and family into research subjects. The "differently complex" (Ortner 2003: 17) nature of this work distinguishes anthropologists who work in their own communities from anthropologists who simply work in their own countries. Though both types have participated vocally in debates over the term "native ethnography," it is telling that its fiercest supporters are those who engage in research in the very communities where they grew up.

Caring from a Distance

Doing native ethnography signals a commitment to transforming a discipline long associated with turning places, rituals, and people into exotic specimens (di Leonardo 1998). In fact, this decolonizing aspect is the common denominator of work being done under this banner: "Foregrounding native in relation to anthropology, or oneself as a native anthropologist, can act as an empowering gesture and critique of the position of natives in the stagnant slot of the Other" (Jacobs-Huey 2002: 792). In fact, most advocates of the category's continued use suggest that focusing on intersubjective, reflexive relationships between the anthropologist and others may help to disrupt the discipline's association with otherness. In this vein, my desire to do ethnography that would mean something to the people who made it possible compels my interventions into the dominant exoticized portrayals of the industry in both academic and popular imaginations.

Coal miners hold a particular space in both popular and academic imaginations as oppressed yet hypermasculine workers. The emphasis on dirt, darkness, and danger—cultural historian David Duke's (2002) three Ds of coal mining—places miners in a discursive space similar to Trouillot's (1991) "savage slot" by portraying them as industrialized and oppressed Others. In fact, in Victorian England these factors coalesced in coal miners being regarded as a separate race and often drawn with stereotypically "black" features (John 1980). In the U.S. media, underground and especially Appalachian coal miners continue to be portrayed as a "breed apart," marked by their speech as well as their unfathomably risky labor (Darling 2009; Puckett 2000). Though miners and their families in the Powder River Basin tend to ignore these representational tropes because they find them irrelevant, inaccurate, and offensive, they creep into conversations each time someone makes a self-deprecating joke about being "just a dumb coal miner" or criticizes stereotypes about the industry. This book represents our shared efforts to disrupt these stereotypes, though final responsibility for choosing the material to be included and analyzing it has been mine.

In the chapters that follow I endeavor to make three interventions into dominant representations of mining and miners. The first two challenge the reductive stereotypes about gender relations and working-class politics that pervade mining studies. The third intervention is to assert that the Powder River Basin miners are a key part of an industry that is crucial to the everyday functioning of everyday life in the United States. The almost exclusive focus on Appalachian workers in popular accounts of mining, while vital for understanding and critiquing the industry, nonetheless obscures the role that Wyoming miners play in energy production. The greatest frustration expressed by people during my research was that few people around the country realized that they depended on the miners in Wyoming for their everyday electricity. During one of my interviews with Patty, I asked her what she would like people reading this book to learn about the mining industry in the basin. She criticized the negative and "backward" reputation of the industry that is prevalent in popular media. Poking fun at stereotypes of Wyoming as an empty space where people still ride horses to one-room schoolhouses, Patty laughed and said, "We have electricity!" Then she paused and added, "Because we dig coal!"

John, an engineer who works in management, aptly summarized this critique: "Half of every lightbulb in the U.S. is lit by coal . . . but a lot of people can't think behind the wall." People in Gillette, however, can see the power plants, the railroads, the mine infrastructure, the workforce, and the support industries that all make possible the production of the coal that eventually finds its way into power plants around the United States. They know that keeping the coal moving down the railroads to be burned to create electricity requires not just infrastructure but also the second-by-second efforts of men and women miners to work safely and productively while most people are asleep at home. They know that it also requires daily adjustments by entire families in the seemingly most mundane of activities, such as rearranging mealtimes around the shiftworker so that parents and children can eat together or strategically scheduling social activities so that busy children do not disrupt their parents while they are sleeping during the day in preparation for a night shift.

In these wishes for people around the country to recognize Powder River Basin miners as vital producers of national energy, miners and their families construct an organic critique of what Robert Foster (2008) calls disjunctures and misrecognitions in product networks. Foster traces the efforts of both activists and corporate representatives to link spatially distant people around a particular brand-name or category of consumer goods. For activists, "product-centered politics make visible what is hidden in plain view, namely, the shared concerns (as opposed to shared identities) of people linked, however tenuously, by associations with a worldly thing" (Foster 2008: 237). The structure of the coal industry presents a unique perspective from which to study the construction of such product networks. Unlike the corporations and brands studied by Foster, there is no direct interface between mining companies and the people who consume their product in its final form (Kirsch 2006: 204). Consumers buy electricity from cooperatives, local governments, or private utilities, which in turn purchase it from power plants. Even if people know where these power plants are located, it is unlikely that they also know from which companies and which mines the coal originates. By contrast, miners in Gillette keep the network in view (Kirsch 2001) by keeping track of the power plants to which their companies sell coal. These networks, however, rarely attain public representation except in times of crisis and disaster when Americans are reminded that coal miners still actually exist.

When people in the Powder River Basin express their desire for people around the country to recognize them as the producers of energy, they are calling for what Foster calls caring from a distance (2008: 240).[26] This practice first requires moving beyond commodity fetishism, in which social relations between persons are made to appear as relations between things (Marx 1978 [1887]: 321). In the case of the coal industry, relationships between electricity consumers, producers, and coal miners appear as relations between coal, money, and electricity. But the miners and their families are not simply seeking to correct this misrecognition of people and things; they are also seeking acknowledgment of "the moral relations and ethical responsibilities implicit in the movement of products from one set of hands to another." Caring from a distance is an ethical engagement that "hinges on the respectful and serious regard given by people, connected to each other as agents in a product network, for each other's concerns: a politics of mutual recognition" (Foster 2008: 240). Such a politics of mutual recognition is sorely lacking in contemporary debates about national energy policies, which focus on global warming, the environmental devastation of particular mines, or the tragic loss of human life in specific disasters. Although this is vital for national debate, this attention comes at the expense of sustained, careful consideration of the everyday experiences of the thousands of industry workers who continue reporting for shift after shift, year after year.

Thus, in addition to advancing theories about gender and kinship from the perspective of the workplace, this book is also an effort to counteract the disappearance of Wyoming miners and their families from national imaginations and debates about coal, electricity, and energy policies. I do so not to romanticize them like so many Marxists or demonize them as so many critics do. In the words of a fellow anthropologist whose studies also took her back to the rural, white, working Americans with whom she grew up, it is my hope that this book "leaves caricature behind and wades fearlessly into complexity," recognizing the mining families as "real people, worthy of a good argument rather than reduced to a facile parody, heroic or demonic" (Darling 2009: 32). Clichéd images of miners covered in filthy black coal dust are found everywhere the industry is discussed and debated, from cable news television to the covers of academic books. Everywhere, that is, except for the mines, homes, and public spaces of the Powder River Basin, where people prefer to hang pictures of smiling family members, well-scrubbed crews, or perhaps a particularly impressive bounty from hunting or fishing trips. My greatest concern is that images of filthy, otherworldly miners wearing headlamps emphasize the difference between them and their audience, daring people sitting in their armchairs to ponder what strange breed of people could resign themselves to such unbearable work day in and day out. This book takes greater inspiration from the deceptively ordinary images and stories from the everyday lives of miners in the basin. These are not only more reflective of the miners' everyday hopes and challenges but they invite the empathy, understanding, and sense of connection necessary for the world to take the lives of contemporary miners and their families seriously.

Outline of the Book

Chapter 2 continues the reader's orientation by sketching a history of labor relations in the basin. The Wyoming miners are not unionized and identify themselves as working members of the middle class, a development that confounds popular and academic associations of coal miners with working-class activism. The chapter situates this positioning in relation to the emerging and contested corporate responsibility movement, in which businesses commit to reconiling the pursuit of profit with the protection of people and the environment, which shaped the coal industry's expansion into the Powder River Basin.

Part 2 illustrates the time-based notions of kinship that emerge in the crew and home families. Chapter 3 traces the work of kinship: the ways in which miners craft crew families by collectively embodying the spatial and temporal demands of rotating shiftwork. Chapter 4 examines the translation of time-based notions of kinship and gender from the workplace families back into the community and the miners' homes.

Part 3 examines the moments and configurations in which gender is done and undone at work. Chapter 5 examines everyday talk as a key site for the push and pull of gender difference and similarity. Chapter 6 examines the significance of a distinctly blue-collar work ethic for gender and the creation of workplace relatedness. Miners posit their work ethic as ostensibly gender neutral since it is achievable by both men and women. Though men and women alike successfully embody those ideals, particular workplace features and cultural ideologies make it differently difficult for them to meet those expectations, be considered core members of the crew families, and therefore maintain positions of authority and respect in the workplace.

A brief conclusion synthesizes the book's major arguments in light of the dramatic 2012 coal market collapse, which brought the miners' critiques of the industry and their hopes for their children's futures into sharp relief.

2

Labor Relations and Corporate Social Responsibility

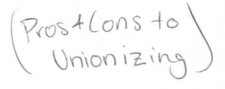
(Pros + Cons to Unionizing)

——————————————————◄○►——

For the past century, mining communities and workplaces have proven productive ground from which to document and theorize the harms of capitalism. As Elizabeth Ferry writes, "The high concentration of capital and labor, territorial isolation, and heavy state intervention make the organization of power and authority, and resistance to it, appear in particularly stark terms in mining contexts" (2005: 6). The legendary danger of mines, infamous examples of corporate negligence, and a celebrated labor movement established miners as icons of working-class struggle. In fact, miners were the only group of workers Friedrich Engels mentioned by name during his 1883 speech at Marx's graveside (1977: 682).[1] In this vein, landmark pieces in anthropology and labor history hone our understanding of the dangers confronted by miners and the limitations of legislation aimed at protecting them (Long 1989; Whiteside 1990); the conceptions and contestations of power that emerge from the mutual imbrication of industrial production in the mines and social reproduction in the home and community (Ferry 2005; Finn 1998; Nash 1993); the differences in age, skill, gender, and ethnicity that contour labor movements (Jameson 1998); the transnational strategies developed by companies to ensure that even labor strife benefits capital (Finn 1998); and the interconnections between environmental and labor history that shape miners' workscapes and possibilities for action (Andrews 2008).

Coal miners in particular dominate scholarly and popular imaginations so much so that the "image of the militant, class conscious coal miner has played a powerful role in constituting knowledges of 'the working class' and 'working-class struggle'" (Gibson-Graham 2006: 208). North American media coverage of the industry reinforces this association, covering the industry's workers almost exclusively during times of tragedy, such as when twenty-nine men perished in April 2010 at West Virginia's Upper Big Branch Mine, the country's deadliest mine accident in four decades. Miners and their families poignantly documented and critiqued the abuses of big business for an outraged audience that was otherwise unaware that the majority of their electricity continues to come from coal. After all, coal conjures up the grit and grime of the Industrial Revolution more easily than the sleekness of smart phones or electric cars.

If ethnography "calls for careful listening to the ways in which people find and make meaning, embody and express feelings, and negotiate their way around the world" (Finn 1998: 233), justly and respectfully engaging the mining families in Wyoming requires moving away from some expectations readers may hold for a book about a mining community. Coal miners in the Powder River Basin consider themselves working members of the middle class rather than working-class people (see also Halle 1984: 203). During the decade from 2000 to 2010 in which I regularly worked and conducted research in the mines, I met only two people who identified as working class; each came from unionized mining families in other states. Although miners have supported unionization in other locations and historical periods, none of the Powder River Basin mines were unionized during my time in Gillette and none of the miners I came to know wanted their workplaces unionized. The two union mines in operation during the 1970s voted to end their affiliation by the early 1980s, and in 1987 the region's only major union organizing campaign ended with the United Mine Workers of America (UMWA) defeated by a margin of three to one.[2] By the time I worked and studied in the mines, stickers with a red diagonal line through the initials UMWA, to indicate opposition to the union, adorned hard hats and lunch boxes. Frustration with cutbacks in health care occasionally provoked threats of unionization to rumble through the ranks, but the majority of the workforce perceived these as strategies to get management's attention rather than as serious calls for organization.

Far from being an anomaly, the nonunion status of Wyoming mines parallels national labor trends. In the decade after World War II, unionization rates of coal miners exceeded 80 percent (Lichtenstein 2002: 56). By 2010, just under 20 percent of the country's ninety-six thousand coal miners and 8 percent of miners overall were unionized, which roughly corresponds with the 11.9 percent national average for all workers in that same year. The decline is even more striking for the over 417,000 people classified as industry support workers, which includes a range from vulnerable temporary contract workers employed by staffing agencies such as Manpower to the well-paid, full-time employees of vendors such as Caterpillar. A paltry 3.2 percent of these workers were union members in 2010 (Hirsch and Macpherson 2011). Even in the symbolic Appalachian heartland of the industry and the UMWA, union membership has withered from the shift to mountaintop removal operations and direct attacks by companies such as Massey Energy (McNeil 2011; Scott 2010). Despite these broad transformations in labor relations, research has been slow to examine the everyday working lives of nonunion miners.[3]

Powder River Basin miners are quick to criticize aspects of their working conditions as well as specific members and policies of management, but they also vociferously defend the industry, including the corporations and personnel within it. This development is unthinkable for observers accustomed to— and more comfortable with—miners serving as the last icons of working-class militancy. Rather than dismissing the miners' everyday thoughts and practices as symptoms of false consciousness, this chapter dives into the cognitive dissonance academics and other observers experience when blue-collar workers actively defend a publicly vilified industry. The miners' defense of the industry, their "precarious economic predicament as well as . . . their contradictory cultural identity" (Darling 2009: 32), can be traced back to the distinct cultural and historical context in which the mines were first opened in the 1970s and 1980s. Labor relations in the basin have been contoured by discourses of corporate social responsibility and decades of negotiation among community members, workers, and companies over what that term means and how it should be practiced.

This analysis elucidates a novel development in the consolidation of capitalism. Contemporary capitalism is defined by the strategic neutralization of critique by corporations that present themselves as responsible actors already monitoring their own performance (Benson and Kirsch 2010). Although internally variegated, the corporate social responsibility (CSR) movement coalesces around the conviction that "doing good" is good for business. The reputation of mining as a harmful industry propelled those corporations to play an especially large role in the CSR movement in order to protect and extend their own operations (Benson and Kirsch 2010; Rajak 2011). Mining companies now publicly commit their operations to minimizing environmental impacts, contributing to local economic development, and integrating the concerns of the surrounding community members into company policies and practices. Grappling with the industry thus requires ethnographic attention to the moral commitments, people, and practices that constitute and defend it (Welker 2009: 166). Filling a gap in scholarship that flattened corporations into monolithic entities, current research fleshes out the lived worlds of mining company personnel and the veritable CSR industry in which they participate. The Wyoming case adds a vital perspective to this research, since rank-and-file workers themselves—rather than just white-collar employees and executives—have become vocal industry defenders.

Starting Over

The mines that would make the Powder River Basin the largest producer of coal in the United States were first planned and permitted in the 1970s, a decade characterized by a growing environmental movement and increased labor unrest. Both developments propelled mining companies to position themselves as responsible corporate citizens; this chapter focuses on the labor dynamics of this process.[4] Wildcat strikes increased throughout Appalachia in the 1970s and culminated with a prolonged 110-day strike in 1977 that was the longest in UMWA history (McNeil 2011: 79). Against a backdrop of the violent repression of those striking miners, company representatives in Wyoming promised a new form of labor relations based on what they called mutual respect. For them, this meant opening and maintaining the mines as nonunion operations. These efforts dovetailed with larger national corporate and government union-busting strategies of the 1970s and 1980s.

Although company representatives went on the public record expressing confidence that the new miners in the basin were too "western" to give up their valuable independence and wages to a union (Brown 1981: A2), they also quietly expressed concern that the region could follow in the footsteps of the historically unionized southwestern section of Wyoming. Even though the state is often characterized as an exceptionally probusiness one, it has a rich history of labor activism. Coal miners in the aptly-named town of Carbon were unionized by 1870. When they struck in 1871, Thomas Wardell, a principal founder of the first major Wyoming coal company, established a precedent for handling labor conflicts in the area: "call on the military for support, fire the troublemakers, and bring in new workers" (Wolff 2003: 23). These tactics were employed by many coal operators throughout the early twentieth century. For example, Patrick Jay Quealy, who operated a collection of coal mines around Kemmerer, often wrote to business associates to warn them of potential union agitators and took care not to hire any known organizers. In 1905, he wrote to his mine foreman: "I have been reliably informed that there is a party of Finlander [Finnish] miners started for Wyoming camps from Ishpeming, Mich., who are iron miners, and expect to work in the coal mines. These men are coming here for the purpose of getting work and then promote Unionism. Will you please make careful investigation of all Finlanders making inquiry for jobs. Find out where they are from before letting them go into the mine, and employ none of these men that you can find out came from Michigan iron mines." Race played a major role in these reorganizations. Like other operators of his time, Quealy brought in large numbers of Japanese workers in order to decrease labor costs and discourage his employees from unionizing. In Rock Springs and Almy, Union Pacific brought in Chinese workers who could serve as a reserve, mobile labor force and divide the workforce (Wolff 2003: 100). Jay Gould, who masterminded Union Pacific's expansion in southern Wyoming, instructed the operator of a new mine at Almy to hire Chinese workers so that "with Chinese at Almy and native miners at the other point, you can play one against the other and thus keep master of the situation" (Gardner and Flores 1989: 43). Dividing the workforce along racial lines led to countless everyday conflicts as well as large-scale race riots, the most famous of which was the 1885 massacre of twenty-eight Chinese miners by whites affiliated with the Knights of Labor in Rock Springs.[5]

The massacre and riot had long-reaching effects for labor relations in Wyoming and nearby northern Colorado. In addition to sparking other conflicts between Chinese and white workers, it increased pressure on the union and the miners belonging to it. Union Pacific used the tragedy to justify mechanizing its mines, reducing the number of employees, and discrediting the unions (Gardner 1990: 32). Immediately following the massacre, the company president wrote a general manager: "Such an opportunity as the Rock Springs massacre is not likely to offer itself again. I shall be greatly disappointed . . . unless this matter is brought to a head. If the Knights of Labor [can] be compelled to stand before the country with their organization in direct alliance with murderers, desperadoes and robbers it would be worth to us almost anything" (Bowers 1999: 49). The Knights of Labor were put in the difficult position of not condoning the violence while still challenging Union Pacific, and tensions increased between the Coal Miners' Amalgamation and the Union Pacific Employee's Protective Association, two umbrella labor organizations active in southwestern Wyoming (Wolff 2003: 104).

Despite these fissures, labor activism continued through the early twentieth century. The UMWA had organized most coal miners along the Union Pacific Railroad by 1907 (Gardner and Flores 1989: 116; Wolff 2003: 222–223). Quealy's personal letters suggest that the furor over the 1913–14 Colorado Coalfield War and the massacre at Ludlow, in which at least eighteen striking coal miners and members of their families (including eleven women and two children) were killed, did not inspire similar revolts and violence in southwestern Wyoming. However, the state's miners did participate in national strikes, including major ones in 1919 and 1922. Labor activity resumed on a large scale once the coal market recovered from a protracted slump to expand again in the 1970s. In 1975, for example, miners in Hanna, Sheridan, and Decker struck against Peter Kiewit and Sons. Evoking previous labor conflicts, the governor promised to use the state patrol to "restore order." Striking miners accused the officers of using tear gas and hitting, kicking, and stomping on the backs of those arrested (Gardner and Flores 1989: 210).

(handwritten margin note: doing everything they could to avoid unionization of workers)

Labor struggles both within and outside of Wyoming thus weighed on the minds of the corporate architects of the industry's expansion into the Powder River Basin. Because the 1960s oil boom in Wyoming had already exhausted the local labor supply, companies had to recruit workers from other areas. Believing that a lack of family history of unionization would dissuade potential recruits from unionizing once on the job, they focused on agricultural rather than mining communities. As one manager who studied the history of union relations in the basin explained, the companies "went and recruited at vocational schools in the Dakotas, looking for young people with good farm values who had no union background, no family union experience. More of what you find in Wyoming, the quote rugged individualist, with all of the point to stay out of a union situation." Company representatives went to great pains to distinguish their responsible approach to labor management with common views of the industry's exploitative paternalism. To back up their claims (and stave off calls for unionization), they offered new hires wages and benefits exceeding those paid in union mines, along with grievance procedures taken directly from union contracts with other energy companies. Unlike the practice in union shops, companies eliminated specialized job titles and positions and classified all hourly employees directly involved in coal processing and equipment maintenance as multiskilled technicians (Smith 2010).[6] These inducements were the foundation of the social contract that companies and employees would negotiate over the next four decades.

While corporate officials discursively positioned their companies as responsible corporate citizens in the early years of the industry, the precise meaning of responsibility and corporate citizenship emerged through negotiations with employees and community members who carried their own expectations for company practice. I trace this negotiation as it unfolded in organized labor conflict and safety management.

Good Neighbors

The Powder River Basin is known throughout the industry for being the first stronghold of nonunion mines, but this status seemed far from inevitable in the 1970s and 1980s. The mine that would become Wyodak, the first surface operation in the region and perhaps the country, was developed in 1924. Employees at the mine and its associated power plant voted to unionize in March 1973. All but four of the qualified employees voted in the election, and the workforce joined the International Brotherhood of Electrical Workers (IBEW) by a final tally of 139 to 86. In May 1984 Wyodak's miners voted to join the UMW. Of the fifty-three workers, thirty-two cast ballots for the UMW, seventeen voted to stay with the IBEW, and four abstained. Power plant employees remained affiliated with the IBEW. Two years later, the forty remaining miners at Wyodak voted to decertify the union, partially because they were earning an average of two to three dollars an hour less than their new, nonunion counterparts in the basin (Smith 2010).

The 1970s and 1980s in the basin were also marked by a major strike and union drive at two of the other new mines. Although this labor activism ultimately compromised the union's position in the basin, it did change the ways in which corporate officials imagined and practiced the responsibility to which they appealed in their engagements with workers and community members.

Belle Ayr, the first of the region's new large surface mines, was opened in 1972 by the Indianapolis-based AMAX corporation. Steeped in traditions from the central and eastern coal regions, management initially tried replicating many of their previous labor practices in Wyoming, for example, by requiring all miners to join a union. In November 1974, miners were committed enough to the union to vote 45–3 in favor of maintaining their representation by the UMWA rather than affiliating with the Progressive Mine Workers.

The region's only major strike began on January 12, 1975, when Belle Ayr miners walked off the job at the behest of the national UMWA leadership. At issue was the company's refusal to pay royalties into the union's welfare and retirement fund and to coordinate the contract of the Belle Ayr miners with those in the eastern United States. After months of stalled negotiations, AMAX reopened the mine in March, announcing that they would take back strikers but would hire new workers if needed. By the beginning of April, thirty-nine out of the fifty-two striking workers opted to return to work under the conditions of the company's final offer, and the company hired an additional six new miners. Miners and their families continued picketing the mine through the summer, and some even traveled to New York in July to demonstrate outside of an AMAX stockholders meeting. In December a labor organization called the North East Wyoming Affiliated Coal Mine Employees (NEWACME) filed a petition for certification at Belle Ayr with the support of seventy-three out of the mine's eighty-three employees. Local UMWA officials publicly speculated that AMAX was behind the new union and urged their former coworkers not to join and lose the bargaining power that stemmed from affiliation with an established national union. The election was postponed because of existing negotiations between AMAX and the UMWA. In the years that followed, the UMWA, NEWACME, and the International Union of Operating Engineers engaged in a three-way battle until the National Labor Relations Board allowed representational elections to take place in 1979. Of the 405 votes cast in the election, the unions collected only thirty-three votes, including sixteen contested ballots. The few community members who remember the strike speak about it producing or exacerbating tensions among the workforce without reaching its goals.

While the strike ultimately diminished the power of organized labor, it did prompt significant changes in corporate discourse. When the mine first opened, the company's public relations campaigns reflected a paternalistic attitude. During the strike, the company ran an ad featuring a sketch of the country singer Loretta Lynn and the title of her popular song "Coal Miner's Daughter": "I'm Loretta Lynn. You know, my daddy was a coal miner in Eastern Kentucky. Coal has always been a part of my life . . . a tradition. But what is breaking that tradition is the way coal is mined today. Companies like AMAX Coal have made things different for the miners. It's still hard work. But there's better pay, shorter hours, and more concern about health, safety and protecting our environment. America needs coal more than ever before. I'm proud of the mining business, and still proud that I'm a coal miner's daughter." Beneath this text, Lynn suggests that people wishing to learn more about how AMAX is meeting the needs of "Energy, the People and the Environment" should write to the company for a free brochure. The ad is striking for its paternalistic form of kinship: not only is Lynn a coal miner's daughter, but the company is portrayed as taking care of its miners. She attributes better working conditions and pay to the benevolence of the company instead of the long history of activism by miners and their families. Run during the only major strike in the basin, it suggests that miners should be grateful for what the companies have given them instead of seeking more.

After the strike was settled, the company's public relations officers moved away from the paternalistic messages of years before. For example, the following ad from the late 1970s evidences a key change in phrasing: "A vital industry is a good neighbor too. . . . We are equally committed to the proposition that we can produce more coal in this country without exploiting labor or spoiling the environment. Advanced technology has turned the coal miner into a highly paid, highly skilled professional. His health and safety and the welfare of his family are of vital concern to us." In the updated version, the miner is a highly paid and skilled professional rather than a beneficiary of corporate goodwill, and the company implies at least a limited partnership in portraying itself as a good neighbor—a term that would become ubiquitous throughout the region.

The companies who followed in AMAX's footsteps took the lesson of the strike to heart. In advertising campaigns, they presented themselves as members of the community and their companies as a less paternalistic family. For example, Kerr McGee ran an ad from the late 1970s through the 1990s that declared, "We're mining folks too!" Underneath a collage of pictures of people who are presumably employees the text reads: "We're proud of our Wyoming people who are an important part of the Kerr-McGee family . . . Our Wyoming mining operations, purchases, and conservation programs make us partners with all of the people of Wyoming in putting natural resources to work for all of us." Similarly, a 1980 Carter Mining ad featured a large picture of what appears to be a husband and his wife with a set of children's puppets they use in their community volunteering. The text states: "Our people are people you know. That's because they're your neighbors, and they share the community you live and work in. Some may be better known to other members of your family . . . to your children, your parents, or your grandparents." It then introduces the couple as employees of the company who are committed to volunteer work because they, "like the rest of us at Carter Mining, know that it's just as important to produce good neighbors as it is to produce coal." Finally, Caballo Rojo ran ads in the 1980s with the motto, "Working with the people of Wyoming to effectively manage and market Wyoming's natural resources while protecting its environment." In these ads, the companies portray themselves as a distinctly local partner that provides the state a needed service: successfully managing the public's natural resources.

Though AMAX's opening appeal to residents of the Powder River Basin was grounded in good corporate citizenship, the meaning of that responsibility changed from outright paternalism to softer partnerships as workers and their families pushed back against the company during the strike. These changes in corporate discourse were grounded in a symbolic shift of the industry from Loretta Lynn's Appalachia to an idealized West. Even if actual partnership is ultimately limited by the financial power of the industry in a nondiversified economy, the language of partnership provided a symbolic resource for employees to challenge future company officials and policies. These developments are clearly illustrated in the region's other major organized labor event: the 1987 UMWA drive at Black Thunder Mine.

Cowboys or Coal Miners

In 1987, Black Thunder Mine employees turned to the UMWA when they became frustrated with decisions being made by a management team undergoing personnel changes. Many miners were upset that they had been left out of decisions to change seniority policies, and some believed they should be receiving daily overtime pay for working twelve hours in a row (instead of eight) rather than receiving it only after they had worked over forty hours in a week. They were also concerned that the mine's turn to contract labor in the midst of a soft coal market would put their jobs at risk. Labor tensions in the basin were high, as miners in the southern end read daily stories about a violent strike ongoing at the Decker mine near the Montana border. Union organizers collected sufficient cards to order an election, and the entire community became embroiled in discussions about the benefits and disadvantages of unionizing. Though the cards had been collected by late summer and early fall, the election was postponed until after the fall hunting season, which gave the company more time to present their position to the miners. When the votes were finally tallied, all but eleven of the 374 workers had participated in the election and had voted against the UMWA by a six-to-one margin.

Considering that union officials said that they would not conduct an election without the commitment of 60 to 70 percent of the workforce, the eventual decisive defeat of the union merits close attention. Letters to the editor published in the local newspapers during the campaign and interviews with former and current miners reveal that while job security ostensibly occupied a central role in the conflict—with both company officials and miners arguing that nonunion worksites were more secure since they were also more profitable—questions of personhood underlined the debates. The stances taken by organizers, company officials, and miners were informed by distinct conceptions of work, personhood, and workplace relationships that were crystallized in the competing imagery of ranchers and coal miners.

In speeches and letters, Black Thunder's president emphasized themes of trust and partnership, the proposed pillars of new labor practices at the mines, in comparison to the antagonism he and other executives attributed to union operations. During the campaign, company president Jim Herickhoff published an open letter to mine employees in the local newspaper:

> The people of Campbell County, the state of Wyoming, and the West have established a proud tradition of standing tall and then facing and beating whatever hardships might come their way. From the early days to now, Wyoming people still hold these values steadfastly and place a premium on dealing person to person, eyeball to eyeball and honoring a handshake which closes a deal.
> ... We built into our employee programs opportunities for employees to grow and develop into the kind of person who stands on his/her own two feet and is proud of the ability to operate and repair some of the largest machinery in the world. [Herickhoff 1987: 5]

He then argued that the solution to the problems at the mine can be found in their own history: "Proud Westerners have fiercely defended their right to deal straight on with a person when a problem develops—not through some third party who takes their money and really can't deliver."

The images painted by the company president linked miners with a western history of hard work and perseverance rather than the labor history of mining. He referred to the employees as technicians, not as miners, and highlighted the technical aspects of operating and repairing heavy equipment.[7] He also argued that western workers have no need for unions or other mediating parties to settle their problems because they were strong enough to do so themselves. He portrayed the miners as enjoying relationships of mutual trust and respect with the managers, with whom they can stand "eyeball to eyeball," obviating the need for unions and contracts. The letter is similar to more general corporate discourse in its emphasis on the themes of trust and partnership, the proposed pillars of the "new" labor practices envisioned by corporate officials.

Likening Powder River Basin miners to ranchers was a long-established practice in the basin. As corporations began opening mines in the late 1970s and early 1980s, their representatives began publicly highlighting the distinctive "westernness" of the new operations. For example, a 1981 *Washington Post* article focused on the companies' efforts to "best unions at [the] benefits game." The author quoted E. H. Lovering, the employee relations manager of the Carter Mining Company, explaining why the nonunion approach was appropriate for the new workforce: "The individuals out here seem to be open, free, primarily rancher-types from small-town backgrounds. They've battled the elements all of their lives and survived. They don't take too kindly to being organized" (Brown 1981: A2). Likening miners to ranchers rather than cowboys is significant, since the former evokes western independence in the context of responsible capitalist ownership and management, whereas the latter can be more easily compared with exploited proletarians.[8]

What both the *Post* article author and the coal company president failed to mention was that company officials simply did not "find" such a fiercely independent workforce already in Gillette, but actively created it to support their own business goals: they specifically recruited workers from rural, nonunion farming and ranching communities both locally and in nearby states to decrease the chances that they would unionize and potentially interrupt production. As Lovering explained in the article, "The union-free approach is a very practical thing. . . . For one thing, we don't have strikes or other work disruptions." He explained that with more flexible work rules, companies have better control over production since they can move employees into the positions where they are needed the most (see also Gardner and Flores 1989: 213). Portraying the mines as uniquely western operations helped corporate officials downplay potential labor conflicts, since dominant popular portrayals of "the West" erase the class dynamics that give shape to it. Idealized western labor resonates more closely with ranchers rather than industrialized, wage-working miners.[9]

These images of miners as independent ranchers stand in stark contrast to the tropes utilized by union organizers in speeches and letters. They most often emphasized the image of "union brothers and brotherhood," in which men would work together to achieve common goals in the face of oppression from management.[10] The main UMWA organizer, Keith Barnhart, saw his role in the community as an educational one, stripping away the images of unions as corrupt strongmen and replacing them with images of family-oriented workers who want to help others protect themselves against corporate greed. He was quoted as saying, "We're going to be here. We've made that commitment. The coal companies have the Wyoming Mining Association, and the miners will sooner or later realize they need us. It's a matter of unity" (D. Daly 1987: 13). Very few miners adopted this language of mutual assistance and brotherhood, even though they often spoke about their coworkers as being "like family." Believing that unions would threaten the job security on which they depended to raise their families, they rejected the union's family-like class of workers because they thought joining it would imperil their nuclear families at home.[11]

Rather than critiquing corporations for pursuing profit, miners partially aligned themselves with them in order to boost their own financial earnings. During the union drive, for example, one miner went so far as to write that it was the "duty of a company to make money" and that the miners would become wealthy if they supported the companies rather than the union. Another wrote that since the union could not guarantee that strikes would not take place or that they would deliver on their promises to improve working conditions, unionizing would be a "high-risk investment. . . . We cannot put everything we have on the line for vague promises of a better return." Miners employed market logic to assess their best chances of financial security, concluding that the union was "just another business" that would threaten their jobs by decreasing the profitability of the company. This reasoning paralleled the official company response to the union drive. President Herickhoff publicly speculated that the UMWA was searching for new members because more efficient nonunion operations were outproducing their unionized counterparts, putting the union in financial trouble. He argued, "The only time a person has a job is if you have a profitable company. If you don't have profits, you don't have a company and you don't have jobs" (Smith 2010: 108–111).

This parallel market reasoning emerged not because miners blindly swallowed the company line but because it resonated with their own work histories and hopes for their family's future. With no family attachments to unions, they viewed security as better guaranteed by affiliation with profitable companies rather than other miners around the country. Miners in the basin continue to view their jobs as the bedrock of their families' financial success. Production employees in the pit, plant, and shop are paid hourly based on their skill level, with annual salaries ranging from about $65,000 to $100,000 and above for senior technicians who work overtime. As a longtime equipment operator summarized his career: "In defense of mining, I've never missed a paycheck in twenty years. I have good credit and a good 401(k). It's always paid the bills." Because salaried personnel are not paid for overtime, all but the highest-level managers frequently make less than the rank-and-file.

Miners' substantial wages facilitate their participation in the national expansion of the folk category of the "middle class" to include Americans from the working poor to the very wealthy (Descartes and Rudd 2008; Ortner 2003). Miners own their own houses in the same neighborhoods as doctors, lawyers, and mine managers; drive new trucks and SUVs; travel around the country and the world on vacation; and send their children to college and to trade schools. Since most companies have shifted their retirement plans from pensions to 401(k)s, many are avid investors who religiously follow the ups and downs of financial markets, setting down their lunch pail at home after work to watch the financial channel CNBC or look up ticker prices on the Internet. As employment in the United States and around the world becomes increasingly precarious, these miners may represent one of the last groups of blue-collar workers able to achieve historically middle-class living standards and consumption practices.

The defeat of the 1987 union drive therefore consolidated a distinctly regional identity for the Powder River Basin mines as well as a particular form of middle-class identification among miners and their families. Positioning themselves as *working* members of the middle class allowed miners to bring together their pride in working a demanding blue-collar job with their pride in providing the key elements of the American dream for their families.[12] Although this complex class positioning benefits mining companies by dissuading identification with working-class people and movements, it also benefits mining families who are able to send their children to college and save for retirement while living comfortably. Continued high wages and sizeable benefits thus became a key component of the social contract between miners and companies. Responsible companies were profitable enterprises that paid miners generously, bluntly illustrating the idea that the confluence of "moral mission and market rationalism is not only central to the performance of corporate social responsibility, but fundamental to the production and expansion of corporate capitalism" (Rajak 2011: 31).

This accord, however, would have been fragile without the other major component of the social contract that the union drive renewed. One of the reasons miners voted against the union is that they perceived a shift in company officials' willingness to listen to them. As one miner articulated:

I believe the mine manager is sincere in trying to help the employees regain a higher morale and an improved workplace. I am thankful for having a job that not only pays good wages, but has a superb benefit program, and especially so in these economic times. I have been able to voice my opinions to management in the past, and I will continue to do so. I may not get everything I want, but I have been listened to, and some results were achieved. As long as management will respect my opinions, and me as an employee, I will respect management. Therefore I do not feel the need for a union here at this time. [Whetstone 1987: 2]

Management's perceived willingness to listen to employees and take their concerns seriously continues to weave through miners' evaluations of companies and personnel. One miner recalled that whenever his coworkers started talking about unionization, management "stepped up to the plate and started listening to the concerns people had. . . . They took more of an involved approach. I think things did get better. Before, you couldn't hardly get anybody to listen to you if you came up with an idea." This notion of "listening" to employees is a hallmark of the new labor relations and a crucial element of the industry's appeals to corporate social responsibility. The extent to which companies changed practices based on employee input can be seen in recent negotiations over safety programs.

Responsibility for Safety, Safety for Responsibility

The ethnographic and historical context of the Powder River Basin mines requires a distinct approach to studying mining as a fulcrum of capitalist power, since the negotiation of power between miners and managers rarely takes the form of entrenched battles with clearly divided camps, but manifests in struggles over the interpretation of company policies, especially those related to safety. Since the mines first opened in the 1970s, safety has figured prominently in the companies' appeals to corporate social responsibility. First, the region's labor shortages made it a key issue for companies in their labor and community relations. Because potential employees entertained multiple job offers, they asked friends and acquaintances about the actual attitudes and practices of companies on the worksite and chose to work at the mines whose commitment to safety in the workplace matched or exceeded their public promises. Second, the mines were opened during a national reevaluation of mine safety regulations. The 1977 establishment of the federal Mine Safety and Health Administration (MSHA) strengthened state regulation of the industry's labor practices and increased public pressure on the industry to improve its dismal record of workplace accidents and deaths.[13]

The Powder River Basin mines are some of the safest in the entire country. From 2000 to 2010 5 miners died in the basin. Totals for the same period were 349 nationally, with 129 in West Virginia, 86 in Kentucky, 18 in Pennsylvania, 17 in Virginia, and 5 in Ohio. The Powder River Basin fatality rate is low even when controlling for the fewer number of employees and production hours worked. Since 1983, the year for which MSHA data becomes available, the highest incidence rate (including fatalities, nonfatal days lost cases, and medical treatment cases) per mine in the basin was 4.4 in 1987, with the lowest being 0.73 in 2008. For all mines east of the Mississippi, in contrast, the highest rate was 11.74 in 1988 with lowest being 4.0 in 2011. From 1983 to 2011 the average rate was 2.14 in the basin and 7.9 in the East.[14] This accomplishment is traceable to decades of negotiation between miners and management over company responsibility for dignified and effective safety management.

Discipline and Punish

Longtime miners remember the early years of the industry for being joyfully free of bureaucracy. "All of us—managers, operators, everybody—were figuring out how to do this together," explained Roger. "We didn't have any paperwork or anything because we didn't need it. We made our own systems for handling everything, from training people on equipment to safety." During this time miners developed an informal system in which they would publicly identify and discuss how to mitigate immediate hazards without pointing blame at specific crewmembers, saving those critiques for private conversations. These strategies preserved each other's dignity since they did not question each other's competence or intelligence in front of others. This collective responsibility for each other's well-being underlined the intense sense of kinship and camaraderie developed among crewmembers (this is discussed in detail in chapter 3).

These informal strategies came under pressure as the mines were bought out by larger companies and employees found their everyday actions increasingly constrained by policies emanating from boardrooms rather than the mine itself. Companies instituted formal safety programs that tracked incidents and linked them to individual offenses. For instance, to identify and then address patterns of risks, management encouraged employees to turn in reports that explained the details of accidents and "near misses," including the names of all involved parties. People identified as engaging in unsafe behaviors were then punished according to the severity of the infraction: formal warnings, temporary expulsion from the worksite, and permanent dismissal. Most mines offered incentives to employees who would voluntarily turn in these reports. The humorous yet pointed criticism of this type of program is evident in the nickname crews assigned to a program in which employees who turned in unsafe coworkers were eligible to receive a free meal at a local restaurant: Squeals for Meals. These programs also increased tensions between miners and their immediate supervisors, who were responsible for implementing the programs despite pushback from their crews. As Jack explained, "We were like brothers and sisters; we would always cover each other's butt. We were taking care of each other. If somebody did something they shouldn't be doing, you didn't tell the foreman. You'd tell them . . . I would tell them, 'Hey, this isn't right.'" Jack was like most miners in minimizing his participation in official programs because they contradicted crew camaraderie and their collective— rather than individual—responsibility for managing risk.

A conflict between a supervisor named Wally and his crew underscores the tensions generated by this style of safety program. One summer morning Wally became embroiled in a heated argument with Tim, one of the crew's most experienced members. Afternoon temperatures were routinely reaching over one hundred degrees and even the most well air-conditioned equipment cabs were hot, prompting most people to shut down and refuse to operate equipment with faulty air conditioners. Mack, a temporary employee, had revealed the previous evening that the haul truck he had driven all day lacked air conditioning. Word spread quickly, and at the preshift meeting the next morning, Tim announced that no one should operate equipment without air conditioning because it could dehydrate the operator, putting them as well as the entire crew at risk. Wally countered that it was an individual decision, but Tim persisted. Raising his voice, he argued that it was the supervisor's responsibility to make it an official rule since temporary workers seeking to get hired on full-time felt pressure to demonstrate their productivity and would therefore avoid shutting down equipment at all costs. "We're a family, we have to watch out for each other," he said. Referring to his previous experience as a supervisor, he said, "That's the way we did it on my crew." Wally also raised his voice and ended the discussion by repeating that anyone who felt the need to shut down equipment should make that call individually. After the meeting was officially over and the crew started filing out the doors to go out to the pit, Tim announced that no one should operate unsafe equipment. "No one will blink an eye," he said. "Just do it."

The supervisor, presumably acting on behalf of the company to obey safety regulations while maintaining high production levels, sought to individualize risk; he argued that it was the choice of each operator to determine the safety of equipment. Conversely, Tim sought to socialize the risk by pointing out that each supposedly individual choice affected the entire crew; he argued that it was the responsibility of the crew family—including its supervisor—to protect the safety of the more vulnerable temporary worker.[15] Tim's assertion of collective responsibility echoed the more informal, nondisciplinary strategies miners had historically used to protect one another in the workplace: miners watched out for one another because they were a family, not because it was a rule. Note that Tim made his appeal to safety not by engaging company policy, but by disrupting it. Moreover, he eventually asserted himself in the interstitial space and time between the supervised meeting and start of the workday. This vignette shows how miners during the 1990s actively socialized responsibility for mitigating workplace risk by going outside the companies' official safety programs.

Collectivizing Responsibility

Three fatal accidents took place between 2002 and 2003, prompting companies in the basin to rethink their existing measures for safety management. Most instituted behavior-based safety programs in which employees, rather than managers, would formally monitor their crewmembers' practices as well as their own. Workers' advocates criticize these programs because "instead of management's taking responsibility for eliminating hazards and providing safe working conditions, blame is placed on workers who make mistakes" (Barab 2003: 13). These programs are also problematic in viewing injury "not as a structural premise of capitalism and a condition of its possibility but as an accidental side effect—a problem that can be rectified at the level of the individual and the particular facts of her case" (Jain 2006: 3). Succinctly, these programs transform workers from potential victims to offenders (Gray 2006, 2009).

Miners initially approached the new programs with skepticism. On my first day of research at one mine, I attended a preshift meeting along with the rest of the crew to learn about their new safety program. The miner in charge of the volunteer committee overseeing the program began by asking how many people were satisfied with the current state of safety at the mine. Only half raised their hands. The crew's normally high morale was waning because of the accidents that had occurred at the mine, prompting many to seek work at neighboring mines or in the booming coalbed methane industry. The committee members promised that the new program would make the mine safer because it would correct the underlying practices that caused accidents. The miner who introduced the new safety program to his crew acknowledged his coworkers' frustrations and promised that the new program was a long-term strategy for making the mine a safer place to work. He then compared their current "reactive" practice of raising hazard awareness after an accident occurred with the new "proactive" approach that would address the underlying behaviors leading to such accidents. Like many other safety personnel in the basin, he spoke about the false sense of security that came from engaging in unsafe behaviors without any negative consequences: "Once you get away with it once, twice, three times you start thinking that it's safe and that it's not a risk anymore." According to him, the new program was designed to identify and correct such entrenched behaviors.

The program encourages miners to monitor their peers and internalize a critical perspective on their own behavior through a system of formalized peer observations. Miners volunteer to be trained as observers who spend a few shifts away from their normal duties observing their coworkers' work behaviors. As they are watching, they fill out a form that categorizes and rates the observed person's behavior according to specific areas of concern identified by the committee based on a survey of incident reports. After ten minutes, the observer shares their findings with their coworker, taking particular care to emphasize the good practices they noted first before discussing the potentially unsafe ones. The two miners then discuss and evaluate the degree to which the safest behavior was or was not enabled by the surrounding conditions. For example, when touching a shovel cable, miners are always supposed to wear hot gloves that have been tested for holes because of the cable's high voltage, but some routinely do not. The safer behavior would be considered "enabled" if the hot gloves were tested and available in pickups, "difficult" if the gloves had been moved and the miner would have to drive back to the shop to pick them up, and "non-enabled" if there were no gloves available on the worksite. Crucially, miners are expected to use the points raised in the discussion to continue monitoring themselves and improving their own work habits. The information from these sheets is then compiled so that the committee can identify patterns of problems and brainstorm solutions for them. In turn, the managerial "barrier removal team" evaluates and possibly facilitates the implementation of these solutions.[16]

Yet as the miners quickly noted, these programs potentially placed responsibility for the mitigation of risk squarely on individuals who were expected to monitor their own practices and decisions on a second-by-second basis. After the committee's speaker finished speaking at the introductory meeting, the mine manager took the floor for the first time and asked the crew to be patient and open-minded, promising that results would come but not immediately. He then reiterated his and management's commitment to the program before opening up the floor to questions. The first response was a request for clarification on what constituted a "behavior." The speaker distinguished the concept from "attitude" and said that it was something that could be captured in a picture. One of the most experienced miners then suggested that the program did not fully address the problem of unsafe working conditions and gave examples of accidents that were the result of tools or equipment being in bad condition. The committee's speaker responded that choosing to use unsafe tools and equipment was a behavior and therefore encompassed by the program. Another miner pointed out that the "S" curves in one of the pits were so tight that haul trucks nearly touched each other, and the manager promised to look into the situation. He also promised to consider adding more light plants (portable light towers used to illuminate work areas at night) to the dump after a request was made for them to provide better visibility on the roads during night shifts. The miners' initial responses can all be viewed as attempts to deindividualize the program, drawing attention away from behaviors to external conditions. For them, the collective responsibility for managing risk encompassed management as well as the rank and file.

When the miners actually put the new program into practice, they further diminished its individualizing potential by embedding it within the already existing framework of crew kinship and collective responsibility for safety. "It's not hugely different from what we were doing before," explained Nate. "Sure you have to fill out the paperwork and officially do so many observations throughout the year, but the heart of it is the same: people watching out for each other in a respectful way. We're helping each other be the safest we can be." Like most of his coworkers, Nate did not place ultimate responsibility with the individual, but with the entire crew. "Of course safety starts with the individual. We all have to do our best." He then clarified, "But it's more than that. Nobody is out there on their own: we're all watching out for each other."

The introduction of paperwork into the collective process of creating safe workplaces ideally would not threaten their close-knit relationships because it is anonymous, unlike the previous disciplinary-focused programs that punished workers exhibiting questionable practices. The observed miners remain nameless: only the observer's name appears on the evaluation form, and supervisors are not supposed to know or ask who has been observed.[17] Crews appreciate this anonymity and liken it to the types of conversations they had previously. Brad said, "There's some guys who take safety the wrong way and think, you know, they need to belittle people when they're telling them to be safe. They do it in front of a whole bunch of people and say, 'Hey, you're not doing this or that or wearing your seat belt.' But I think a one-on-one with somebody is the best way to do it, and the new program covers that real well." Brad's evaluation of the program is significant because he draws a parallel between the new safety program and the informal one that crews previously established in contrast to the official disciplinary one. For him, both encourage safety by building on, rather than threatening, the crew's kin-like relationships.

At the heart of the negotiation between the rank and file and management over the implementation of the safety program therefore is a contestation over company responsibility for workers' well-being. In the face of a program that potentially placed responsibility for safety on the individual, the crews asserted a long-standing collective responsibility for safety that included management's obligation to provide a safe workplace: individual "choices" were constrained by management's allocation of resources, such as light plants, and engineering decisions, such as the shape of haul roads. Significantly, this framing was supported by members of management, who also maintain their commitment to enacting the concrete changes in working conditions suggested by the safety committee. "We're all in this together," explained one safety manager, adopting the collective framing. "Everybody out there is doing whatever they can to make this mine safe, and I'm going to do the same from here. Whatever it takes. It's all of our responsibility. We've got to watch out for our family out here to make sure that everyone goes home to their family at the end of the day." When managers discussed the program, they willingly adopted the miners' language of collective responsibility, suggesting that they felt compelled to engage the miners' already existing informal safety management strategies in the new program.

The extent to which management would implement that collective framing in practice was a source of debate at the beginning. Echoing concerns that audits are nothing more than "rituals of verification" (Power 1997) that monitor the auditing process rather than substantial improvements in practice, the primary worry of most miners was that the so-called barrier removal team might not actually put into practice the changes suggested by the committee—especially if these changes could decrease profit margins. The first hint of resistance to implementing miners' safety suggestions was clear at the initial meeting when the manager hesitated to comply with the request for more light plants. As one seasoned miner wryly commented to me later, "I'll guarantee that we'll never see them make any big changes because it'd be too expensive. You know what we need? Enough mechanics, parts, and time to fix all of this old, broken-down equipment. You know what we'll get? The same old promises. Nothing ever really changes with these things." Other miners, though skeptical, retained confidence in management's commitment to following through with the program. The opinion of one relatively new miner was typical of this view: "I believe in the program. I think if we give it a chance it'll work. And I guess I trust that management is actually going to do something about it."[18]

Although miners are still critical of some management decisions, the collective orientation of the safety programs remained in place five years after the programs were first implemented.[19] An indication of the program's success is the improved safety record of the mines instituting them. Both the MSHA and the Wyoming Mine Safety and Inspection office recognized one of the mines under study for having a perfect safety record in 2007, the first year of the new program. According to MSHA records, the mine also decreased the number of nonfatal days lost from around fifteen in 2006 to under ten in 2007 and under five in 2008, despite continuous increases in the number of operator hours worked. The mine's MSHA citations also dropped from around seventy in 2006 to less than fifty in 2007, less than forty in 2008, and less than thirty in 2010. Other mines in the basin show comparable improvements. The average incidence rate in the basin as a whole (including fatalities, nonfatal days lost cases, and medical treatment cases) has decreased since the programs were instituted, from 1.253 in 2006 to 0.799 in 2011. The negotiations over the safety program shows that rather than being handed down in final form from company public relations offices, "responsibility" is actively debated and constructed in the workplace.

Constructing an Anti-Appalachia

In the Powder River Basin the significance of region weaves through the discourses and practices of corporate social responsibility from the earliest years of its development in the 1970s through the first decade of the twenty-first century. This finding underscores Dinah Rajak's argument that the practice of corporate social responsibility rests on the twinned processes of abstraction and recontextualization: corporate actors appeal to the universal salience of moral and market values but must embed and engage them in resolutely local frameworks. The first company to open a large-scale mine in the basin initially engaged residents and workers with a public relations campaign steeped in imagery and discourses more characteristic of Appalachia than Wyoming. The paternalism evident in the Loretta Lynn ad disappeared after a lengthy strike and public debate about the role of the company in the community. The companies that opened mines after the strike self-consciously grounded their campaigns in idealized images and values associated with Wyoming and the American West. This representational work played a large role in company actions during the 1987 union drive, which found a company president enjoining miners to identify with specifically western ideologies of hard work rather than broader labor histories of coal miners' struggles.

Distinctions between the imagined West and an Appalachian Other continue to animate the ways in which the rank and file and managers alike defend the Wyoming mines in public statements, ethnographic interviews, and informal conversations. These positive appraisals are grounded in perceived economic as well as cultural differences between the two regions. The case of West Virginia is emblematic of energy development failing to benefit local populations, especially as mechanization has increased. As coal production and profits have risen, the population has actually become more impoverished. Anthropologist Brian McNeil reports that from 1996 to 2001, Boone County led a surge in production unmatched in the state's history; in that same period the county's unemployment rate doubled (from 5.6 to 10.4 percent) and the rate of students classified as low income increased 7.6 percent to reach 57 percent of the population (2011: 114). The state as a whole ranks at the bottom of all states in economic indicators such as household income, education, and access to the Internet (McNeil 2011: 116).

Aware that this economic hardship underlines popular stereotypes of miners as exploited victims, Wyoming miners take pride in their ability to comfortably support their families with their substantial wages. In 2010 Wyoming's median household income ranked in the top twenty in the country. That year the state's unemployment rate hovered around 5 percent, with Campbell County (home to most of the mines and employees) at 4 percent. From 2006 to 2010 in the county, the median household income was $76,576 and the home ownership rate was 75.7 percent. In 2010 households headed by the main cohort of miners (people aged 45 to 64) had median incomes of $90,821. The state as a whole also benefited financially from the industry. In 1974 Governor Stan Hathaway established the Permanent Mineral Trust Fund to invest a percentage of taxes collected from the coal as well as oil and gas industries for the welfare of future generations. The fund specializes in promoting educational opportunities, primarily by offering college scholarships, building new schools and libraries, and expanding the University of Wyoming (Gardner and Flores 1989: 199–203). In 2010 the balance reached over $4.5 billion despite expenditures on major infrastructure and scholarship projects.[20]

In the minds of Powder River Basin residents, the economic divide between Wyoming and West Virginia is laminated on top of perceived cultural differences.[21] People in the basin disavow potential occupational relatedness with Appalachian miners, though their understanding of the region is grounded in stereotypes rather than firsthand experience. Wyoming miners boast about the technological sophistication and enormous cost of the equipment they operate (and often even repair) in the outdoors. Tellingly, equipment operators point to their ability to spend all day outside, watching wildlife and appreciating the scenery, as one of the things they loved most about their jobs. Gary reported telling his distant family that he "saw nothing but blue sky all day." Jack said he originally needed more details before taking a job at the mine, because "I ain't no groundhog. I wanted to know if I could see the stars instead of a hole." Since he had moved from Kentucky and had family working in the mines there, he enjoyed comparing the two regions. "It's the difference between daylight and dark," he said, referring to underground mining, but then noted that "back there they've been doing strip mining for the last fifteen to twenty years." Gary and Jack, like other Americans, reinforce popular understandings of Appalachian mining as underground work, even though the industry there also increasingly relies on mountaintop removal methods (McNeil 2011; Scott 2010). Across the country and the globe miners are statistically more likely to operate multimillion-dollar equipment in the open air than swing a pickax in a tunnel, but the dominant stereotype of underground manual labor is difficult to dislodge.

Crucially, the distinction between Wyoming and Appalachia also underlines the appeals company representatives make to the social and environmental responsibility of the Wyoming mines. In a meeting recruiting college engineering students to work for one of the companies, a midlevel executive expressed frustration that "people don't understand how differently we operate here." In an interview, Patty, an equipment operator who worked her way into safety management, expressed a common criticism of the negative and "backward" reputation of the industry that is prevalent in popular media: "We do so much to protect the land. We're supplying power basically to the country. We do it well. We are careful with the land, the animals, and the people. I would like people from other parts of the country to know that it's clean, safe—not the *Coal Miner's Daughter* mentality. I don't know how you say all that, but we're pretty normal out here." To defend the industry in Wyoming, Patty references a film iconic of Appalachian culture and mining, marking Appalachia as the Other by describing Wyoming as normal. Susie, an environmental engineer, is similarly proud of her company's efforts to be good environmental stewards and wanted to be sure that my research reflected that commitment: "That's not the company line. I don't want to sound like a corporate billboard, but we do want to do the right thing because all these people who live in Wyoming live here because they want to. They enjoy the outdoors in some regards more than others. We don't want to trash our environment because this is where we play and work. What family would want to do that?" Even the annual reports of mining corporations whose primary operations are in the West self-consciously feature western discourses of innovation and freedom from tradition, along with imagery ranging from mountains and ranches to rolling plains and charismatic wildlife happily coexisting with markers of industry. An environmental manager could not have been blunter: "We are not Appalachia. When people think coal mining, they think Appalachia, but we couldn't be more different from them." Asserting the environmental and social responsibility of the Wyoming mines rests on portraying the Appalachian mines as archetypes of irresponsibility.

Conclusion

Scholarly and public debates about CSR too frequently dissolve into polarized appraisals of the practice, with critics portraying it as a vast public relations sham and supporters praising it as a hallowed solution for reconciling markets with morality. In this chapter I join a growing effort to move away from this polarization to see what CSR discourses and practices actually do in particular ethnographic contexts. In the Powder River Basin, appeals to responsibility smoothed the expansion of the coal industry into a region initially skeptical of development. This observation corroborates Rajak's argument that CSR sustains capitalism by providing corporations with "a moral mechanism through which their authority is extended over the social order" (2011: 13). In Wyoming, the companies' moral authority was publicly negotiated through their responses to labor activism as well as on-site contestation over safety management. The specific form of responsibility espoused by representatives thus emerged from direct dialogue and confrontation with their critics, as is prevalent throughout the CSR movement in general and the mining industry in particular (Benson and Kirsch 2010; Rajak 2011; Welker 2009, 2012). The interplay of labor relations in the basin demonstrates that even if CSR initiatives are imperfectly realized, they nonetheless transform social relationships and imaginaries, providing a discourse through which miners and managers alike assess corporate practice and position themselves in relation to other sectors of the industry.

Although CSR facilitated the industry's expansion on terms largely favorable to it, mining families and the wider community also benefited financially from this development without sacrificing their safety or dignity at work. A large part of the miners' loyalty to the general industry and specific companies stems from their solid middle-class standing, especially as they watch opportunities disappear for people without college degrees to find well-paying, steady employment. Their ability to provide their families with homes, health insurance, and educational opportunities exceeds the expectations they held as young adults. Al's thoughts on the significance of his job were common. "I've been able to pay for my home," he said. "You know, I can remember that when I was first working, I never even dreamed that you would ever even own a home, let alone own one free and clear."

Thus, crucial to the Wyoming case was the companies' facilitation of a partial alignment between their interests and those of the rank-and-file employees they specifically recruited to ease the task of building the industry in the basin. Miners heartily resist policies that endanger the safety of themselves and their crews and boldly criticize managers who insult their integrity. But they also invest themselves in the companies' financial success. This finding shows that labor relations, while overlooked in scholarly research about CSR that focuses on NGOs and communities, forms a key aspect of the movement. In South Africa, for instance, Rajak (2011) shows that Anglo-American Corporation's wellness programs—couched in a language of care for employees—actually extended previous forms of industrial discipline by monitoring the intimate details of workers' nutritional, familial, and sexual practices. In Wyoming, miners were able to leverage their position as skilled workers in the midst of labor shortages to compel companies to distance themselves from paternalistic models of labor relations in practice as well as discourse. Although they and managers alike remain cognizant of power differentials on the worksite, miners have been able to protect what they hold dear, as is especially clear in the evolution of safety programs.

Development in the region therefore also echoes Marina Welker's (2009) finding that the practice of CSR can create unlikely alliances between corporations and their would-be critics. Much like the strategic advantage she found for the mining company Newmont enrolling communities as a first line of defense for a controversial project in Indonesia, companies in Wyoming view their employees as an army of potential defenders in what they perceive as a war of public relations. "Look," explained a manager named Dwayne, "you've got hundreds of people working for you, and who better to make sure that the rest of the world hears your story? These guys have firsthand experience. It's compelling. So if we do our job right, then they'll go out there and tell people that all of these negative portrayals of the industry are wrong, that we do a good job out here." An executive was blunter, saying, "We're engaged in a war of public relations here, and so far we're losing. The entire industry is painted with one brushstroke, so we have to defend not just our operations here but mining in general. Our employees can help with that, starting from below." For officials, treating miners well and encouraging them to identify with a regionally grounded company rather than the larger national community of miners are strategies to drum up support for an otherwise beleaguered industry.[22]

Casting the miners as corporate pawns and writing off this partial alignment as a symptom of false consciousness impoverishes our understanding of both the Powder River Basin and an entire industry shifting to nonunion workplaces. After all, even in the home base of the UMWA, the miners working in the Appalachian mountaintop removal operations are nonunionized young people who benefit handsomely from large paychecks and expensive perks from companies (McNeil 2011: 127). As Welker (2009: 166) writes of the Indonesian community members who defended a controversial mine, these miners are "social actors and commentators in their own right" with the capability "to interpret and morally evaluate their situation and to formulate projects and try to enact them." This recognition is sorely lacking in portrayals of rural, working Americans as either "the down-home, salt-of-the-earth, stalwart backbone of democracy" or the "the ignorant, backward, benighted castoffs of progress" (Darling 2009: 18). Wyoming miners strongly critique some industry practices as well as particular high rollers within it, but they maintain their jobs and nonunion status because they have been able to forge an enduring social contract with companies that recognize the benefits of a remarkably productive and stable workforce. Their relationship with the industry challenges both romantic views of blue-collar workers' resistance to structures of exploitation as well as simplistic CSR rhetoric of employee empowerment. As explored in the book's conclusion, their social contract was not publicly questioned until 2012, when the coal market deteriorated in the wake of lower prices and demand, due to increased natural gas production, an unseasonably mild winter season, and increased national public pressure for cleaner sources of domestic energy.

Part II

Putting in Time

3

Shiftwork as Kinwork

◄○►

The most difficult part of their jobs, according to Powder River Basin miners, is not operating some of the world's largest machinery in an inherently risky environment, but attuning their bodies and relationships to a demanding shiftwork schedule that requires them to switch continually between day and night shifts, each of twelve hours' duration. When talking about their work, all but the most cantankerous point to two things that inspire them to rouse themselves out of bed while their families are sleeping: their ability to provide financial stability for their families at home and their close relationships with crewmembers at work. In fact, decades of working a demanding shiftwork schedule have brought coworkers so close together they consider themselves to belong to a crew family of their own. Talk of crew families signals egalitarian relationships based in shared respect for hard work and points to the interdependence that underlines specific job tasks and ties each person's well-being to the actions of their coworkers (cf. Andrews 2008: 147, 173; Dudley 1994: 45, 132; Richardson 2006). Miners use the generic term "family" to refer to these relationships likely because the otherwise egalitarian terms brother or sister would evoke the unions they voted against. As the main cohort of middle-age miners reach retirement and are being replaced by younger workers their children's age, exceptions to the generic family rule are made for mentoring relationships that mimic parenting: novices refer to their guides as being "like a mother" or "like a father" to them.

Throughout my initial employment as a technician and later ethnographic research as a graduate student, I witnessed and participated in myriad activities that created, reinforced, and transformed this sense of relatedness in the workplace. Some of these were embedded in the routines of everyday life that often go without note, such as sharing food, exchanging tools, or talking through a stressful situation. Others stood out by being momentous, such as mourning the death of coworkers. On my first day at one mine, for example, a small group sat down with me and shared that a well-liked member of their crew had recently died on their days off. They spoke at length remembering him for always smiling and asking everyone how they were doing. They told me that because they were such a close-knit crew everyone attended his funeral, and many found the eulogy his daughter gave particularly meaningful. "She said that we knew him as well as their family did because our crew is a family too," said Daisy, a relatively new hire who was raising her son as a single parent. She explained, "She's right. We spend more time with each other than with our families at home. We become our own family."

Like Daisy, most miners in the basin consider their crews family because they spend so much time in the same space together. A conversation I had with Jack one cold winter night made this point clearly. He seemed to enjoy having someone to talk with on night shifts, perhaps because he was feeling reflective as he approached retirement, but also probably because talking simply helped to keep him awake as he drove in circles between the coal shovel and the processing plant. At two o'clock in the morning, as I sat beside him in the training seat of the ancient electric haul truck he was driving, we began talking about what he would miss the most after he retired. Without hesitation, he said he would miss his crew family. I took the opportunity to ask him about what made the crew a family. He deftly maneuvered the truck so that it lined up with the shovel's bucket. As he threw on the parking brake and the cab jostled with the weight of the first bucket of coal hitting the truck bed, he furrowed his brow and rebuffed my question by offering an organic theory of what Pierre Bourdieu (1977) would call practical knowledge: "You have to go through it. I can't explain it." As we waited for the shovel operator to finish loading the truck, he explained what he could. "They're not family like your kin, but they're family because you live with them, spend half your damn life with them." For the next few hours, he guided our conversation from the funny practical jokes he and his crew used to pull on each other to their mutual support in times of personal crisis.

In this conversation, Jack brought together the major themes related to workplace families in the basin: they are distinct from but analogous to relatives by blood and marriage, and they are created over time through shared experiences of working, joking, and eating together. This perspective on workplace relationships is not unique to Wyoming or the mining industry; workplaces that demand close coordination among coworkers or present particularly hazardous conditions have been shown to foster close relationships among blue-collar workers. As historian Alf Ludtke writes of workers in Imperial Germany: "On the job, factory workers did not simply operate their tools and machines, or cooperate with each other in various ways—they also, literally, lived together for long hours at a time. This physical contact, this 'being-together-in-the-same-place,' must be related to the rest of life on the shop floor, to those endless uncertainties that constantly molded workers' experiences" (1985: 309). Ludtke's identification of shared time and space for creating a sense of closeness and belonging also rings true for Wyoming. The miners spend most of their waking lives in a workplace that is geographically distinct from the community (up to sixty miles away from their homes) and off-limits to visitors, and they also move through a distinct time regime. In fact, ethnographic evidence suggests that the extreme temporal mismatch between miners and their communities, spouses, and children intensifies workplace relationships and prompts this group of workers to understand these ties not simply as close friendships but as a type of kinship.

These types of worker-initiated relationships are distinct from the more infamous top-down form of workplace family critiqued by interdisciplinary scholars: corporate paternalism, in which executives and managers utilize idioms of kinship, specifically parent/child relationships, to frame their interactions with workers.[1] This management style has been rightly criticized for the dependent and subservient roles company patriarchs assign to workers who are likened to children, the condescension inherent in management defining the best interests of their employees, and the crosscutting of solidarity by vertical identification with managers instead of coworkers. Even though the mining companies operating in the Powder River Basin consciously sought to move away from paternalistic models of labor relations, key differences remain between the visions of workplace family imagined and brought into practice by managers and technicians in the pit, plant, and shop (Rolston 2010b).

In this chapter I explore how the Wyoming miners craft crew families through the everyday practice of work. As such, it offers a twist on anthropologist Micaela di Leonardo's (1987) influential conception of kinwork. She originally coined the term to capture the unacknowledged work that Italian American women did in maintaining relationships with extended kin networks, including mailing holiday cards, making phone calls, hosting parties, and buying presents. If di Leonardo's concern was to show that practicing kinship is a type of labor, mine is to show that laboring can be a form of practicing kinship. Doing so requires tracing the time regime of rotating shiftwork and the ways it permeates everyday details of waking, sleeping, eating, and resting. Shiftwork intensifies a sense of belonging to crew families, and this kinship provides miners with the tools to make their work meaningful and enjoyable. At the same time, the stresses it places on miners' bodies and social relationships points to an asymmetrical dimension of the politics of embodied time: gendered disparities in levels of physical exhaustion traceable to women's increased burden for household responsibilities.

I begin by laying the theoretical foundations for studying kinship at work and viewing time as a key building block of relatedness among crews. Turning to the ethnographic material, I then describe the labor process of the mines and show that the difficulties of embodying the shiftwork schedule foster a sense of empathy and relatedness among the miners, who share daily and monthly rhythms of everyday life with their coworkers rather than their spouses and children. I then consider the gendered dimensions of this time regime and the workplace families that emerge from it. Miners argue that shiftwork greatly minimizes differences between men and women because it induces bodily stress and exhaustion for both. Although this assertion holds true in many cases, close attention to a few key issues reveals that the stress of shiftwork makes different demands of men and women, as single mothers routinely sacrifice their own sleep to raise children and women technicians in general modify their liquid intake to minimize bathroom breaks while on the clock. This analysis advances the larger argument of the book by showing that practices such as these that produce and reproduce gender difference nonetheless exist alongside and in tension with those that would otherwise diminish it.

Workplace Relatedness

Workplace families may seem like a contradiction in terms for Americans who view family as a "haven in a heartless world" (Lasch 1977) and an antidote to a "contemporary political and economic system based on values of competition, instant gratification, and amoral calculations about persons as well as things" (Gillis 1998: xvi). Although these cultural ideas are commonly associated with the western European and North American middle classes, Marx himself famously described alienated labor as that in which the worker "only feels himself outside his work, and in his work feels outside himself. He is at home when he is not working, and when he is working he is not at home" (1977 [1844]: 74). Marx references the dichotomy between home and work to reinforce the contrast between the types of persons and social relationships typically associated with these two social spheres: work—especially in its industrialized form—with the competitive, economic rationality believed to be characteristic of the public sphere; and kinship, in contrast, with the belonging, altruistic love, and identification attributed to the private sphere.[2] When workplaces are regarded as bastions of the self-interested competition characteristic of the public sphere, little conceptual space remains to imagine other types of motivations and relationships.

Studying kinship and relatedness in workplaces is vital because these are key contexts for the construction of gender, senses of self, and relationships with others. The few studies that begin to analyze relatedness and kinship from the perspective of western workplaces have already made significant contributions to anthropology. Bridging the spheres of home and work in her ethnography of Italian family textile firms, Sylvia Yanagisako shows that "people think and act in ways that crosscut institutional boundaries" (2002: 6; cf. di Leonardo 1987; Dudley 1994; Yanagisako and Collier 1987). Additionally, ethnographers have traced the work that idioms and practices of kinship do in the workplace. While these kinship practices provide companies with a strategy to gain workforce loyalty and preempt unionization and state regulation (Finn 1998; Kalb 1997), they also offer workers an alternative frame with which to value themselves and the products of their labor (Dunn 2004: 143; Ferry 2005) as well to craft more egalitarian relationships with coworkers (Richardson 2006).[3]

Though the Wyoming workplace families may initially confound popular Euro-American understandings of relatedness since they are fostered in the public sphere, they appear perfectly logical when considered within the framework of contemporary studies of kinship. This innovative research roots relatedness in shared time and space rather than simply shared biogenetic substance, the dominant American folk theory of kinship. Time figures largely in the creation of relatedness in a variety of cultural contexts, including the Powder River Basin, because both concepts are based in practical, embodied activity. As Janet Carsten (1995, 1997, 2004) powerfully argues, kinship and relatedness are processes based in and emergent from shared activities and space—in her Malay case, living together and eating from the same hearth. One of the main insights offered by anthropologists of time is that it, too, is based in and emergent from shared activities and space. The classic case is Evans-Pritchard's account of Nuer "oecological time" which emerges from the "distinctive rhythm [of the] backwards and forwards movement from villages to camps, which is the Nuer's response to the climatic dichotomy of rains and drought" (1940: 95).[4] This concept of time as motion even finds its way into more static notions of time as collective representations; Nancy Munn argues that even Émile Durkheim's categorical notion of time still "looks ever behind itself at social 'rhythm'—i.e. time as process constituted in the unfolding of activities" (1992: 96). Munn's own influential theory of "spacetime", based on her research in Gawa, Papua New Guinea, is grounded in meaningful action. She suggests that people create their lived worlds and produce themselves as spatiotemporal beings through everyday embodied practice (1986: 11; 1992: 94, 106). In the Powder River Basin, the distinct rhythm of the rotating shift schedule creates the unique spacetime of shiftwork.

Marking Time, Embodying Shiftwork

Anthropologists document the distinct notions of time characteristic of extractive industries such as mining, from periods of excessive consumption that follow those of isolated and intense production (Wilk 2006) to cycles of union contracts, negotiations, and strikes that shape the everyday activities of entire families and communities (Finn 1998). Moreover, the introduction of mining activities to places where there were formally none can change the way in which communities view place, time and their relationship to the world around them. Stuart Kirsch (2001, 2006), for example, traces how the Yonggom of Papua New Guinea shifted from spatial to temporal representations of past and future experiences after the Ok Tedi Mine began dumping tailings waste into the local river system, and thereby destroyed the places that had formerly anchored memories of persons and events.

In the Powder River Basin, the most salient rhythm of time is the rotating shiftwork schedule designed to maximize production. Heavy machinery, such as draglines, shovels, haul trucks, scrapers, blades, and dozers, represents one of the largest capital investments by mining companies. Novice equipment operators, including the most helpless temporary summer students discussed in chapter 4, begin their training on the least expensive equipment: haul trucks originally purchased for a paltry sum of three million dollars. This cost pales in comparison to draglines, the largest equipment on-site. The size of these machines dwarfs most single-family homes, and their cost easily reaches forty to fifty million dollars. To derive the most profit from this investment, companies aim to keep equipment running as close to twenty-four hours a day, seven days a week, as possible. Doing so requires part of the workforce to be on-site both night and day as well as on the weekends, which are designated as leisure time for Americans with more conventional schedules.[5] As such, most mines in the basin employ the rotating schedule of shifts described in the introduction: four nights on, three days off, three days on, one day off, three nights on, three days off, four days on, seven days off.

For miners, the twenty-eight-day rotation often trumps other ways of tracking time. It is telling that memorable occasions are marked by their position in the rotating schedule more often than by specific dates.[6] During a conversation about one of the few fatal accidents that had occurred at one mine, the equipment operator began her remembrance of the day by saying, "It was the Wednesday of our day shifts. I'll never forget it." For her, the fact that the accident happened while on day shift, only two days before their stretch of seven days off, was more significant than the actual date. Her coworkers remembered the incident in the same terms. Why might this be? For shiftworkers, it is easier to talk about and make plans for the "Tuesday of our four days" rather than "April first" because it is not immediately apparent what *kind* of day April first would be. The first in a stretch of night shifts? The "short-change" or day and a half in the middle of hell week? The end of seven days off? The differences in sleep patterns and time availability among these points in the schedule are dramatic, including nighttime versus daytime sleep, and fifteen-hour periods at work versus entire days of leisure at home. Identifying a point in time by the shift schedule rather than its date tells miners and their families where they will be (at home, at work, or on the bus) and when they will be eating, sleeping, working, and relaxing.

The other reason why the shiftwork schedule trumps more conventional ways of marking time is because miners map varying levels of bodily energy and the speed of movement through space according to each shift's placement in the rotation. Time for miners is not uniform: bodies and clocks alike are perceived as moving more slowly at the beginning of a block and more quickly toward the end. A Wednesday day shift, no matter what week or month it takes place in, *feels* different from a Monday day shift because the highly anticipated stretch of seven days off is only one shift away. The longest shifts by far are those at the beginning of hell week, the part of the rotation in which three night shifts follow three day shifts with only thirty-six hours off in-between to readjust their sleeping and eating patterns. "When you're staring down six shifts with only a day off in the middle, man, that is depressing," explained an equipment operator named Bob. "It seems like it will never end. You gotta slow yourself down otherwise you'll be spent by the time it's over." Moreover, the deeper into a block a shift is—the third night versus the first night, for example—the more likely it is that miners feel more energetic because their bodies have had a chance to adjust to the sleep cycle. "I don't know, I just have more get-up-and-go the closer I get to those days off," explained Dave. "At the beginning of a block, you just have to take it easy, go slow, you don't want to wear out right away. And of course you're dragging because you don't want to be back to work, especially that first night after a week off. But I tell you what, that last Thursday before our seven off, I have a little hop in my step."

Miners manipulate time by making efforts to move their bodies and equipment more quickly. For example, truck drivers are assigned to haul either dirt or coal. Each trip from the shovel or loader to the material's final destination is called a run, and dirt runs tend to be much quicker than coal runs. Dirt is normally removed from a new pit that is just being opened and then transported to one that has been mined out and is being refilled for reclamation. Coal, on the other hand, must be hauled from the pits back to the mine's central processing plant. While the pits extend farther and farther away from the mine offices to reach the coal, the processing plant is immobile, meaning that those runs take increasingly longer amounts of time to complete as the mine expands.[7] Dirt runs are also faster because those shovels tend to be larger and more powerful.[8] The larger and more powerful the shovel, the less time it takes to load trucks, and the shorter the run cycle is. Whereas coal runs can take up to twenty or thirty minutes each, dirt runs can be as short as ten. Depending on their mood and position in the shiftwork cycle, truck drivers strongly prefer hauling either dirt or coal. Daisy usually liked dirt because "you get in two or three times as many runs as on coal. You're always busy, going back and forth, always moving. The time just flies by." On the other hand, those seeking to relax would rather run coal. Nick said, "You can just take it easy, drive down those smooth roads and listen to some tunes." Miners characterize each shift and each block of shifts, therefore, by how energetic or sleepy they feel.

Despite the salience of the shiftwork schedule, miners are also bound to the dominant time regime of families, doctors, churches, and schools, in which Monday through Friday mornings and afternoons are reserved for school and business and evenings and weekends are ideally spent relaxing with family and friends and catching up on household maintenance. This mismatch creates tension in the home, as described in greater detail in the next chapter. For now, I note that to navigate the mismatch and attempt to translate the two regimes, miners and their spouses carry small, laminated cards coded with blue, yellow, and white boxes to give a visual representation of a particular crew's schedule. Spouses and shiftworkers pull it out of their purses and wallets when making plans with friends, setting up medical appointments, or deciding which of their children's extracurricular activities they will be able to attend. Sometimes the mismatch is insurmountable. For example, participating in church activities assumes regular weekends off from work. "I would have loved to have worked with the youth group," explained Dave, "but it just wasn't possible with my schedule. I work two weekends out of every month, and I don't always have Wednesday night off either." At other times the shiftwork schedule is advantageous, such as when shiftworkers on their seven days off can pick up a sick child from school while their spouses would find it difficult to leave their workplace.

The rotating shiftwork schedule is so significant for miners and their families that in telling their life and work histories, they bound off entire periods of their life based on the particular schedule being worked. For each phase, miners clearly remember what time they would set their alarm to go off in the morning or afternoon, when they would eat, and when they would walk through the front door on their arrival home. Spouses remember strategies for preparing meals that could be eaten at different times by their children and their husband or wife. Children remember how the schedule impinged on their own activities, such as if it allowed opportunities to host weekend sleepovers or if the house needed to be designated as a quiet space.

Miners and their families vividly remember the moves from eight- to ten- and then twelve-hour shifts because they greatly altered the details of their everyday lives. For the earliest years when the mines first opened, employees enjoyed the fact that the eight-hour shifts allowed them plenty of time to drink together at the bars after work. At the same time, they had to report to work five days a week instead of three or four, which cut down on the time they would otherwise spend hunting, fishing, or riding four-wheelers with family and friends. Eight-hour shifts also meant that three crews worked during each twenty-four-hour period, and each crew rotated weekly between day, swing (late afternoon to evening), and night shifts. They remember feeling active and energized, partially because they were younger, but also because they received sufficient amounts of regular sleep and did not work long enough hours to reach the point of exhaustion.

People also fondly remembered the following years that were characterized by a ten-hour schedule. "Man, that was great," explained Bob. "That was the perfect schedule. You still had time for a life after work, but you weren't going in all the time like you did with eights." Four shifts per week, rather than five, opened up a large block of leisure time without taking too much away on a daily basis. "Once I'm out there and I've made the drive, I want to work," said Mary. "Ten hours is just right—you're not too tired, but feel ready to go home, like you did a good day's work." The move to the current schedule of twelve-hour shifts presented greater difficulties for many miners, especially with the majority approaching middle age, with the trade-off of more days off in a row.

Making Family by Sharing the Bodily Experience of Shiftwork

The large amounts of time, characterized by distinct bodily states and rhythms, which miners spend together helps to explain why they view their crews as more than mere coworkers. When pressed to explain what makes people family, people in Gillette point not simply to shared biogenetic substances like blood or genes, but also to shared time and space, whether that be in homes, mountain cabins, bars, or outdoor venues for entertainment and leisure. Members of the same crew not only spend all of their working lives together but they also share a unique sleeping and eating schedule and are likely to frequent the same places on their days off—such as grocery stores, restaurants, or the nearby lake—even if they do not intentionally plan on doing so because there are limited places to shop and relax in town. If family is who you spend your time with, eating together and sharing space, fellow crewmembers fit this definition more easily than do families as they are conventionally understood.

Keeping track of time by the shiftwork cycle is meaningful in part because, as the previous section shows, the basic details of everyday life—when miners work, when they enjoy leisure, when they eat, when they are awake, when they sleep, and when they see their friends and family members—revolve around it. The rotating shifts represent not simply a schedule with reference points and categories, but embodied patterns of movement and orientations to the world. Every three to four days, miners must dramatically alter not simply their work schedule but the daily routines of sleeping, waking, and eating that those who do not do shiftwork take for granted. Anne pointed to extreme dislocations engendered by shiftwork by saying, "It's hard to be a normal person because no one else has the same schedule." She found that her friends and family who did not do shiftwork or were not married to a shiftworker found it difficult to remember and be considerate of her schedule by, for example, refraining from calling her on the phone during the days when she needed to be sleeping in preparation for a nightshift.

On stretches of day shifts, miners go to bed and wake up slightly earlier than people with nine-to-five jobs. Those employed at the mines closest to town can sleep the latest. Getting up an hour before the designated start of a shift gives them time to eat a small breakfast while watching television or scanning a newspaper, pack their lunch, and drive twenty minutes or so to work. Dave, a plant mechanic, boasted that if he made his lunch the night before and waited to eat breakfast until the first break of the morning, he could sleep an extra half hour and arrive at work just in time to pull on overalls, grab his hard hat, and slip into the morning meeting with just moments to spare. Others prefer to arrive early, fix coffee or tea, and relax and visit with coworkers before the official start of the shift. On the other hand, those who work at the most distant mines must wake up much earlier to meet the bus that drives them about sixty miles southeast of Gillette. The trip takes an hour and a half each way, but most weary commuters try to use the time to nap in order to catch up on their sleep. Al, for instance, woke up each morning at 4:30 and did not return until 8:15 that evening. His wife normally had leftovers from her meal with their daughters ready for him to eat when he walked in the door. After dinner, he cleaned out his lunch box and began prepping for the next day by placing all of the nonrefrigerated food inside and making a small pile of food in the fridge he could quickly grab in the morning. By the time he showered, he was lucky if he could go to bed by 9 o'clock, leaving him seven and a half hours to sleep. Any time spent doing anything else, from watching television to making a phone call, cut into that sleep. He succinctly summarized the challenges of the schedule by saying, "We lived on our days off."

While the day-shift schedule is exhausting, it is not as disorienting as night shifts since miners on the day shift sleep and eat at roughly the same time as they would on their days off. Stretches of night shifts require them to sleep during the day, while the sun is out and spouses or children may be in the house. As much as they love their seven days off every month, most miners are frustrated by the quantity (little) and quality (poor) of sleep they get while on nights. "I'm lucky if I get four hours," Gary told me as we did a walk-through of the plant at the beginning of a night shift. "And even then I'm waking up all the time because the room's bright or because the kids are being kids or whatever. It just feels like I should be awake, even if I'm dead tired." One of his coworkers liked to critique the prevalent local gripe that miners were spoiled because they made good money but only worked fourteen out of every twenty-eight days. "They look at our schedule and think that we've got fourteen days off, but anyone who's done it knows it's not true," he explained. "You've got to spend a lot of them catching up on the sleep you lost while you were working. You miss your sleep while you're working, so you sleep on your days off." Another shiftworker summarized her sense of disconnection from her own family and more general rhythms of family life by describing how she would drive through the neighborhood on her way to a night shift, feeling demoralized as she watched the lights in each house turn off in anticipation of sleep.

In addition to drastically altering their sleeping schedules, shiftwork also upsets miners' eating preferences and habits. At the end of a twelve-hour night shift, they come home to their families eating breakfast, but may be hungry for the heartier foods associated with dinner. After sleeping for part of the morning and afternoon, they may feel hungry for just eggs or cereal while their family prepares a more elaborate dinner. And sometimes miners are so disoriented that they are not hungry for anything at all. "The whole thing is screwed up," said Greg, who had been working rotating shifts for twenty years. "It hurts my stomach to have a big meal right before I go to sleep, but I've gotta eat! Sometimes the food that my wife fixes makes my stomach turn just smelling it. I mean, I'm in the mood for something light, like toast, and there she is making lasagna." Many shiftworkers, especially those who operate equipment, find themselves snacking more during the shift in order to stay awake, which also throws off their more conventional division of eating times into three or four distinct periods.

Although their eating habits often distinguish them from their families and communities, miners do share an eating schedule as well as particular meals and celebrations with their coworkers. This finding is significant since a long trajectory of cross-cultural ethnographic research suggests that food sharing is a powerful way to recognize the personhood of others and create relatedness with them. Although the majority of these studies have been centered in homes, a few suggest that such practices might result in comparable outcomes in workplaces.[9] In his study of a small group of naturalized American factory workers, sociologist Donald Roy (1959) identified a variety of "times," characterized by the sharing of food and drink, which helped the men manage the tedium of their jobs. These included the "coffee time" that marked the beginning of the working day for the earliest arriving workers; "peach time," which accompanied the last worker's arrival; the entertaining "banana time," in which one worker consistently "stole" the fruit out of another's lunch pail; "lunch time" initiated by a practical joke of tampering with the clock; "fish time," in which the two workers who originally shared coffee then took a break and shared pickled fish; and finally "Coke time," in which the workers took turns buying canned soda for one another. In this research, Roy's primary concern was theorizing the link between group interaction and job satisfaction.

Anthropologist Don Handelman (1990) subsequently reinterpreted Roy's original ethnography to account for the ways in which the different times served as dynamic frames for social action. Following Roy, Handelman argues that through these "times," "the protagonists reinvented the working day as an integrative framework of sociability" (Handelman 1990: 104). Whereas Roy's account gives the impression that these "times" were implemented somewhat mechanistically, Handelman argues that the sequence of activities "contained its own power of reproduction" and should thus be treated as a "synthetic framework for action that reproduced itself through time" (1990: 104). Most significantly, he argues that the frame of the integrative times established a "master context of reciprocity, mutuality, and solidarity for interaction in the workplace" that framed the ways in which conflict and opposition were to be interpreted and handled (1990: 109). For example, the daily sharing of coffee set the frame for the rest of the day's interactions that included mock conflict, such as the stealing of the banana and the tampering with the machines and clocks.

A similar process is at work in the mines. Many miners arrive at work early, due to either their own preference or the company's bus schedule. After a trip to the locker room to put on coveralls and gather tools and safety gear, most proceed to a common area, either a hallway or room. Without fail, someone has started a pot of coffee that is shared among the group, except perhaps for those who prefer to sip tea, soda, or an energy drink. This time provides the crew with a chance not just to strategize the working day but also to socialize face-to-face, a rare opportunity given that for the rest of the shift most of them will be confined to their own pieces of equipment. Using Handelman's vocabulary, this "integrative" time frames the rest of the day's activities, which include similar times of solidarity (lunch and coffee breaks) as well as those characterized by conflict, both mock (such as practical jokes) and real (such as serious arguments). Before the mines switched to twelve-hour shifts, many miners also marked the end of the working day by drinking a beer during their routine carpool home or at a local bar. These events made them feel like family. "We were just like family back then," remembered Jack, who was nostalgic for the early years of the industry. "We'd just pull our trucks over wherever we were and get out and have lunch together. Sometimes we'd even cook things on the engines since they were so hot! And then we'd drink together on the way home." Laughing, he explained, "People would bring six packs [of beer] in the morning and hide them outside the gate or along the road, and we'd pick them up on our way home."

This integrative framing process also animates the much-loved ritual of "bringing doughnuts." At all but the largest mines, operators who get their equipment stuck in the dirt and require assistance from their coworkers to free themselves are expected to bring in doughnuts for the entire crew the next day.[10] Jokes and self-deprecating humor infuse the rescue and its subsequent retelling as the doughnuts are shared. A few supervisors and operators interpret the custom negatively as punishment. As one supervisor explained,

"I don't support that whole doughnuts deal. It's hounding people. A lot of the guys don't like it. It hurts their feelings. You think they're cast iron but everybody's still human."[11] Many others, however, make a dramatically different interpretation. "It's just a fun little thing we do," said a middle-aged equipment operator. "It's not meant to embarrass anyone. If we give you a hard time, that means we care about you." He then pointed out that everyone, even the most experienced people on their crew, had brought doughnuts in at least once or twice in their career: "Everybody's done it. You just do it, smile when people give you a hard time, and then everybody moves on."

Handelman's interpretation of Roy's ethnography helps us to understand this practice. When equipment becomes stuck, it introduces potential conflict into the minesite. Not only do the stuck operators fall behind in their own tasks but the people who come to their rescue have to temporarily abandon theirs as well. These situations also raise the possibility of assigning blame for the mistake. Did the shovel operator ask the stuck truck to back into a soft spot, or did the truck driver miss the shovel's mark? Did the dozer operator fail to take care of a soft spot on the dump, or did the truck driver fail to take proper evasive maneuvers? Bringing in doughnuts to share with the entire crew provides an overarching frame of integration to ameliorate the potentially disintegrative situation, even as it singles out one person for blame.[12]

Crews also share food and drink to mark major transitions. Each time someone retired from a crew I worked on or studied with, their supervisor brought in cake or ice cream for everyone to share on that person's last day. Their coworkers usually brought in additional treats, such as breakfast foods on day shifts or desserts on night shifts. The size of the mine conditions how elaborate these celebrations are. For example, during my first summer as a temporary employee, the mine where I worked had only two crews made up of fewer than ten people each. On my last day, the entire mine shut down to come together in the main office to eat cake and ice cream, socialize, and tell funny stories about my time there. Such an event would be unimaginable at larger mines. In fact, by the time I returned two summers later, the mine's workforce had almost tripled. Many of my coworkers brought in muffins, doughnuts, and coffee cake the morning of my last shift, but the bigger celebration took place off-site when they all took me out to a local bar after we had clocked out. One of my coworkers had taken me under his wing that summer, making sure that I stayed safe and had a good time. As he slid a bottle of Bud Light to me across the bar, he said, "We're going to miss you, kid. You're just like a daughter to all of us."

Sharing food and drink also played a major role in marking and mourning a major reorganization that would split up one of the crews I worked with at another mine. On the last night before what people referred to as the "busting up" of the crew, the supervisor asked his wife to bring in pizza for the entire group during our midnight lunch break. Sitting down together in the office for a hot meal instead of eating sandwiches alone in equipment or in a trailer in the pit provided a welcome break from the night shift and an opportunity to talk about the impending changes. After people had told their favorite stories of funny things their coworkers had done and began preparing to go back for the rest of the shift, Nick, the crew's unofficial leader, summed up the mood of the room: "It's been a pleasure working with all of you. I know we've all had our moments, but you guys really are family to me."

Ethnographic evidence thus suggests that this sense of workplace related-ness in the basin emerges from the crews sharing distinct rhythms of everyday life. Miners are acutely aware of themselves as people whose basic rhythms of everyday life—eating, sleeping, waking, working, and playing—are dictated by a unique and challenging shiftwork schedule. They quip that except for their seven days off, they have very little sense of the outside world, including what day of the week or time it is. This sense of confusion stems from irregu-larities in fundamental practices most people take for granted: sleeping and eating. Sharing the bodily stresses of shiftwork therefore fosters an intense sense of empathy and common understanding among miners that forms the basis of their crew families.

Gendered Politics of Exhaustion

In addition to sharing bodily rhythms of eating and working, miners all experi-ence a chronic exhaustion that is difficult for those who do not do shiftwork to understand. Constantly switching between day and night shifts reinforces the profound sense of disorientation described above. It also creates distinct cycles of weariness, as miners "rest up" on their days off only to push them-selves to exhaustion while working, especially at night. Sleep deprivation and a sense of eeriness of working while the rest of the community and their fami-lies sleep make twelve-hour night shifts drag on for even the most enthusiastic employees. For most, night shifts are so exhausting that work is dominated by mechanical, utilitarian movements that lack the energy and finesse required for the entertaining yet safe practical jokes that otherwise enliven social rela-tions at the mine. "The witching hour, that's between three and four in the morning," said Ray. "Nobody talks because they're so tired. It's eerie, you're like a zombie, just trying to make it through." A shovel operator named Roy described night shifts by saying, "I know I become mentally slow, my coordi-nation's bad, and I have incoherent conversations. At four A.M. I'm not think-ing. I'll blink my eyes and it will be two hours later and my load count is still going, but I'm thinking, 'Where have I been?'" He relies on "memory motion," which is when "you follow routine and don't think about it if you get trained right and don't have any bad habits."

Men and women miners alike argue that this chronic exhaustion draws out similarities between men and women. Men and women shiftworkers do move through the same shiftwork schedule, and the majority of miners argue that men and women face the same challenges and stresses in attuning their bodies to the demands of the rotating shift schedule. For example, chapter 1 opened with the provocative comment by the shovel operator Mary, who told me that gender was not the most important part of her day or something very interesting to talk about. When I asked her what was most important, she said "human" needs. Later in our conversation, she said one of her biggest challenges was figuring out "how to work this schedule and not turn into a horrible person." She explained, "These twelve-hour shifts bring out the worst in everyone, and it doesn't matter if you're a woman or a man. A tired miner is a tired miner, period." Like many of her peers, Mary argued that men and women alike struggle to sleep during the day, stay awake at night, and find food that is appealing to them to eat at strange hours. Men and women alike bring in food to work to share with their crewmembers, such that preparing food and feeding others is not exclusively associated with femininity as it can be in other contexts. Men and women alike also celebrate the end of a rotation or particularly stressful block of shifts by drinking together at a bar in town or barbequing at the lake or in someone's backyard.

The labor process itself would also seem to minimize bodily differences between men and women.[13] First, technicians at most mines are required to wear the same standard, company-issued denim coveralls that make it difficult but not impossible to discern the male or female form of the bodies underneath. At others, miners uniformly wear jeans and T-shirts in the summer and flannel shirts and sweatshirts in the winter. Women usually wear loose-fitting clothing that is similar to, and sometimes indistinguishable from, those worn by their male coworkers. In fact, women and men who wear tight clothing that shows off curves or muscles, thus emphasizing their masculinity or femininity, find themselves the targets of scorn rather than admiration, for reasons elaborated in chapter 5. Similarly, women who wear noticeable makeup or fingernail polish also find themselves subject to gentle teasing or more serious scrutiny. Second, the machinery mediates interactions among miners, especially in the pit. The large size of the equipment makes it difficult to identify the person driving it unless there are noticeable clues, such as a particular truck driver who always wore a bandana that could be seen from the road, or unless people make efforts to remember which operators are assigned to which numbered pieces of equipment. When looking at haul trucks circling around a shovel or a group of dozers pushing dirt into an empty pit, especially at the larger mines, it is easier to see machines than gendered operators.

Yet as much as the shiftwork schedule can undo gender by drawing out common bodily states for both men and women and crafting them as similar types of persons, men and women miners also recognize that the demands of raising small children and adjusting female bodies to the mine workplace present particular challenges for women that increase their exhaustion.

Pregnant Bodies and Shifting Expectations

Pregnancy is the most salient of these processes that foreground gender difference, as it almost always requires women to modify their regular work assignments to accommodate their expanding bodies. Most women resist these changes for as long as possible, seeking to maintain their standing within the crews as well as their financial stability. Melissa was able to continue driving haul trucks until she was eight months along and could no longer fit behind the steering wheel. She humorously explained, "I thought if the fat guys with their big stomachs could do it, so could I, so I watched them get into their seats. But I learned that my stomach didn't move like theirs did. They could move theirs around to make it fit, but mine stayed put." Noting that she also rode horses until the eight-month mark, she distinguished herself from the "sissy pregnant ladies" who transfer to what is called light duty at three or four months along. Light duty consists of office work or unstrenuous tasks around the shop or warehouse. These tasks are less physically stressful and they offer the added convenience of always being close to a "real" bathroom—not an insignificant factor for women experiencing nausea or more frequent urination. At some mines, the disadvantage of moving to light duty is that employees make only 60 percent of their wage while working (as well as during their leave), instead of the full pay they would receive if they were able to stay on the heavy equipment until their last day of work before leaving. The other disadvantage is that light duty is viewed as "easier" work, which calls into question the dedication and skills of people who accept it too readily.

Even if women seek to minimize the influence of their changed condition, their male coworkers reproduce more conventional notions of masculinity and femininity in their attempts to protect such women in the name of crew care. Daisy found out she was pregnant while I was spending time with her crew. When she made the announcement at a morning meeting, she adamantly said that she did not want special treatment. Everyone congratulated her warmly. Against her wishes, the crew supervisor said that they were all going to "treat her with kid gloves" and immediately reassigned her from the regular haul trucks to the water trucks, which were perceived as offering a smoother ride and less stressful work demands. Perhaps sensing her discomfort, one of the guys poked fun at the situation, saying, "I'm coming to work tomorrow with a pillow in my belly so that I can get a nice truck too. I'll be more pregnant than you!" His coworkers roared with laughter, especially after someone else advised him to "watch those hormone fluctuations" and to watch out if he "started spotting heavy." Daisy laughed along with them, appearing relieved that everyone could laugh about the situation.

A few weeks later the mood turned somber after Daisy announced that she had miscarried. Speaking privately with me, she assured me that continuing to operate equipment had played little or no role in losing the pregnancy: "I don't think it was anything I did or the equipment or anything." She spoke at length about her family history of miscarriages, and I heard her telling a group of guys the same thing the next day. She further diminished the significance of her miscarriage by saying that without the contemporary tests that can detect pregnancies at their earliest stages, she might not have even realized it and simply thought she had her period. Her mother, Wanda, who also operated equipment, took a markedly more critical view, as I learned from a later conversation. "Women shouldn't do this job if they're pregnant," she explained to me. "The roads are so bumpy that it can't be good for the fetus." As proof, she pointed to the decision Daisy's supervisor made to move her off the haul trucks. Soon after our conversation, I shared lunch with them, and Wanda tried pushing Daisy to commit to quitting if she really became pregnant again. Wanda asked her what she would do if she got morning sickness while driving truck, and Daisy put a quick stop to the conversation by saying with an air of bravado, "I'd just puke out the window."[14]

Daisy's matter-of-fact response to her mother is representative of the desire held by a majority of women miners to downplay any potential differences that pregnancy could introduce into workplace relations. They would rather puke out the window, like Daisy, or strategize ways to squeeze behind the steering wheel, like Melissa, than be accused of receiving special treatment. It is telling that the special treatment they resist is a particularly gendered one. Daisy was upset when her supervisor paternalistically enjoined her coworkers to treat her with "kid gloves," even though she recognized his good intentions to translate the crew's care for one another to her new condition. Receiving special treatment in the form of changed assignments is troubling for most miners but especially for women because it raises questions about their competence, dedication, and skill—evaluations that are central to membership in the crew families and tied up in the local work ethic, as I describe more fully in chapter 6. This evidence shows that "protection" can be a form of discrimination used to deny women access to well-paying jobs (Lahiri Dutt 2011b: 13).

Sacrificing Sleep

In conversations and everyday practice, pregnancy raises questions about bodily differences between men and women. These do not end with giving birth, but continue in slightly changed form as parents—and especially single mothers—adjust to the demands of raising small children. Many women miners are also single mothers, and single mothers with small children sleep less than their coworkers.[15] Nicole averaged only three hours of sleep per twenty-four-hour period while her children were young. Her coworkers with spouses or live-in partners counted on them to watch their children while they slept during the day in preparation for the night shift, and many fellow single moms arranged for babysitting outside of the home.[16] Nicole, however, wanted to spend the day with her children so she stayed awake. As such, the only sleep she got at home was the hour when she napped along with her children. To compensate, she slept on the bus to the mine for an hour each on the way there and back, which gave her a daily total of three hours of sleep. She also tried sleeping during the thirty-minute lunch break. She did not get much more sleep while working days. "Six hours a night was good," she explained, because she had to dro\ p the kids off at the babysitter early in the morning and then pick them up at night. After she put them to bed, she still had to shower and pack her lunch for the next day. "But you do what you got to do sometimes," she said. "And I was surprised I was able to do it." This extreme form of sleep deprivation becomes gendered because men rarely face it, unless they find it impossible to sleep during the day, work a second job, run their own business in addition to their mine employment, or take on major home improvement projects. Very few men raise children by themselves because they rely on their wives, girlfriends, and other family members to watch over them, and single fathers are rarely awarded custody in divorces. This finding supports research showing that working women more often suffer sleep disruptions and deprivations than men (Maume et al. 2010). Yet even women find that this lack of sleep eventually passes: once Nicole's children were old enough to attend school, she began sleeping during the day like the rest of her coworkers.

Many men also find themselves chronically sleep deprived during particular periods of their lives. Fathers with small children, for example, often put in more overtime in order to accommodate extra household expenses and establish themselves as a breadwinner. Since most miners catch up on their missing sleep on their days off, extra overtime means much less sleep. Some men also attempt to work second jobs or complete additional training on their days off. Roger, for example, worked night shifts and then went to school during the day to train to become a mechanic. He had so little time to sleep during the day that he worked out a clever routine to sleep when he could during night shifts. He figured out exactly how long it took each shovel to load the truck he was driving. After he pulled in and set his parking brake, he set a small kitchen timer from home for that time and attempted to accumulate sleep, every few minutes by every few minutes. However, he never got the type of deep, relaxing sleep his body needed. "It's not good for you," he summarized, "but it was what I had to do to support my family."

These ethnographic materials show that sleep is not the domain of autonomous individuals, but people embedded in relationships infused by power, as

Maume, Sebastian, and Bardo eloquently argue: "It is perhaps more realistic to view sleep as embedded in a network of gendered sentient responsibilities, and as such the bedroom is contested terrain where partners with unequal levels of power and obligations to family members vie for rights to a restful sleep" (2010: 755). Although ethnographic data shows that both men and women can become sleep deprived at particular points in their life, it does suggest one concern: unlike women, when men undergo sleep deprivation it is more likely due to their attempts to advance their careers and receive additional training.

Everyday Bodily Regulation

Pregnancy and raising small children draw out differences in the way men and women miners embody the demands of their work. On a more everyday basis, bathroom use is a site in which differences between male and female bodies can become salient, especially in the pit (Lahiri-Dutt and Robinson 2008). Although some corporate personnel frown on the practice, men almost always simply pull their equipment off to the side away from traffic, park it, and then urinate off the side. Women cannot. They must locate a port-a-potty, park, enter a computerized code into the dispatch system to signal and categorize their delay, climb down off the truck, chock the wheels, pull down half their clothes, use the bathroom, unchock the wheels, and climb back up into the cab. In the time it takes to do so, their male coworkers have completed an entire extra run. This discrepancy bothers established women less than their novice counterparts or those seeking a promotion, since signs of productivity, efficiency, and dedication are scrutinized by management. Laura, who was a relatively new temporary employee the first day I spent with her in her truck, clearly described what was at stake in something as seemingly insignificant as bathroom breaks. After explaining how grueling shiftwork can be because "you only sleep on your days off," she linked the chronic exhaustion and her ability to go a good job while at work: "I try to give my full effort when out here [at the mine], but I just give up when I get behind in the load count because of a blue house [port-a-potty] or mechanical delay." She was upset that the supervisors have to care about production and look at all their load counts, and the guys do better at them. "I think there should be a leveling mechanism between men and women when we have to hunt for a blue house." She did appreciate that the female supervisor on her crew tries to create parking ditches by all of the blue houses, so that equipment operators do not have to chock their tires when they park.

Feeling the pressure of production numbers, women try to shorten their bathroom delays by going to the bathroom while hiding behind the dual wheels, rather than locating and then entering a port-a-potty. This practice is not only uncomfortable, but also potentially embarrassing since they risk being seen by coworkers. Whereas some women shake it off and take pride in being able to not care if others see their exposed bodies, others blush just thinking about the possibility. Women who are the most worried about getting behind in their load counts—the number of runs completed—and thereby risk looking like a less productive worker often reduce the amount of liquids they consume so that they do not have to urinate as frequently. This all-too-prevalent practice is dangerous because it dehydrates women.

Menstruation adds more pressure, since women have to regularly change pads and tampons.[17] A minority attempt to avoid getting off the machinery at all; horrified truck drivers at two different places regaled me with stories about finding bloody tampons hidden under the seats or sitting on the floor of the cab. Experienced women miners try to discourage new hires from doing so, even if it means taking extra time on the runs. As a part of her socializing strategies, Mary explained that she always talked to new women about "period stuff." She said, "They need to know that it's okay to stop, that you can't help it, and that people will understand. I try to give them pointers about how to time it so that it's less obvious." Married men and those with daughters tend to more understanding of women who make frequent bathroom stops every month at about the same point in the shift cycle—the twenty-eight-day shift rotation mirrors the standard twenty-eight-day menstruation cycle, after all—but it is not unusual for frequent bathroom use to be brought up in grumbles about coworkers who routinely fail to pull their own weight.

Disparities in sleep, debates about special treatment during pregnancy, and conflicts over bathroom use demonstrate that "power is inscribed on and by bodies through moves of social supervision and discipline as well as self-regulation" (Grosz 1990: 65). Production regimes aided by sophisticated computer software compel compliance from workers in their attempts to regiment the inconsistencies of individual bodies into routine, predictable, and measurable performance indicators. More vulnerable workers, especially novice women, feel this pressure more acutely and seek to mold their practices to the ideals prescribed by the production process. Yet even the most disciplined bodies are not machines, and the need to rest and relieve oneself pushes against demands for production. These practices gesture not simply to how women and men sometimes differently embody work, but also to how the expectations of this embodiment can privilege men in some blue-collar workplaces (J. Williams 2000: 65). Women miners in Wyoming have mitigated many of these features in their own efforts to adapt to the workplace and adapt the workplace to them, but the few problem areas discussed here remain under contention.

Conclusion

Shiftwork is not unique to mining or other extractive industries. Like the rest of the United States, large numbers of shiftworkers in Gillette are found in the ranks of janitors, nurses, doctors, and emergency medical technicians; train engineers and their support staff; and employees of stores such as Wal-Mart and K-Mart. The work schedules of people who work in bars and restaurants also depart from a 9-to-5 schedule, since they frequently work either very early in the morning, slinging coffee and eggs to the early risers or people who were up all night, or they work very late in the evening, serving beer and bar food to people who are just waking up or are hungry from a full day's work. In fact, shiftwork is such a prominent feature of the country at large that an estimated one in five Americans works at night and attempts to sleep during the day (Maume, Sebastian, and Bardo 2010: 751). The unique stress of the mine schedule is its continual rotation; rather than consistently working nights or swing shifts, miners switch between nights and days every three or four days.

If the shiftwork schedule stresses people's social relationships and bodies, why have they stuck with it for so many years? In part, working rotating shifts seemed inevitable, a necessary element of work in the industry that cannot be avoided even if they desired to do so. This pragmatic orientation holds true for other blue-collar workers who do not question shiftwork because it seems out of their control (e.g., Perucci and MacDermid 2007). In fact, a Bureau of Labor Statistics survey found that while some people cited personal preference or childcare arrangements as their primary reasons for working nights and evenings (ranging between 11 and 20 percent of the sample), over half did so because it was the "nature of the job" (Bureau of Labor Statistics 2005: 3). A further and more specifically local explanation for the acceptance of shiftwork is that miners came to love the freedom of the seven days off they get once a month, using the time to travel, hunt, fish, work on home improvement projects, or even take on a second job. When management gave employees at one mine the option of switching from a twelve-hour schedule to a ten-hour schedule, which would have given them more time to be at home with their families and sleep, they overwhelmingly voted against it because they did not want to lose the seven days off. The twenty-one days of exhaustion were the price to be paid for seven days of freedom.

Perhaps even more important, the miners' close affective bonds made the demanding schedule bearable. When miners consider their crews to be family because they share the intimate experiences of working, joking, and eating together, they offer an organic theory of kinship—in the sense that it emerges from their lives—as what Marshall Sahlins (2011) calls the "mutuality of being." His description of these relationships echoes the observations of generations of labor historians and shop-floor ethnographers: "To the extent [kin] lead common lives, they partake of each other's sufferings and joys, sharing one another's experiences even as they take responsibility for and feel the effects of each other's acts" (Sahlins 2011: 14). Sharing time and space in the Wyoming mines creates exceptionally strong bonds of relatedness due to the extreme spatial and temporal separation of the miners from the physical community and its temporal rhythms. Rather than going to bed each night at the same time as their spouses and children, they move through a constantly rotating schedule with their coworkers. Rather than regularly sharing meals with their spouses and children, they share meals with their coworkers, both on-site and in the community.

The significance of gender partially diminishes in the face of this larger differentiation between miners and nonminers, since the demanding shiftwork schedule prompts crewmembers to view themselves as having more in common with each other than with men or women in the community. What is paramount for them in thinking about their lives, for example, is the fact that they have to dramatically alter their patterns of eating, sleeping, and working every four days.

Though chronic exhaustion draws out similarities between men and women's bodily states and their ways of thinking about them—a tired miner is a tired miner, to recall Mary—it also places a heavier burden on women at particular points in their lives. In other words, men and women miners face remarkably similar challenges in attuning their bodily rhythms to the industrial time of the mines, but particular moments over the course of both single shifts (such as bathroom use) as well as entire life cycles (such as pregnancies and child raising) bring gender difference to the fore—and usually to the detriment of women.

Shiftwork thus turns coworkers into families, and these crew families help miners inhabit a potentially alienating workplace and mitigate the stresses it presents. In the process of recognizing one another as family, the miners also recognize each other as persons rather than as extensions of machines. Anthropologist Kathryn Dudley's eloquent observation of Wisconsin autoworkers rings true for the Wyoming miners: "Out of the experience of collective reliance comes an appreciation of coworkers as individuals who can have good days and bad days, a concept of work as a set of enduring social relationships that transcend the bad days, and a strong feeling of loyalty toward others like you" (1994: 112). The ritual of bringing doughnuts succinctly encapsulates this perspective in reassuring people that the crew will continue to support, love, and joke with everyone despite their momentary missteps.

These ethnographic materials therefore suggest that by making work seem more like home, workplace relatedness helps miners create the dignified workplaces they desire and deserve. After all, anthropologist Tim Ingold reminds us that "the worker does not cease to dwell in the workplace. He is 'at' home there. But home is often a profoundly uncomfortable place to be" (2000: 332). Ingold and the miners alike critique Marx's famous assertion that workers are "at home" only when they are not working. In so doing, they point to the overlap between the spheres of home and work that tend to be separated in popular discourse and academic theory. At the same time, however, miners carefully construct limits on how much work can be like home, since they do not want their work to supersede their dedication to their spouses, partners, and children. In the next chapter I turn to examine this tenuous balance for the miners and their families.

4

Interweaving
Love and Labor

———————————————◄o►——

Traces of the mining industry are found throughout Gillette, even if the mines are located between ten to sixty miles outside of town. Driving into town from the north or east requires driving past active mines and power plants located alongside the highway; travelers pull over to watch shovels, draglines, and haul trucks in action from the road, sometimes stopping to take pit tours that companies offer tourists and schools as a part of their outreach efforts. Approaching from the south or west requires driving past the offices and warehouses of equipment vendors and the giant machinery they park alongside the road. Outside of a major events center that hosts national rodeos and conferences, concerts and dance performances, and the county fair, lies a park displaying old mine and railroad equipment—a train engine, drill, haul truck, truck bed, and huge tires—over which teenagers and children crawl. The whistles of coal trains passing through at all times of the day and night can be heard throughout the neighborhoods. Except for the historic downtown, residential subdivisions can all be traced to a specific boom, the houses bearing the telltale signs of the 1960s (oil), the late 1970s and early 1980s (coal), or the 2000s (coalbed methane) in their construction style and paint. Trucks parked outside of those homes hint at their occupants' occupations: buggy whip antennas and mud signal a vehicle that enters the minesites.

The industry also permeates the homes' interiors, from the presence of lunch boxes and boots left at the front door to the absence of miners at dinner tables. One afternoon Linda and I were sitting in her living room, discussing what it was like to be married to a longtime shiftworker, when she said, "We didn't see Roger for two years." Family photos of their four sons hung on most of the walls, and crafts that she had made perched on windowsills and bookshelves, but the house seemed empty to her. Like so many afternoons, Roger was at work at the mine. In years past, her boys would have filled the house with their constant conversation, school projects, and dirty laundry, but now they had all graduated from high school. Not having children to cook for, clean up after, or taxi around town seemed strange, since she had spent most of the past two decades caring for the pack of them. In thinking about her life, she remembered the early years as being the most challenging because she was "basically a single mom." When Roger first started at the mine, he worked at night and then went to school during the day to train to become a mechanic. "I was always so busy with the kids, being pregnant and busy, that there was sometimes where it was just wearing me down," she said. "During those two years he was driving truck and going to school, I was pregnant and raised two kids. He was always gone."

The demanding, constantly rotating shiftwork schedule described in the previous chapter brings crews close together and cements a feeling of relatedness on the worksite, but it simultaneously imperils family ties at home. Dual-earner couples can go days without seeing one another, their only communication being over the phone or through "notes left on the butcher block," as one miner put it. This finding supports the sociological literature on the familial lives of shiftworkers, which documents increased stress and decreased marital satisfaction leading to higher divorce rates.[1] The literature on extractive industry booms also points to shiftwork as a key cause of high divorce rates among those workers in particular, though further research has questioned the research methods and conclusions of the studies forming the basis of that literature.[2] In Gillette, divorce is found among mining families, though not in dramatically larger numbers than the population as a whole. The great majority of miners I met were happily married. To add a missing perspective to the existing literature on the family lives of extractive workers, in this chapter I focus on the experiences of mining families headed by couples who have maintained satisfying marriages.

Exploring the everyday family lives of the Wyoming miners also adds a unique perspective to the wider sociological shiftwork literature, which points to the schedule's potential to increase the time parents and children spend together. Existing research suggests that for blue-collar families, working night shifts can be a strategy for spouses to ensure that someone is at home with children during the day or before and after school, making paid childcare unnecessary.[3] Men who regularly work nights, for example, can shuttle children to and from school, and those who work days can cook dinner and put children to bed. For women, working nights allows them the benefit of being at home and available to children during the day, thus enabling them to claim the symbolic time and space of stay-at-home mothers (Garey 1999). The downside of these arrangements is that, in order to maintain a smoothly running household, the shiftworkers regularly sacrifice more sleep than day workers (Garey 1999: 132–133; C. Williams 2008).

The populations forming the basis of the literature on shiftwork are people who regularly work the same nonstandard hours, such as nurses who always work nights or plant technicians who always work evenings. The Wyoming miners, on the other hand, work both days and nights over the course of a single week. It is crucial to distinguish between regular, rotating, and irregular shifts, since these structures have very different implications for family life (Preston et al. 2000; Presser 2003). Rotating twelve-hour shifts for miners in the basin, coupled with daily commutes that can stretch up to three hours round-trip, do not allow the same dependable opportunities for workers to spend time with their children. Whereas a nurse working nights will always be home at 10 A.M. to pick up a sick child from school, a miner could be working days, sleeping off a night shift, or relaxing at home when they receive a call from school to pick up their children. Whereas a plant technician who works nights can depend on eating breakfast with children in the morning, the only time miners are able to share meals routinely with their families at home is on their days off. While working nights, miners are gone by the time their spouses and children gather around the dinner table, and they return too late in the morning to share a bowl of cereal or see them off to school. While working days, their alarms go off hours before anyone else wakes, so they get ready for work while the rest of their family sleeps. They return much later than the preferred time for dinner, so they usually eat warmed-up leftovers from their family's earlier meal while everyone else relaxes around the television, does homework, or gets ready for bed. Spouses and children look forward to weekends as time off from work and school, but miners work at least two weekends out of every month—more if they work overtime. Most of their days off fall during the middle of the week when everyone else is away from the home, leaving them alone to watch movies, go to the gym, or do home improvement projects. Though the schedule is patterned, repeating over each twenty-eight-day cycle, it feels erratic to children who are never sure if the shiftworking parent will be at home and awake at the same time as they are.

The efforts made by miners to overcome the distance the schedule creates between them and their children and spouses shows that "relatedness is not solely about the genealogical relationships between people but about the practices of connection—and disconnection—through which people maintain and contest the emotional, social, political, and material parameters of their daily lives" (Van Vleet 2008: 26). In this chapter I examine miners' parenting practices by exploring the disconnection that the shiftwork schedule engenders between parents and children, as well as the strategies families have developed to mitigate it. These strategies encompass deceptively mundane everyday household activities, from reading books to sharing chores, as well as a popular rite of passage in which the college-age children of mine employees temporarily work at the mines themselves during summer breaks. The ethnographic materials show that the families' efforts to mend relatedness are imbued with attempts to diminish gender differences in their growing children. Moreover, analyzing the summer student work program in the larger context of parenting practices and their dreams for their children reveals the miners' criticisms of working conditions (primarily the rotating shiftwork schedule), the industry in general, and a national job market that is increasingly hostile to blue-collar workers.

Gendered Divisions of Household Labor

Before analyzing parenting practices in particular, it is crucial to examine the wider context of how couples manage household responsibilities. All of the miners, spouses, and other significant others I came to know espoused an ideal of companionate marriage that is consistent with dominant North American notions of the phenomenon (Cherlin 2009: 68). Husbands and wives think of themselves as best friends and confidants in addition to romantic partners who love one another. It is significant that none of the couples who maintained their marriages subscribed to the other dominant model of North American marital patternsidentified by Cherlin: expressive divorce, in which divorce is a vehicle for self-fulfillment and self-expression. If miners and their spouses believed that marriage was primarily a strategy for greater self-realization and self-satisfaction, the stresses of shiftwork likely would have caused them to divorce decades earlier.

Mining couples enjoy each other's companionship. Outside of their children and their children's activities, the common thread uniting most of those whom I came to know was their shared love for the outdoors. Like Jerry and Cindy, many appreciated northeastern Wyoming summers because the long days, sunny skies, and warm weather made for excellent conditions to ride motorcycles. Others preferred camping at the local reservoir or nearby mountains. Al and Sandy trekked westward to the Wind River Mountains, where they camped in car sites or went on extended backpacking expeditions. "It's such a beautiful place, and we both feel relaxed just being there, being outside, and being with each other," Sandy explained. And while most urban, middle-class Americans would view hunting as a decidedly masculine ritual, women like Carrie joined their husbands on their annual fall trips in search of deer or elk. Wanda enjoyed it all, saying, "I hunt, fish, camp, everything. I go elk hunting with my husband every year. I used to always fish with my brother, but now I fish with my daughter and her kids." Fishing was so important to her that she kept her parents' ancient fishing boat in top condition so that it will stay in the family.

Mining couples were also content to stay at home and work on the house. Like most of their friends, Jerry and Cindy enjoyed "piddling" around the house on their home improvement projects. When I asked him what he liked to do on his days off, he smiled and listed off activities that all included his wife: "Work on the house. Go to church. Hang out on the deck when the weather's warm. Watch the birds. Ride the scooter. And that's about it." Although couples did appreciate some time apart—and there were a few women who always chose to go shopping at the mall in Rapid City rather than fly-fishing along a creek—the dislocations of shiftwork brought out an appreciation for time spent together. Activities such as camping, fishing, hunting, and motorcycle riding may be associated with manly men and masculine expertise for many middle-class Americans, but for rural western families like the ones in Gillette these were viewed as enjoyable and proper endeavors for women and men alike.

In discussing their marriages both individually and together, the couples viewed each other as equals and partners even if they also joked about one of them ruling the roost. But except for couples without children, the actual division of household labor was much more unequal when both spouses worked full-time or one (usually the wife of a male miner) had chosen to stay at home. Recall Linda's statement from the introduction that she was "basically a single mom." Cindy also decided to stay home to be able to raise her and Jerry's kids without regularly hiring a babysitter. It was important to her to be able to "be home with them and do things, go to school activities or sports that they were involved in, and be able to shuttle them around for all that instead of depending on somebody else." She said she would have wanted to do those things anyway, and somewhat sheepishly admitted that she had "always enjoyed being a homemaker." She enjoyed activities such as mowing the lawn or doing housework because it meant that when her husband's days off came around, they could spend that time together. "We spend time working on our house and on the yard, and we spend a lot of time with our friends," she explained, and then her eyes lit up. "We do motorcycle trips, vacations with our friends in the summer when we take blocks of time off and just get together, whether we just go out of town or play cards for an evening or something like that." For Cindy, being able to share leisure time with her husband was worth taking on the bulk of day-to-day chores around the house.

Dual-earner couples also had difficulty arranging what they perceived to be an equitable division of labor. Dave, for instance, appreciated that his wife's schedule as a school teacher allowed her to take care of their daughters. Drawing on the language of teamwork, he said that shiftwork is "not all bad, but it makes you realize the importance of a two-parent family. Sue worked a regular eight-hour, five-day, pretty much forty-hour week, and that helped. If we'd both been working my schedule, it'd be a lot harder." Sitting on their couch, savoring a glass of wine after dinner, they enjoyed a lively debate about household chores. They agreed that whoever cooks dinner does not have to clean up, so usually Sue ends up cooking and Dave ends up cleaning. She plans the menus and does laundry once a week, but he mows the lawn and does his own laundry when he needs it. Sue said that when her daughters were living at home, they lightened the load for both of them. "Now that they're gone," she said, "I have got their chores." She and Dave both started laughing in anticipation of what she was going to say next: "So I think we need to renegotiate." On a roll, she shared another funny story about such negotiations. "I'd get up every morning and I'd make him bacon and eggs and toast for breakfast. I'd make him his lunch sandwiches." Emphasizing the effort it took her to get out of bed before dawn just to take care of him, she said, "So I'd get up and I'd make him his lunch, but he *complained* one time." Dave chuckled and sheepishly looked at his hands, which bore the telltale marks of a mechanic. She continued, "He said, 'You think you could make this sandwich a little thicker?'" She paused for effect. "So I looked at him, I said, 'You can make your own from now on. I'm done with this.'" Without missing a beat, Dave delivered the punch line: "So I've been making my own lunches ever sense. But I know what I get." The negotiation animating Dave and Sue's approach to running their household threads through the remembered experiences of many couples in the basin, supporting Francine Deutsch's (1999) identification of everyday interactions and adjustments as crucial for understanding household divisions of labor.

Despite the structural constraints of shiftwork, couples did make efforts to find more equitable divisions of labor. "Whoever is home watches the kid or does the laundry or mows the lawn," said Gary. "It's not like Mom has her jobs and Dad has different ones. We all gotta pull together to make this work; you can't be stuck with some outdated idea of who does what." The equipment operator Diane was equally clear, saying, "There's no reason for a husband not to help. If the wife is working full-time, why wouldn't the husband think he could help?" Since her husband, also a miner, is a good cook, he often prepares their meals as long as she plans them out in advance. He also does all of their dishes, but she takes care of the laundry and vacuuming because she is "particular" about how she likes it done. Carrie also pointed to the importance of her husband's sharing chores with her, saying that because they both worked shifts, everyone in her house helped out raising livestock and taking care of the house. Patty thought that her ability to advance in the industry was directly related to her husband's willingness to take on jobs in the home that would otherwise fall to women. She is thankful that while she was on shiftwork, her husband had a straight day job that allowed him to do the primary caretaking for their daughters: "He was and still is a very hands-on dad. We had daycare. If I was on nights, he'd pick them up when he got off work, feed them, change diapers, and pack them and haul them and away they went. Never would have made it without him." These couples, which included male miners as well as male partners of female miners, all attempted to share household responsibilities.

Other couples, especially those in which the husband was the shiftworker, found it too difficult to integrate him into routine family responsibilities. These arrangements were clearest in the cases of stay-at-home mothers, such as Cindy and Linda described above, who took almost sole responsibility for the everyday work of running the house. Even some women who worked full-time outside the home (but not at the mines) found it easier to take care of domestic duties themselves. Sandy, for example, expressed a common sentiment in her preference to have a standing arrangement in which she drove their children to their after-school activities. She said, "You'd have to think, is it my turn to take them to swimming lessons this week or his? I'd rather just do it myself." For her and other wives, it was "too complicated" to constantly switch back and forth even though she also worked full-time. She did appreciate that shiftwork meant that her husband regularly did their grocery shopping when he was home by himself and could be called on in emergency situations, such as when their children were sick and needed to be picked up from school while she was working. But like other women, she recognized that she did more of the every-day work of maintaining the house and raising the children since her husband was simply not available to her and their children when they were home.

There are clear limitations to the sharing of household duties, including parenting. As sociologist Arlie Hochschild (1989) found in her pathbreaking research on women's "second shift" in the home, men's contributions to the household activities in the basin are often viewed as "help" or "support" rather than a primary responsibility. Gender divisions also linger in how men "pitch in." Even though Carrie was proud that her husband and kids all "did their part" to keep their small ranch running and their house clean, she later quali-fied the rosy picture she initially painted. Referring to herself, she said, "Mom does extra chores." A particularly clear example immediately came to her mind. "One night I came home from work just exhausted, and they were all sitting there watching TV. They asked, 'What's for dinner?' I was so tired that I just took out a jar of peanut butter and a jar of jelly, slammed them on the counter and said, 'Dinner is served!'" Carrie's action was a protest against the linger-ing assumption that she would ultimately be responsible for feeding everyone, even though her children and spouse were equally competent and available.

The couples reporting the most egalitarian and gender-neutral division of household labor were those without children, supporting Risman's (1998: 94) finding that these efforts are most successful when both spouses work and are childless. Mary and Doug have both worked rotating shifts as technicians at the same mine since the early 1980s. She said, "I'm lucky because he does 90 percent of the cooking and I do all the cleaning. And he occasionally does laundry, and he does all the oil changes." Jo enjoys a similar situation with her husband: "He dusts and vacuums so he doesn't have to do the bathrooms, which he hates, and I clean the kitchen." When it comes to cooking in that kitchen, though, she laughed and said that he did the heavy lifting. "I'm the luckiest female in the world because his uncle is from Denmark, and he worked in his bakery and then did KP duty in the guards [National Guard]." Jo is proud of her work at the mine and looks to her aunt as her biggest role model. Jo considers her a "female innovator" and "the Gloria Steinem before Gloria Steinem was around" because she was able to forge a successful career. Mary and Jo divided chores with their husbands based on personal preference rather than gender stereotypes.

Women like Jo and Mary realized that it would be more difficult to do their job and take care of children. "If we had kids, I don't know if I'd be out here," Mary said. "I don't know how we'd do it, since we're so busy without them." In fact, a significant number of women in their twenties and early thirties who have reached positions of leadership in the pit doubt that they could raise children while working the rotating schedule, so they have decided to delay or completely abstain from having children. "My husband and I both have strange schedules so I don't think we could raise our kids the way we want to," said Joanne, who runs the dispatch system at another mine. "We could take more menial jobs, but we think the work we do is important." These sentiments echo those sociologist Sarah Damaske (2011) found among American women describing their decision to not have children. They framed their decision in language that privileged the good of the children they did not have: they remained childless, they said, because it would have been impossible to engage in the intensive mothering society demanded (2011: 151). Damaske cogently points out that this language points to the continued dominance of American cultural ideals that leave women primarily responsible for the home and family, even as these expectations have normalized paid work outside the home.

Together with the experiences of the couples with children, these ethnographic materials point to the limits of gender being undone in the mining families' homes. The miners' efforts to craft companionate marriages (and thus collectively enjoy the time the shiftworker does have with their family) and share household responsibilities partially undo gendered work-family arrangements. But having children makes sharing these responsibilities more difficult, though not impossible. In a twist on Gallagher and Smith's (1999) observation that evangelical families exhibited "symbolic traditionalism" and "pragmatic egalitarianism," most mining families are to at least some degree symbolic egalitarians and pragmatic traditionalists. Although their parenting efforts could not be categorized as equally shared—as Deutsch (1999) found among blue-collar shiftworkers in her landmark study on equal parenting—they do manage the time they have with children to create equally close affective bonds with them.

Relatedness Imperiled: Distance between Miners and Children

The greatest irony of mine employment is that while almost all of the men and women sought jobs at the mine to provide for families or secure a foundation for the families they dreamed of having, the demanding rotating shift schedule distances them from the everyday routines of the very people they seek to love and support. This tension between their efforts to provide financial stability and foster emotional closeness is not unique to Wyoming (e.g., Townsend 2002: 130), but the rotating shift schedule intensifies it.

Jerry, who has worked the shift schedule for the past twenty years, eloquently describes the dilemma. In explaining why he wanted to work at a smaller mine close to town rather than supervise a crew at one of the large southern mines, he said: "It was just too much time. With a twelve-hour shift, you had to be there an hour early, then you stayed a half hour after shift, and had two hours of driving time. It was just eating you up. That's how we lived in-between days off. I didn't think it was a good life. If I could get six hours of sleep a night, that was doing good. Otherwise you just worked and slept and waited for days off to come back around." The twelve-hour schedule made it difficult for him to spend time with his wife and children while he was working; he only really saw them on his days off. The two-week, eight-hour shift schedule he initially worked was also challenging. "When you were on swings, you didn't see your kids at all. If you go to work in the afternoon and don't get off until after midnight, you don't see them unless you get up early in the morning. And even if you do, you hardly see the kids at all." Laughing, he admitted, "I was a little grumpy. It took me a while to learn how to deal with it, that sleeping during the day and having those little bitty kids around. It was bad." His wife Cindy vividly remembered the stress from those years. "With a twelve-hour shift plus additional hours for supervising and an hour drive each way," she said, "there were times when it seemed like I didn't see him for several days in a row because he was only home to sleep and eat and then leave for work."

As much as Jerry and Cindy hated shiftwork, being able to provide for the family made a mining job a big draw for both of them. Cindy was thankful that Jerry had a job after having been previously laid off from construction. "It's just provided a good living for us," she summarized. Jerry echoed her sentiments. "It was good work," he said. "It was fun back when you kids were small.[4] Everybody has to work, of course, and mining was the work to have when you were in Campbell County. We raised our families and paid for everything with that job." Jerry and Cindy echo other hardworking on the northern plains for whom life is "unimaginable without working at something" (Fricke 2008: 30). Though he takes pride in his work and his ability to support his wife and children, he is frustrated that the mine job takes him away from those same people on a regular basis.

The stress of shiftwork is palpable when listening to children talk about their own lives and thoughts about the industry. A miner's daughter bluntly criticized the shiftwork schedule and her father's dubious honor of holding the record for overtime by saying, "Obviously we don't see him very much at all." Chloe, whose father had worked shifts for nearly two decades by the time we were in high school together, had limited knowledge of his work when she was growing up. "The only thing I really knew was that it took my father away from home, but I didn't know anything at all about what he did," she explained. "I just knew that he came home late at night, and it was a place where you were married to the job, you always worked constantly." By using the language of marriage to describe her father's relationship with the mine and his coworkers, Chloe suggests that it approximated the singular devotion usually reserved for family in the conventional sense. In this case, her father's "marriage" to the mine family made it difficult for him to dedicate the same time and energy to his spouse and children at home.

Absence also stood out for Callie, the twenty-something daughter of the mechanic Al, as the main reason why mining was, in her words, a "tough lifestyle." She said, "If your dad was a miner, you understood," she explained. "It wasn't tough financially or anything, but, you know, he just wasn't there a lot of the time or your mom wasn't there. They don't work from nine to five and then come home." But Callie did appreciate that her father took time off from work to attend her school events, just as Dave did and my own father did. One of my own earliest memories, in fact, is of my father unexpectedly showing up to see me perform in a kindergarten Christmas play. My five-year-old self knew that he was working and most likely would not be there. Still, I was disappointed. During the play, the gym was dark except for a spotlight shining on my class, all of us decked out with large trees fashioned out of green construction paper taped to our heads. During the middle of a carol, I looked over when the gym doors swung open. There, outlined against the bright light streaming in from the hallway, stood my father. He was holding his giant lunch pail and still wearing the jeans and flannel shirt he usually took off the second he stepped through the door of our house, which meant that he must have hurried directly from the bus to the elementary school without stopping at home to make himself more comfortable for an evening outing.

Whereas rank-and-file shiftworkers experience the most extreme dislocation from their families and community, the long hours put in by managers raise comparable challenges for their families. Sara's husband has worked in management since they first moved to the basin twenty years ago. She appreciates that the job has made it "very comfortable for us to clothe and feed our kids, and have a nice home and vehicles that run." On the other hand, she said, "The negative thing is how much time it takes. He gets up at four o'clock. As he's aged, that's become more difficult for him. It meant that he had less social time with the rest of us. . . . There have been times when he has just not really been a part of the family other than the income, and he just comes through to sleep." Sara's stark assessment of her husband's work schedule points to the importance of time for being a part of the family. If he only came through to sleep, he was taking his meals at the mine or at an empty dinner table because everyone else had eaten hours earlier; he was not able to help ferry their children around town after school; and often did not spend evenings relaxing with them at social events or simply around the television. For her, this meant that he was "outside the circle" except for the few times when his schedule intersected with theirs.

Sentiments like Sara's may seem extreme, but they echo throughout the basin in every conversation about shiftwork. The plant mechanic Dave broached the topic by saying that it had made it difficult to "become a part of something that meets on a regular basis." He had enjoyed being on the church council, but felt bad that he frequently missed meetings for work. Whereas people with nine-to-five jobs know they would always be free on Wednesday night or Sunday afternoon, he does not. "I don't like to take on an obligation unless I can be there and fulfill that obligation," he said, "so because of shiftwork I've not done things that I would have wanted to otherwise." His wife Sue nodded throughout his explanation. She grabbed his hand in a gesture of support and added, "It's been hard on the family, too." Now it was Dave's turn to nod in agreement. "You know," she said, "he was on different schedules so wasn't always there for mealtimes and weekends. He's not home on the weekends." Spending time with his growing daughters was the most important thing to him, he explained, so every night when he got home from work, he immediately sat down with them to read. They were also careful to integrate the rest of the family into his seven days off each month. For example, while the girls were on break from school, they would use that time to go skiing or camping, depending on the season. During the school year, he also used his vacation time to attend swim meets and parent-teacher conferences.

Roger and Linda also made conscious efforts to include him in their family life. Once a week they tried to have a sit-down family dinner, whether that meant pizza on Friday night or a chicken dinner on Sunday afternoon, since most of the time he missed meals. They all spent almost all his days off in the summer at the lake, where they water-skied and raced the speed boats that he and the boys spent time together fixing in the garage. Like Roger and Linda, all of the mining families I came to know made the best of a difficult situation by praising the "toughness" that the schedule ingrains in workers as well as their spouses, partners, and children. Most made an effort to make sure that they were there for parent-teacher conferences, award ceremonies, and big school events such as plays, meets, and games, but it was nearly impossible to re-create the intimacies stemming from day-to-day meals, conversations, arguments, and jokes.

Thus if ties of relatedness and feelings of kinship are "always in the process of being created" (Carsten 1997: 281), the mining families remind us that they are also always potentially in the process of being unraveled. But even as the disconnections of shiftwork stress ties of relatedness in the home, the same families also remind us that kinship is also "an important arena in which to find creativity . . . an area of life in which people invest their emotions, their creative energy, and their new imaginings" (Carsten 2004: 9). Men and women in Gillette have addressed the challenges and potential dislocations of shiftwork with creativity. Arranging for periodic shared, sit-down family meals—an icon of familial closeness in the United States—takes on increased urgency for the families, suggesting that feeding and being fed are as crucial for fostering relatedness for these families as it is, for example, for those in Malaysia (Carsten 1995: 223) or North India (Lambert 2000: 84–85), though specific practices vary cross-culturally. The case of shiftwork is unique, however, because being out of sync expands beyond mealtimes to encompass the most basic rhythms of sleeping, working, and enjoying leisure. Even when sitting down for a shared daily meal is not possible, miners and their families have created other rituals—such as Dave's tradition of reading with his daughters every night—in which they share time and space together. Shiftwork makes it difficult but not impossible for miners to embody and enact the types of family arrangements they value.

Though dominant Euro-American folk understandings of kinship are grounded in marriage and shared blood or genetic material (Finkler 2001; Schneider 1980), the ethnographic materials examined here show that shared space and time is equally crucial for turning "blood relatives" into family as it is for creating workplace kin out of coworkers, as described in the previous chapter. Even though these families view kinship partially in biological terms—they believe they are parents by virtue of conceiving and giving birth to children, and those children are related to them because they share their blood and genes—they also keenly understand the importance of nurturing those ties.

Diminishing Gender Differences While Mending Relatedness: Household Labor

Despite the challenges of the rotating shiftwork schedule, miners take an active role in parenting their children. The practices analyzed above centered on the creation of affective bonds with children through shared family rituals.

In the rest of the chapter I examine the second key arena of miners' parenting practices: their efforts to prepare children to succeed in the job market after graduation from high school or college. This analysis brings gender to the foreground, since the couples consciously attempted to instill gender-neutral skills and dispositions in their children. These activities are certainly not the only elements of parenting, which also encompasses the routine support and care for children through cooking meals, doing laundry, providing transportation, changing diapers of infants and toddlers, and more. This focus is partially due to the stage of life in which most mining families found themselves during my research. Because the majority of the miners and their spouses were middle-aged—they had kept their jobs after first being hired at the mines, leaving few openings for younger workers until the original cohort began retiring in the 2000s—their children were in high school or college, considering and preparing for future careers. This stage provided the frame through which the couples remembered the past and (consciously and subconsciously) selected the experiences and stories most relevant to them.

The language and activities of labor permeate miners' memories and visions of parenting. In discussing their role in family life, most pointed to the importance of instilling practical skills in their children. Roger, for example, included his sons in their many home improvement projects so they could gain experience with mechanical and electrical work, plumbing, and building. While he and his wife were happy if their children discovered a good fit with one of the trades, they were equally pleased if they discovered firsthand the need to go to college to pursue a different kind of work. Roger and Linda were both proud that one pursued a related career in construction, while the others became an accomplished academic, a nurse, and a member of a military special operations force.

Diane also consciously mentored her children in practical skills. She grew up on a multigenerational ranch in southern Wyoming. Her grandparents settled there after they moved to the state, and her grandfather went to work at a nearby coal mine to help pay the bills. Her father owned his own construction business, which frequently kept him in town, so taking care of the horses, cows, sheep, pigs, chickens, and a few donkeys required her and her siblings to pitch in. "We all worked," she said. "We had to use the shovel and pickax, but it was no different for us girls than [for] our brother. We had to learn, so we got trained." As an adult, she appreciated the strength and independence that she felt the experience cultivated in her, so she sought to do the same thing for her own children. "We made the kids work always. They need to know and have to do it." Laughing, she added, "We didn't pay them because they lived there!" Regular chores coupled with being forced to do extra work for money made them hard workers, she said. "If they wanted $60 jeans, they worked for them, shoveling sidewalks, whatever. I told them to go ahead and buy those

$60 jeans and see how long they last." With a satisfied grin, she said that they were back into the cheaper, sturdier, but less fashionable jeans more quickly than they expected. The incident illustrated her belief that "everything in life is a learning lesson."

Even though Diane sought to replicate the lessons of hard work she learned as a kid, she did make a significant departure from her mother's approach. Her mother required the girls to sweat along with their brother outside on the ranch, but he never joined them in the kitchen. Conversely, she makes a conscious effort to ensure that all of her children learn "basic survival stuff." Her sons as well as daughters learned life skills normally reserved for the opposite sex. Unlike her brother, her sons learned to cook, and she bragged, "My boys are better cooks than their wives!" With an impish grin, she added, "They can also sew and crochet, but they don't always broadcast that to everyone." She was also proud that her daughters know how to perform auto mechanic work, which means that they will not have to be dependent on a man to do it for them. "I keep telling them, they may not want to marry and even if they do their husband might not know how to do it." After one of her daughters complained about having to learn how to change the oil in her car, she remembered telling her that she had better learn because her father was not going to be able to rescue her.

Though Diane's mother worried that she puts too much pressure on her kids and is giving them an unduly hard life, Diane is not swayed: "Look, I'm unlike most women because I can change a flat tire. We learned how to do that. But my mom never made my brother cook, and she said that boys were sissies if they were cooking." To prove the superiority of her own approach, she contrasted her sons with her nephews, who did not spend time with their mother in the kitchen: "They got babied and now are pigs. They can't feed themselves unless it's premade junk food, but my kids know how to make nutritional meals for themselves." For her, the main goal of parenting should be to make children independent, and she believes that it is "sexist" to not train them in the full range of life skills. "I think it's survival training, period. I don't care what your gender is. Learn to cook, learn to do laundry, learn to change a flat tire, learn to change the oil, and you'll be fine." Her children seem to be a case in point; they all have found work they enjoy, including her daughter who is a pilot.

Weaving through Diane's stories about parenting is a theme common throughout the basin, in which parents consciously attempted to disrupt the gender stereotypes their children see in the media and reflected in a workforce that is nationally sex-segregated. These efforts expanded beyond daily chores to encompass leisure activities that are nonetheless frequently framed by the same values of hard work and perseverance. Organized sports played a large role in the local social scene, with the nationally ranked high school girls' teams packing in the same number of fans as the boys' teams. Parents supported their budding athletes by driving them to practice, talking with them about their experiences, attending their games or events, and sometimes training or practicing alongside them. According to the families, sports are an important opportunity to learn the values of hard work and dedication that will serve them throughout their lives.

Outside of organized teams, girls ski alongside their brothers and fathers during winter breaks, and a few even surpass them. An equipment operator named Josh, for example, could not be prouder that his teenage daughter is being courted by the professional snowboarding community. "She is awesome!" he exclaimed in the middle of a conversation we were having at the mine. He loved talking about her because it seemed to make the long stretch of road in-between the shovel and the dump a little shorter. They spent a lot of time together on the slopes, where he would give her feedback on her performance. "What makes her great and so promising is that she's conservative, doesn't take risks, so she just learns a skill and then adds on, and that means that she's a good candidate for training." Josh also took an active role in her academic life, keeping informed about her progress and relationships with students and teachers. He appreciated that her spunky personality was also clear at school. Even though she was an honors student, she did not blink when standing up to authority. Thinking that their teacher had been too hard on one of her classmates, she put a wad of gum in the teacher's coffee when she stepped outside the room. Grinning, he said, "I totally understand why she did it, and I think the principal did, too. I have a lot of respect for her." Here Josh drew a parallel between himself and his daughter, since he also imagined himself to be a guard against inappropriate authority, even if it meant he became the target for supervisory discipline at work.

Josh did not take much stock in conventional notions of proper careers or behaviors for men and women in thinking about himself or his daughter. He attributed his open-mindedness to being raised primarily by his mother and grandfather, who was "an old cowboy with a heart of gold." People's first impressions of Josh might fixate on his athletic prowess, which he cultivated both at work and in the gym. He was also, however, a keen intellectual who read Sun Tzu's *The Art of War* during equipment downtime, watched the History Channel more than ESPN, and was just as likely to drink a cup of tea as a neon energy drink. He also shrugged off the manly celebration of dirt and grease that are pervasive in popular views of the industry. Every day he brought a gallon of water to work with him. He drank it, of course, but also poured it on a paper towel to clean his face or wipe off a dusty steering wheel. While we were waiting for the shovel to reposition, he pulled out a Swiss Army knife and used it to carefully clean out the dirt from underneath his fingernails.

Women miners had a special appreciation for the need to spend time with their children and engage them in a full range of activities. Like many, Carrie took pleasure in recounting how she was raising her daughter to be a tomboy, just like she was. As a family, they enjoy going hunting, horseback riding, and camping, just like when she was a kid. She continued: "I enjoy family time with my kids. Since my daughter has been going hunting with us since she was five years old, she's a better shot than her dad and her brother! We call her One Shot. Four bullets, four years, four animals. She also likes fishing and showing her friends noncity life, how to be a kid and get dirty. I was always a tomboy too. I loved doing things with my brothers." When her daughter eventually went to work for a subcontractor at one of the mines, Carrie gave her a set of tools so that she would not have to borrow them from male coworkers. The gesture built on a longer history of the encouragement she gave her daughter to develop her mechanical skills.

Marie, who worked in land permitting (which includes negotiating and managing mineral rights) and grew up on a ranch in northeastern Wyoming, also attributed her daughter's eventual success in the industry to the child-hood experiences she provided for her. Her daughter got a degree in history and taught for a few years, but eventually switched careers to follow in her mother's footsteps. Marie attributes the switch to the excitement of the min-ing industry that filled their home when she was growing up. Rather than separating her career from her family, she talked about her work and brought her colleagues home. Her daughter then "had exposure to people in uranium and gold and coal mining through twenty years of people passing through our home, and that turned out to be pretty exciting compared to what she was doing at the school," Marie said. She also pointed to the practical les-sons she taught her daughter by staying close to the family ranch, saying, "I raised my daughter the same way my mom raised me: if it needs done, do it. It doesn't matter if you're a man or a woman." That can-do attitude, Marie thinks, gave her daughter and herself the confidence to succeed in a histori-cally masculine industry.

Like Marie, all of the women I came to know situated their current, non-traditional careers within the longer trajectories of their life histories, point-ing to fond childhood memories of hunting, camping, and fishing with their brothers, fathers, and mothers. Rather than subscribing to biological notions of inherent differences between men and women, they and their male cowork-ers and partners point to concrete activities through which they developed (and hope their daughters develop) characteristics associated with tomboys, who are locally valued and viewed as women who distance themselves from feminine stereotypes (see chapter 5). These narratives of growing up point to an organic theory of gender as contested, fluid, and emergent through every-day practice. The miners' efforts to parent their children by preparing them for future careers, therefore, are bound up in a desire to diminish gender dif-ferences in their growing children, even if—or perhaps because—they are not always able to do so in their own division of household and parenting responsibilities. The couples who were the most successful in achieving a gender-neutral division of household labor were those who did not have children. Raising children tended to result in a tenacious gendered division of labor even for couples with egalitarian ideals.

Nurturing Relatedness through Working Together: Mine Labor

The mines' summer student program extended and solidified the work in which parents engaged to mentor and mend strained relationships with their children. Some of the college students worked in the office or gave tours of the mines to visitors, but most were employed alongside the rank and file in production as equipment operators, plant technicians, or general labor. They rarely worked alongside their parents directly, but were assigned to a different crew, a different work area, or even different mine owned by the same company.[5] The number of students involved in the program varied according to the size of the mine: their numbers approached forty at the largest but could be less than ten at the smallest. When the graduating senior classes at the basin's largest high school normally comprised about five hundred students, the participation of more than a fifth of these in the summer student program represented a significant pattern for young people in the area. In addition to

FIG. 4 The author and her father standing in front of a loader during her summer employment.

becoming a rite of passage for these young adults, it had also become a greatly anticipated annual event for mine employees who had a chance to get to know their coworkers' children, show them how the mines operate, mentor them, and integrate them into long histories of practical jokes.

The biggest financial incentive for the companies was the ability to draw on a reserve labor force that is cheaper (and presumably more dedicated, given their familial ties to the company) than temporary workers from a staffing agency. The summer students were temporary workers by definition, and they filled crucial spots on the crews during a period in which many of their full-time employees take vacation time. For the students and their parents, the biggest practical advantage was money to help defray the skyrocketing cost of college. When I worked as a summer student, I made $14 an hour, which was twice as much as most of my peers were making in the jobs they could find around town. Other mines paid even more and offered bonuses for good attendance. By the end of the summer, I was able to save around $5,000 to take back to school, while some of my friends managed to put away as much as $7,000.

Perhaps even more important than the financial incentive was the opportunity to bring shiftworkers and their children together in shared time (shiftwork) and space (the mine) after years of moving through very different social worlds. Children actually talked about "really getting to know" their shiftworking parents through working at the mines themselves. Though children did not directly work with their parents, they nonetheless gained understanding of their parents by seeing and experiencing the work their parents did.

In talking about growing up, almost all of the summer students remembered either their father or mother being absent due to their job at the mine. Chloe said that all she knew about her father's work when she was growing up was that he worked far away and got home late at night: "The only thing I really knew was that it took my father away from home, but I didn't know anything at all about what he did." Similarly, Callie remembered that, as a child, all she knew about her father's work was that "he was a mechanic and that he worked out at the mine. It was a different shift. He worked shiftwork, and that was one thing that you had to adjust to. It adjusted our home life. He ate dinner at a different time than we did. He got up at a different time than we did. He just had a different schedule. That was one of the main things you knew because you can't see where he works, you can't go bring him lunch. It's a very removed world from the family." The summer Callie worked at the mine, however, she came to understand and appreciate how hard her father worked and how important his work was to the entire operation. Before working there, "I didn't understand his reputation out there. I didn't understand at all how much people respected his work." During her summer working at the same mine as her father, she gained "a new appreciation for what he did and how big the mine was. Like, he was working on a truck and I got to ride in it. I actually knew what he was talking about and what he was doing." She also learned how stressful that kind of work could be. "You were always in fear that you were going to do something wrong and get fired. I didn't understand that until I worked there, that it was constant, not pressure, but knowledge that if you did something very wrong you'd get fired because you weren't safe." She also thoroughly enjoyed meeting his coworkers. "I looked forward to the days we were there together. He could show me off to all his little buddies and they'd make fun of me." For example, after she told them that she worked in buildings and grounds, a lot of people would tell her that the lawn looked bad, knowing that mowing it was her job. Then they would usually let her in on a funny story about her dad. She understood and appreciated that this joking was a way of showing affection.

Christie also grew up with a father who worked shifts. Like Callie, she never understood his work until she worked at the mine herself as a summer student. "I didn't know what the heck was going on. I mean, we'd have company picnics and stuff but it's never the same as actually doing it." She remembers that her father would come home from work and while they were eating dinner, complain to her and her mother about the stupid things different coworkers had done during the shift. "But you don't have any concept about what he's talking about because you don't know nothing, and you don't know those people." That changed after she started working there. They become closer through sharing knowledge about the mining process and the people who worked for the company. "He was proud of me. He knew I was doing a good job. Like, 'Yeah, this is my daughter!' And every time we'd go talk to someone, it was like they know us both now. Plus I could go home and complain about something and he would know what I meant. That all brought us closer." She also came to appreciate his reputation as one of the nicest shovel operators on-site, especially since he would load trucks even if they had parked crookedly under his shovel.

John's daughter also thought that her work at the mine gave them "something in common." She had always felt close with her mom because she was the one who was around a lot when she was growing up, but her dad could not spend as much time at their house because of his schedule. Once she was at the mine, however, she and her dad had a lot more to talk about: "You're sitting in this truck, all the time, with no one to talk to, and your mind wanders. So you see something in the mine that you didn't have anything to do with, but you'd wonder what's going on. So I'd ask my dad. I'd talk to him a whole lot more about that." He also made an effort to see her when their schedules matched up. He always had a meeting at 6:30 in the morning, so he tried making sure that he would see her when she was coming off of night shifts: "Either he'd see me coming off the line and he'd come talk, or he'd wait in the main building.

Sometimes he'd hang out around there and wait for me to come in, just so I could see him." Laughing with just a hint of exasperation, she said, "He still tells me everything about what's happening at the mine."

Miners share the same positive appraisal of the summer student program. John was happy that his daughter got to see the mines at firsthand: "I think this is true of every parent who has a child work at the mine, especially the same mine. They finally get to see a glimpse, you know, of what you do and the environment you're working in." Al thought the program was important in giving young people an opportunity to "get out and see where their mothers and fathers work, save a few dollars for college, and get out in the workforce and see what's going on." He enjoyed being able to take Callie out to see the loader that he always worked on and introducing her to a few of his crewmembers: "She got a chance to see what a coal mine was like and save some money. I was glad to see her out there. It was fun to see her in a hard hat and coveralls and sunglasses.[6] And I did take her out for a ride in the loader one afternoon." He is proud that her old crewmembers enjoyed working with her so much that they still asked him about what she was doing. Chloe also reported that her father beamed when he could introduce her to coworkers. "Just to have your child there along with you and you can say to your coworkers, to whomever, this is my child, this is my son, this is my daughter, they're going to school in Ohio, they're going to school in Illinois, they're doing whatever," she explained. "This is what I produced, this is the child that I have raised. They're here, they're making some money for the summer."

What was clear in talking with the summer students and their parents was that the newfound closeness and appreciation they feel does not rest primarily in the technical knowledge the children learn, but what could be called the "iconicity of feeling" it generates. Working with Apache on the San Carlos Indian reservation, linguistic anthropologist David Samuels (2004) coined the term to refer to an iconic, or perfectly duplicated, experience of emotion in a separate but recoverable time and place. In terms of his fieldsite, the Apache experience "Apacheness" when they conjure up a feeling of what it meant to be Apache in the past. In terms of my fieldsite, the iconicity of feeling linked the emotional experiences of the new miners with their parents: their initial fear and nervousness, the exhaustion prompted by the rotating shift schedule, their weariness in going to work to do heavily routinized work and yet their pride in a job well done. The summer student program might be so popular because this shared empathy is hard to access without both parents and children actually working at the mines themselves. Furthermore, it also offered children a chance to work at the mines without contradicting the importance their parents place on education, as discussed below. In other words, summer employment offered the potential for miners and their children to reconnect in a way that did not challenge the parents' strong wishes to see their children seek work elsewhere, as the work was ideally temporary. Importantly, these strengthened relationships carried forward beyond the summer.

This shared empathy helped mend the ties of relatedness that the shift-work schedules originally unraveled. In fact, parents and children both speak about "really knowing" or "really understanding" each other for the first time through the work experience. These comments further bring home the point that even though the community generally relies on a biological model of "real kinship" comprising relatives by blood and marriage, they also have a conception of kinship both being continually created through sharing time and space, and being potentially undone when time and space cannot be shared. Instead of viewing their relationships as being completely defined by shared biogenetic substance, the mining families value the creation of ties of relatedness over time and acknowledge their potential fragility. As such, the mining families present a counterpoint to the commonsense notions of biology that most social scientists posit as the basis for Euro-American folk theories of kinship. The miners may believe that relatives are people with whom one shares blood, but they also recognize the importance of nurturing those ties over time.

By reconnecting parents and children, the summer student program also places a more hopeful spin on increasingly alarmed accounts of home becoming like work and work becoming like home. Arlie Hochschild influentially theorizes the mismatch between the ideals and realities of everyday work and family life in North America. In a study of white-collar workers, she observed that although men and women expressed a desire to spend more time at home and with their children, they were putting in more and more hours despite more "family-friendly" workplace policies. Many employees spent more time at work because it was there, not the home, where they found rewarding and comparatively less stressful family-like relationships. At the same time, women's long work hours increased time pressures on everyday family activities so much so that parents have imported Taylorian time efficiency from the factory into the home (Hochschild 1997: 45–49). In this scenario, home becomes the locus of stress about organizing and completing onerous tasks, compelling many workers to seek rewarding kin-like relationships at work (44). Companies (perhaps inadvertently) encourage this flight from the home by promoting positive family-like work relationships as strategies to recruit and retain workers, increase production, and gain an edge over their competitors (42–43).[7] For Hochschild, this development is troubling because private life may become ever more "devalued" as Americans increasingly find at work the emotional satisfaction usually associated with the family (198, 44).

This paradox would seem to be especially pertinent for thinking about social relationships in Gillette, as this book shows that miners experience stresses in maintaining their family relationships at home and create much-loved crew families at work. The mining families' thoughts and experiences of the summer student program, however, offer a more hopeful spin on the work and family dilemmas. My research confirms that the home has become subject to the stresses of time efficiency usually found in the workplace in the form of assembly-line meals, rigid activity schedules, and feelings that chores are never fully done. However, it also suggests a more optimistic corollary: the retranslation of meaningful kin-ties from work to the home. One of the biggest appeals of summer work in the industry is the possibility to reconnect with the parents who were largely absent or grumpily sleep deprived due to shift schedules while their children were growing up. In other words, work becomes not just an escape from the pressures of home but an opportunity to mend otherwise disrupted and stressed family relationships in the home.

Whatever She Wants to Be: Gender and Mine Labor

The miners' attempt to diminish the significance of gender difference while mentoring their children in household labor finds parallels in the ways they sought to diminish the significance of gender difference through mine labor. They hoped that the job would show both daughters and sons that if they work hard they can be successful in whatever career they choose. This lesson seemed especially important for the shiftworkers' daughters, who would be the most economically disadvantaged by pursuing a career in a female-dominated field (Hegewisch et al. 2010; Mastracci 2004).

The mine job was viewed as a crucible in which weathering a summer of toil predicts their ability to persevere in a demanding future career. "Think about it," prompted Sandy. "It's an awesome accomplishment, working out there. It's not easy. You're probably outside all day in the hot sun or pounding rain, and on night shifts I know the people out there get growly. If you can get along there, you can get along anywhere." For Sandy and most others, the social achievements of learning to develop good relationships with sometimes cantankerous coworkers was equally if not more important than the technical skills they learn at the mine. Her daughter Callie enjoyed telling stories about all of her coworkers and the funny jokes they ended up playing on each other. Those friendships pleasantly surprised her, she said, because of the initial trepidation she felt when she first walked on-site.

Students in all areas of the mine had to become proficient in their jobs to avoid a miserable summer, but production work in the pit, shop, and processing plant was the most intimidating. The scale of the mines can be hard for the uninitiated to imagine, since haul trucks look like houses, shops feel like airplane hangars, and plant silos tower as high as skyscrapers. Christy vividly remembered the first time she saw one of the haul trucks she had been assigned to drive her first summer. "Dang, that thing was huge!" she exclaimed. "I just stood there, little old me, and didn't even reach the axle. I thought, you might as well send me home, there is no way I'm going to be able to drive that thing. It's bigger than my apartment!"

My first days at the mine made a similar impression on me. The first summer I spent at the mine I worked in the processing plant. In addition to loading mile-long coal trains so that my coworkers could catch a nap with a roll of paper towels propped under their head like a pillow, my most routine job was washing down the vast machinery that crushes the coal into smaller chunks before dropping it on a conveyor belt to be sent to the silos. The plant apparatus is located underground, with the coal moving downwards through a series of machines that crush it into smaller pieces that can be burned by power plants. The process produces a fine dust that settles on the machinery, which requires washing thus once or twice every shift to avoid accumulating into a fire hazard. Powerful fire hoses are stationed throughout the plant for that purpose. The toughest part was learning how to tame the hoses into doing what I wanted: one wrong move and I would quickly find myself, and my coveralls, drenched in a murky mix of coal mud. The second most difficult part was trudging back up three stories of grated stairs after wrestling with a series of six of those hoses underground. At the end of the summer, my crew presented me with an award they constructed to remember my time with them: two fire-hose nozzles welded to a sturdy piece of metal emblazoned with the mine's name.

The moving belts and clanking machinery in the plant were terrifying to a nineteen year old whose previous work experience consisted of typing up engagements, marriages, school lunch menus, and bowling league scores for printing in the local newspaper; it was nothing, however, compared to driving a 290-ton haul truck, my assignment for the following summer. On the first day driving by myself, without the trusty trainer beside me, I tried to act cool doing the safety walk around the underside of the machine. Nothing looked disastrously wrong, so I checked off the boxes on the form we all had to fill out before turning on a piece of equipment. I shimmied up the ladder, praying that my carefully packed lunch box would not fall to the ground and leave me hungry for the seemingly interminable shift. I settled in and prepared to turn the key. The machine roared to life beneath me, seeming to taunt me with a reminder of its power to crush literally everything in its path, from a wayward rock to a full-size pickup, without so much as a bump. I took a deep breath, closed my eyes as I honked the horn to signal that I was about to back up, and threw the truck into reverse. I maintain no illusions of my performance that day. But with every hour that passed without incident, I became more comfortable, even to the point of daring to turn on the radio. (These were the days before satellite radio became popular and affordable, so we were all stuck with either the country or classic rock stations for a musical distraction. The unrelenting repetition of the songs cruelly paralleled the monotony of driving around the pit in circles.)[8] By the end of the summer, I felt invincible. The picture a friend took of me dwarfed beside my trusty truck sat on my desk for the rest of college and graduate school.

Chloe also pointed to the confidence that driving the giant haul trucks gave her. She brought a picture of her posed with her truck back to her dorm and loved showing it to her friends and random people who would stop by. "I'm still called coal miner to this day by probably eighty people on campus," she said. What made the picture so funny to her and her friends was that it brought out a different part of her personality. At college she participated in speech and debate and did well in all of her classes—so well, in fact, that she went on to an advanced degree directly after graduation—and had a reputation for wearing designer clothes. "They see pictures of me standing next to the tires of the truck, in an absolutely appalling outfit because you're going to get so dirty, with a hard hat. . . . They just can't believe it because it's such a different part of who I am." Although her coal mining experience may not seem to mesh well with her academic persona, she is clear in saying that it is still a part of who she is. "There are times when I've really struggled with that, but it's a big part of who I am and why I do what I do. It's made me a stronger person."

Parents see the value of the lesson that people who succeed at the mine can succeed anywhere. John thought the summers his daughter spent at the mine were "invaluable" preparation for her eventual career as an engineer. Not only was she was able to see engineers at work and get a feel for the business side of operations, she got a sense of what it was like to work in an industrial context: "That can be a rough crowd, it's a real-world crowd out there. I know she got good exposure to all of that uncensored behavior." At the same time, he said, she also learned each of the crews is their own family. All in all, "I think that proved, you know, that she's very adaptable. There was a host of very foreign experiences that she had success at. So, I think as a parent, that's what we try to do. You know, you try to do what preparations you can, for what you can provide so that you know your kids can run off and be successful." He chuckled, making a mine analogy: "Give them the tools! That's what we're trying to do."

John's daughter shared his perspective. She remembered her first week driving trucks as being scary because the shovel operator was loading quickly. "The truck wasn't even completely stopped when he dumped the coal in, and the trucks feel unstable to begin with. I wasn't used to that," she said. The shovel was also one of the largest on-site. When the sixty tons of coal dropped into the bed, "the whole truck just shook. And the guy I was training with slammed on the brakes all at the same time, so the whole truck just shook and I thought, 'Oh, God, there's no way I can do this.' And really that night I came home and I said, 'I'm not going to be able to drive the truck.'" Part of her fear came from knowing how dangerous the trucks could be. "It's scary at first because you've just watched all these safety videos about how they can run over a truck and you can't even feel it." (My friends and I fondly referred to the first week of training as "death week" since we had to watch so many reenactments of industrial disaster.) After two weeks, though, she "got the hang of it" and did not have to think through every single move she made. Driving the truck started feeling like driving a car, just like "second nature." In addition to the feeling of accomplishment working at the mine gave her, it also turned out to be a boost to her career. In part, she thinks it helps people remember her since it "obviously sticks out on a résumé." Her recruiter and eventual supervisor loved talking about the mines when she was applying for the internship that would eventually lead to a full-time position at a major corporation.

Conclusion

The interweaving of labor and love threads throughout the remembered experiences of both miners and their children. It was through shared work around the house or at the mine that shiftworking parents and their children connected. For the miners, nurturing appreciation for challenging work was a way for them to nurture affective bonds with the children they missed. This emphasis underscores the cultural importance that families placed on a strong work ethic as a marker of good character as well as a positive force in the practical arrangement of their lives, which were dominated by the mines' shiftwork schedule. Because many of the miners were men, the Wyoming case builds on a growing body of research that draws attention to the affective rather than simply economic dimensions of American fatherhood (e.g., Deutsch 1999; Han 2009; Tomori 2009).

The miners' efforts to nurture relatedness with their children revolved around labor both in the home and at work in the mines. The miners made a conscious effort to diminish the significance of potential gender differences in both arenas. At home, they required sons and daughters to learn practical skills commonly associated with the opposite gender. At the mines, they encouraged their daughters to take pride in conquering tasks associated with macho masculinity in the dominant American cultural imaginary. Their explicit desire to discourage and diminish adherence to dichotomous gender norms in their children exists uneasily beside their own gendered divisions of household labor, as women miners and wives of miners maintain primary—but not sole—responsibility for the day-to-day care of houses and children.

The summer student program underscores the overarching argument of this chapter and the last: relatedness can be both nurtured by sharing time and unraveled by being separated by it. The demanding shiftwork schedule brought crews so close together that they viewed their sense of belonging to one another in kinship terms: they were a crew family. On the other hand, the shiftwork schedule left the miners out of sync with things that most people take for granted, such as sharing a meal, going to bed at the same time, or having shared opportunities for leisure and rest. Far from espousing commonsense notions that family is defined solely by shared bodily substances like blood or genes, this community resolutely pointed to time as central to the creation of kin-ties.[9] If miners were not home except to sleep, as Sara bluntly pointed out, they were not really a part of the family. The summer student program's popularity was grounded in large part in its reconnection of miners and their children, as both parents and children say that finally experiencing shiftwork together creates a shared empathy that was impossible to re-create any other way. It was by sharing the shiftwork schedule that originally unraveled kin-ties during the children's early years that miners and their offspring cemented their feelings of relatedness as adults.

Together the two chapters in this section also suggest that social processes that draw out differences between men and women exist in tension with those that diminish those potential differences. In the crew families, shiftwork crafts men and women miners as similar temporal beings whose differences with the community are often more significant than gender. At the same time, gender becomes salient when women face greater exhaustion and bodily pressures in adapting to the workplace. In parenting their children, miners attempt to nurture gender-neutral values and qualities in them to counteract the stereotypes that permeate the world around them, even though miners' wives often end up taking on more household responsibilities in order to keep the family running while their spouse is working shifts. The two chapters in the next section examine the contested and incomplete construction of gender neutrality in greater depth, specifically as it emerges and becomes debated in the workplace.

Part III

Undoing Gender at Work

5

Tomboys and Softies

———————————————◄○►———————————————

Miners in the Powder River Basin are not immune from evoking dominant stereotypes about men and women as they make sense of, comment on, and debate issues and events both in the workplace and outside of it. This observation is not surprising given that they watch American television shows and movies that play up differences between men and women and naturalize them in biological differences. Their own family histories or personal experiences sometimes confirm truisms about women's supposed innate drive to nurture children or men's helplessness to resist watching professional sports broadcast in high definition. But the miners and their families are also quick to point out the numerous mismatches between dominant gender ideologies and their own lives.

In this chapter I explore the ways in which the miners think about and talk about gender, both directly and indirectly. I examine everyday talk as a key site for the undoing and consolidation of gender difference. In interviews, casual conversation, and talk on the public mine radio, miners position themselves and others as particular types of gendered persons by referencing a series of cultural categories: tomboy, lady, bitch, softie, sissy, and macho. While these may seem familiar to many North Americans, they take on meaning specific to the local context. Miners recognize that these categories are not static descriptions of the way people "really are," but ideal types that people reference when thinking about themselves and others. In fact, people shift between categories over the course of a lifetime, a working day, and a single conversation, which complicates any simplistic understanding of their gendered personhood.[1]

The pages that follow trace the linguistic moves through which miners assign, adopt, and deflect these designations, which I show are all distinguished by distinct attitudes toward gender and work. This analysis follows a well-worn path of feminist theory that critiques dichotomous notions of gender by exploring multiple femininities and masculinities. I extend this work a step further by showing that the two most highly valued categories—tomboy for women and softie for men—are grounded in strikingly similar personal qualities: hard work, support for others, and platonic emotional intimacy with coworkers of the opposite sex. This convergence points to more gender-neutral ideas of personhood that exist in constant tension with those that would highlight gender difference.

This ethnographic material also refines the notion of workplace relatedness developed in chapter 3. The insulting labels (bitch, sissy, and macho) point to the social pressures of conformity and coercion that animate the workplace families alongside love and safekeeping. Euro-American anthropologists were slow to recognize these aspects of kinship, probably because their own cultural imagination of family is steeped in warm and fuzzy feelings about belonging (Edwards and Strathern 2000; Weston 2001). But the process of turning people into kin and similar types of persons is steeped in coercion (Carsten 1997; Van Vleet 2008). Though the miners as a whole have developed an enviably egalitarian and supportive work environment, its smooth functioning depends on people living up to the dominant ideals for how crewmembers should treat one another. People who fail or refuse to conform to these expectations fall to the edges of the crew families, though they are rarely excluded entirely; conflict stresses but does not negate relatedness. Because even well-intentioned pressure can chafe, the crew families, like other forms of relatedness, are characterized by conflicts, coercion, and hierarchy as well as intimacy and solidarity (Van Vleet 2008: 9, 188–190).

Undoing Gender

The two chapters in this section share the feminist predilection for examining how gender is "anchored in the structures and relations of production that underlay workplace cultures" (Canning 1996: 286), since this perspective critiques the sources of inequality, disrespect, and alienation in the crew families. But it also traces the processes through which everyday practices can become unmoored from expectations of gender difference, both because these cases form a significant part of everyday life in the Powder River Basin and because they add nuance to debates about women's participation in nontraditional fields.

Paying attention to the undoing of gender hardly seems radical to anyone familiar with feminist or queer theory, which hold that gender is something one does instead of as something one intrinsically is (e.g., Butler 1990; West and Zimmerman 1987). Studying how, when, where, and why gender difference comes to matter is exciting and promising for scholars and students alike. After all, the central message is that if gender is socially constructed in particular times and places, it can be reconstructed and transformed to more egalitarian and open ends.

What is troubling is that when research turns to the actual details of everyday life, especially when it concerns work and family in the United States, the luster of liberatory theory fades as ethnographic case after case seems to prove the inescapable tyranny of binary gender difference (Deutsch 2007: 110). As sociologist Francine Deutsch argues, this focus "undermined the goal of dismantling gender inequity by, perhaps inadvertently, perpetuating the idea that the gender system of oppression is hopelessly impervious to real change and by ignoring the links between social interaction and structural change" (2007: 107). Scholarship analyzing the reproduction of gender difference, Barbara Risman points out, creates a tautology in that "whatever groups of boys and girls, or men and women, do is a kind of gender" (2009: 81). As a corrective, they call for more research on the processes through which "the essentialism of binary distinctions between people based on sex category is challenged" (Risman 2009: 83)—what they call degendering or undoing gender.

Two of the most influential scholars behind the shift to studying "doing gender" caution against the turn to studying undoing gender, arguing that the cases offered as examples represent a shift in the norms to which men and women are held accountable rather than the abandonment of those norms entirely (West and Zimmerman 2009: 117). Because West and Zimmerman believe that men and women are held accountable to gender norms, even if these norms change, they argue instead that "gender is not undone so much as redone" (West and Zimmerman 2009: 118).[2] In this chapter and the next I advance the debate about undoing gender by precisely documenting and theorizing the sometimes momentary, and at other times enduring, loss of accountability to differentiated gender norms. The ethnographic materials demonstrate that some of these cases were tentative and quickly quelled by the strong reassertion of difference; others were more durable and resistant to dispute; and in the most heavily contested contexts the construction of gender difference and similarity occurred on a moment-by-moment, turn-by-turn basis. Even when such moments of undoing gender are fleeting, their existence in the heart of an industry otherwise infamous for difference and discrimination calls out for analytic attention.

In this chapter I show that to take undoing gender as a critical facet of everyday life does not require turning away from the problematic entrenchment of difference. Nor does it mean ignoring gender or averting the analytic gaze from the masculine basis of many organizations, practices, and ideals that cloak themselves in the language of gender-blindness (Acker 1990; Britton 2000; J. Williams 2010). Rather, undoing requires taking the construction of similarity as a potential, serious, and complementary social process to the construction of difference. Studying the undoing of gender means analyzing how difference both comes to matter and fades away as people engage in everyday practice, interpret each other's behavior, and make sense of their own experiences. Everyday talk is a particularly rich arena for analyzing this push and pull of accountability to gendered norms.

The Interactional Emergence of Gendered Identities

Commonsense logic holds that people's linguistic practices emerge from, and can be attributed to, a preexisting identity, whether related to gender, age, ethnicity, region, or other characteristics. At the mines, statements such as, "Women talk too much and too fast," or "He came in here with a drawl, like he was straight out of West Virginia," suggest that types of talk simply reflect people's inner psyche or demographic placement.

Linguistic anthropology reverses that logic, showing instead that one's social positioning—what most people call identity—emerges over the course of interaction and only appears to solidify over repeated interactions.[3] In other words, talk does not reflect an already existing identity, but actively constructs it. This insight holds true as well for gender, as multiple generations of scholars have shown that dominant notions of masculinity and femininity, as well as the fit between these categories and particular people, are actively constructed and renegotiated in talk.[4] My analysis draws on Mary Bucholtz and Kira Hall's lucid framework for studying the interactional emergence of identity. These moves include overt references to cultural categories, such as when a woman says she is a tomboy, as well as more indirect implicatures, such as when a man insinuates that a woman is a lady because she wears impeccable nail polish. These moves also encompass stance-taking, such as when a woman positions herself as one of the guys by acting like a prankster, as well as the use of language typically associated with particular groups, such as when women seek to minimize their femininity by letting loose a barrage of curses.[5] These practices show that "even in the most fleeting of interactional moves, speakers position themselves and others as particular kinds of people" (Bucholtz and Hall 2005: 595).

Analyzing cases in which people assign and deflect these cultural categories underscores Bucholtz and Hall's (2005: 598) argument that identity is relational on two counts. First, the cultural categories invoked by the miners only take on meaning in relation to others, such as when people argue that tomboys and ladies represent opposite ends of the social spectrum. Second, exact matches between people and categories are not necessary for them to become meaningful; rather, they "must be merely understood as sufficiently similar" (599). Likewise, attempts at distinguishing people and categories need not rest on complete differentiation (600). In both cases, people suppress the

ethnographic details that would complicate simple attributions of similari
or difference. In describing herself as a tomboy, for instance, Carrie spoke at
length about being a tomboy who loves everything to do with the outdoors.
Only later did she also divulge that she is also an artist at heart who loves
being a "bake-cookies-for-your-kids kind of mom," which are qualities that she
would otherwise associate with ladies. Bucholtz and Hall therefore offer adequation and distinction as more precise theoretical tools that capture this suppression better than the typical designations of similarity and difference. These
concepts will prove essential in the last part of the chapter where I examine
the cultural categories in relation to one another. For now, I examine each of
the key categories in turn, with special attention to the ways in which people
invoke, ascribe, and deflect them in a variety of social contexts of talk.

Tomboys

Tomboy was the one of the most frequently invoked categories in both conversations among crewmembers and individual interviews. It almost always refers to
women whose attitudes and practices depart from conventional notions of femininity.[6] Women attributed it to both themselves and others, especially in discussions about how and why particular women did well at the mines. Recall from
chapter 4 that Carrie, for example, took pride in describing both herself and her
daughter Mandy as tomboys who were "like one of the guys." On her days off she
enjoys going hunting, horseback riding, and camping with her kids, just as she
did as a child growing up in a farming community in north-central Wyoming
and just as her daughter currently does. Reflecting on her own childhood, she
said, "I was always a tomboy too. I loved doing things with my brothers."

Carrie then shifted our conversation to talk about Mandy's new job as a con-
tractor at a different mine. Mandy was discouraged because she did not enjoy
the menial tasks she was assigned, but her mother thought she would eventually be fine because "she's a tomboy and understands, look, you have to start
off with shit jobs before you get moved up." To boost Mandy's spirits, Carrie
said, for Christmas she bought her a set of tools that would help her at work.
Carrie then drew another parallel to her own life, saying she was thankful for
her first job at the mine because she had worked a string of low-paying jobs in
her hometown before moving to Gillette: "I didn't want to look a gift horse in
the mouth. And I think it's good for kids to work a shit job so they appreciate a good one when it comes along." The first few years at the mine were not
easy, she said, but she met the challenge head-on: "I was the only woman on
my crew for a while, but I pulled my own weight. I threw language back at
them and fueled my own equipment, so I proved myself and everything turned
out." She hoped that Mandy's own resolve, cultivated over years of living in the
country, would propel her through her current job to a better position.

Jo, the loader operator from Wisconsin, also believed that the most success-ful women at the mines were those considered tomboys. To prove her point, she gestured to a new truck driver named Fay: "Look at her. She rides bulls. She's a tomboy. She's making it out here." Jo may have looked approvingly at Fay's ranching background because she herself lived and worked on a ranch when she first moved to Wyoming from the Midwest. For her, ranch work offered an opportunity to continue her love for physical activity and the out-doors: "I just loved getting out there and getting dirty. You can't be prissy and do that kind of work. But I'm a tomboy and sports have always come naturally to me. I played softball my whole life before I got old and worn down by this equipment." She appreciated the fact that the job at the mine allowed her to spend so much time outside. While we were making our circles between the shovel and the crushers that afternoon, she pointed out all of the wildlife we saw along the roads and in the distance—pronghorn antelope, eagles, and a few rabbits—and regaled me with stories of seeing deer at various places on-site. One time, she said, a whole herd of them was hanging out near where the shovel was working, so one of the guys on the crew gently followed them with his pickup to cajole them to move out of the way of traffic. She concluded the story with a laugh, saying, "I told him he was a regular ranch hand. Head 'em up, move 'em out, Rawhide!"

The love Carrie and Jo described for spending time outdoors weaved through many women's memories of their childhood and their thoughts about their current favorite pastimes. Wanda clearly linked her childhood experiences and her current life: "I was raised tomboyish with boys. We were always hunting, camping, fishing, whatever. We had a woodstove in my par-ents' home. And that's the kind of stuff I still do now with my kids and my grandkids." The note about the woodstove may seem out of place, but she may include it to highlight the unique physical demands and practical knowledge that characterized her childhood. Unlike the common furnace, woodstoves do not heat homes with a simple push of a button and electronic sensors; their users must stock them with chopped wood and periodically clean out the accumulated ash—a task that is incredibly dirty, as anyone who has done it will attest.

Carrie, Jo, and Wanda all gesture to the social significance of dirt in think-ing about their lives and careers. In fact, dirt continually appeared throughout my conversations and interactions with women who considered themselves tomboys. Molly, a mother of two in her late twenties, loves operating equip-ment and boasts about the mess she gets into while doing it. Bored during a shift in which she was assigned to the water truck but had very little to do since it was cold and snowy, she posted photos from her mobile phone to her online profile periodically throughout the day. They included shots of the truck in a giant mud pile, her muddy galoshes, and the mud splattered across her face and hard hat. Some of her friends gave her a hard time about how difficult her job must be if she has the time to be online, and she immediately returned their teasing with well-placed barbs of her own that real work requires getting messy.

In a conversation I had with her later, Molly expressed annoyance with women on her crew who tried to avoid getting dirty while they were at work. She thought that they were shirking their responsibilities and taking away from the sense of camaraderie on the crew. At a different mine, Melissa made that point clear during a conversation she had over lunch with her crew. They were discussing the interview process for new hires, and she brought up the story of one woman who was particularly ill suited for the work. "She said that she didn't want to sit on the chair we brought for her because it was dirty," she said incredulously. "I asked her, 'Do you know where you're applying, lady?! She did not get hired.'" For her and her coworkers, the woman's discomfort with dirt meant that she would never make it in the mines, not only because dust infiltrated offices as well as equipment cabs but because she would be too uptight. A coworker named Trish agreed and summed up the importance of dirt by saying, "Tomboys like myself are like one of the guys. They don't mind getting dirty. That means they're mellow and don't get worked up about stupid shit. They don't mind joking around."

In addition to making overt references to tomboys, women and men also indirectly assign certain women to the category. A key way this is accomplished is by referencing agricultural backgrounds, as did many of the women above. The miners who spoke of the importance of agricultural backgrounds all implied that women who grew up on farms or ranches were tomboys because they loved working hard, being outside, and getting dirty. For Patty, what was significant about growing up on a farm was that she was "very used to physical labor" and did not mind getting dirty. She said, "You didn't wuss out, wimp out, or worry about your fingernails." Peg said that growing up on a ranch meant that she was comfortable working with men without asking for special treatment: "It was egalitarian; you just grow up doing everything. You're just another one of the hands!" Marie also said that there were not strict gendered divisions of labor on her family ranch, so women had to do the dirty work of animal husbandry and equipment operation if that is what needed to be done. Finally, in the next chapter, men such as Jerry, Greg, and Tom argue that the physical demands of agricultural lifestyles cultivated grit and toughness in women who grew up alongside their brothers and cousins.

One of the common threads in all of these assertions of tomboyhood is dirt, likely because people equate it with hard work. But dirt does not signal just any type of hard work, but the physically demanding kind typical of working men (Halle 1984: 203). This association was made clear every time someone covered in mud, dust, or grease would enter the office, step onto the bus, or walk up to the lunch shack. They would be greeted by a chorus of laughter and good-natured teasing about how they must have "really worked" that day. These jokes were especially funny when made to a visiting anthropologist best known for voluntarily spending a bewildering eight years in university class-rooms, which most people viewed as undeniable proof that she had never really worked a day in her life. The most entertaining episode of this kind was the day I spent with the utility guys Josh and Taylor at one of the smaller mines. The spring had been wet with heavy snow, so their job for the day was to move around the pumps to make sure that the water was being prop-erly moved out of the pit. They made a big show of outfitting me with giant galoshes and plastic coveralls at the warehouse, where the coordinator helped me duct tape the top of my galoshes to the coveralls to prevent mud from seeping into them. He snapped a picture of me with his cell phone before we ventured out into the pit. When I returned that afternoon, completely cov-ered in sludge, he laughed so hard that no sound escaped from his lips. He composed himself just enough to take another picture, which I later learned he showed to everyone who made an appearance at the warehouse window to tell them about the time an anthropologist visited the mine. He and Josh and Taylor exchanged high fives and spent the next twenty minutes—while I attempted to free myself as gracefully as possible from the duct-taped galoshes and coveralls—talking about my stint of hard work. Their consensus was that I should keep the picture to remind myself what "real work" looked like. I did, even though I did not need the picture to remind me of the summers in which I witnessed Q-tips turn black while attempting to clean out my ears, saw Kleenexes turn black after blowing my nose, or pulled out crusty black eye gunk from my eyes after rubbing them as I wearily swung my feet out of bed to get ready for another shift of driving truck or washing down the plant as a summer student.

Dirt is also significant in the ways miners evaluate what type of person their coworkers are because it requires a sense of humor if one is to last more than a day on-site. Trish explained that was because it was so ever present that if you got upset each time something spilled on you or dust blew on your face, you would be a miserable, grumpy person who could bring down the morale of the entire crew. In the quote above, she also made an equation between peo-ple who take a laid-back approach to dirt and people who are not likely to be offended by verbal or practical jokes, most of which involve "matter out of place" (Douglas 1966): butter in hard hats rather than in lunch boxes, grease on door handles instead of conveyor belts, Kool-Aid in boots instead of pitchers, or dead snakes in inconspicuous paper bags in the lunchroom rather than safely along the side of the road. In this way, being able to manage dirt helps women integrate themselves into the crews, as the next chapter describes in greater detail: hard work and being able to at least appreciate, if not engage in, joking practices is a key mode of crafting relatedness in the crew families.

Ladies and Girly Girls

When describing the social universe of the mines, people always contrasted tomboys with "ladies" or "girly girls."[7] Nicole, a self-identified tomboy, was clear in distinguishing the two, when she told me, "I don't want to be a lady out there. I want to be one of the guys." In fact, most of the women considered tomboys took pride in being accepted as one of the guys, which meant that they were recognized as pulling their own weight and enjoying a good joke. On the other hand, they and other miners consider women to be ladies when they attempt to avoid hard work or purposefully emphasize their femininity at the expense of forming friendships with the guys: "They're prissy," complained Trish. "They have nice nails, they wear makeup all the time, and they can't take a joke."

It is telling that long nails and makeup stand out as markers of inappropriate femininity, as they also hinder people from doing the job that is expected of them. After all, women who wish to preserve their makeup or painted nails must avoid the tasks associated with being a good hand, such as using your own tools and climbing around the equipment to diagnose a potential problem with it. Greg frequently complained that one of the women on his crew never pulled her own weight. As evidence, he described her long red fingernails and said that he looked at her hands during their meetings, but the polish was never chipped: "Now you tell me, if you're out there doing your job like you are supposed to be doing, do you think your nails are gonna stay pretty like that? I don't think so. So that must mean that she's sitting in her truck all day and can't be bothered to check her own stuff." When he made the observation, we were standing around with Laura waiting for the blast to clear the coal pit, and she nodded and recalled that she stopped wearing her nails long after she broke two of them during her first week at the mine. As a relatively new temporary worker at the mine, Laura was anxious to be hired full-time. Making the statement was likely a strategy to "prove herself" to Greg and the rest of the crew that she was a dedicated coworker. As McElhinny (1994: 168) found during her research with women police officers in Pittsburgh, critiques of women's long nails in the basin are not simply about appearance; they are a way to critique women perceived to be overly feminine and thus unable to do a demanding job.

Women are also labeled as ladies and girly girls if they give the impression that they are above their coworkers. The following two snippets of conversation are representative of common interactional styles at the mines. They occur at the end of a shift, as people were coming into the office to change clothes and get ready to go home. The first involves Sue, a woman who was famous on her crew for listening to only Christian radio and refusing to engage in most, if not all, of their joking activities.

Example 1:

1 Sue: How was your night?
2 Colleen: Amazing as always.
3 Don: Just dandy.
4 Colleen: I suppose yours was fantastic?
5 Sue: Fine.
6 Don: How was that 542 for ya?
7 She can act up sometimes.
8 Sue: Fine.
9 It's just like any other truck.
10 No difference.
11 Colleen: Really?
12 You're not thinkin' they all have their personalities
13 Just like we all do I guess [laughs].
14 Sue: Nope, it's just a machine
15 You just have figure out how they work.

In this conversation, Don and Colleen respond sarcastically (lines 2 and 3) to Sue's question about how their night went. When they ask her in return, she answers curtly with a simple "Fine" (line 5). Don pushes her to engage in the crew's beloved ritual of complaint by pointing out that the truck she was driving has a reputation for causing trouble (line 7), and after she rebuffs him (lines 8–10) Colleen doubles his efforts by making a joke about how the people on their crew can misbehave as well (13). Sue again refuses their invitations to joke before walking away to swipe her timecard out for the night. In a few key linguistic moves, she positions herself as an employee who takes her work seriously and does not form emotional attachments to either the equipment or her coworkers.

A conversation earlier that day at lunch between Mike and Kelly, a woman who is known for being easygoing whether on the minesite or out at a bar after work, is different in revealing ways.

Example 2:

1 Mike: Looked like you were havin' a peachy morning.
2 Kelly: Yeah [chuckles] we got to really clickin' after a while.
3 Mike: That 176, she can be kind of a beast sometimes [laughs].
4 Kelly: That thing can definitely be a beast sometimes [laughs].
5 Mike: If you're not careful I guess.
6 Kelly: Yeah if you're not careful,
7 If you don't know what you're doin',
8 But I think I got it figured out.

9   We were just purrin' along.
10   Mike: What do you think the deal was with that thing?
11   Kelly: Think it was a hydraulic leak
12   Got down underneath and saw some fluid,
13   Looked pretty fresh,
14   Gonna talk to a mechanic about it.
15   Mike: Yeah, makes sense.
16   Good call.

As in the first example, Mike invites Kelly to complain about her shift by ironically describing her morning as being peachy (line 1). She responds by laughing and acknowledging that things were difficult at first since it was not until "after a while" that things improved (line 2). She repeats Mike's joke (line 3) about her truck being a beast (though she does modify the gendered pronoun he used to describe it) and also affirms his assertion (line 5) that care is required to get it to perform properly.[8] But Kelly then takes the floor to demonstrate her own technical knowledge and achievements in getting the truck to purr along (lines 8–9, 11–14). Tellingly, she highlights the physical demands of making the diagnosis: suspecting a hydraulic leak, she stops the truck and makes a dirty firsthand inspection of it before calling the mechanic, rather than simply calling them to investigate (lines 12–13). In contrast to Sue's precise pronunciation that distinguishes her from her interlocutors, Kelly drops the "g" sound from the "-ing" morpheme like the majority of miners in the basin, a practice associated with the speech of industrial workers (Huspek 1986) as well as a casual country ethos (Silverstein 2003). Their conversation ends with Mike's positive appraisal of her actions. On a turn-by-turn basis, therefore, Kelly positions herself as a competent operator who enjoys joking around, tries to fit in with others, and does not mind getting dirty to fix her own equipment—all key characteristics of tomboys.

Some women act like ladies or tomboys so much that they become strongly associated with the category, leading people to casually remark that someone *is* a lady or tomboy rather than simply *acting like* one. Sue, for example, rarely deviated from her prim and proper behavior, while Melissa was so committed to being one of the guys that she bragged about riding horses eight months into her pregnancy whereas "sissy pregnant ladies" go on light duty at only three or four months.

The vast majority of women, however, vacillate between the two social positions over the course of a workday, between their time on and off the worksite, or over a lifetime. Trish, for instance, loved swearing and hanging out with the guys but said, "You still have to watch yourself, like not swear too much. And you can't get away with some of the jokes that they can. You aren't a guy: you're *like* one of the guys." She clarified the difference by saying, "On my days off I like to go out and get dressed up and look nice so that you'd never know I was a coal miner, but when I'm out here it's just jeans and dirt." Molly, who also self-identified as a tomboy, highlighted the strategic importance of being accepted as one of the guys. "Out here you have to act like a guy to make it," she said. "If you're girly you won't make it because no one will respect you." She likes acting tough at work and at the small ranch where she lives with her husband and young son, but brings out her girly side when she deems it appropriate. "I'm still a girly girl, I dress up and put on makeup," she explained, "but you have to adjust to it while you're out here. We can cuss out people like the guys but still act like ladies." She took particular pride in acting so girly on her days off along with other women on her crew that people could not guess their occupation: "You'd never know we're coal miners!"

Another group of close women coworkers spends some of their days off doing what they call girly things together, even if they all are happy to be accepted as one of the guys while at work. They meet once a month to do crafts together, and when they are really exhausted in-between shifts they gather at someone's house to collapse on the couch to snack and watch (and make fun of) soap operas together. Once a year, though, they venture out into the wild to camp at the local reservoir by themselves, with no husbands or kids. They drive their four-wheelers around, drink, talk, and laugh around the campfire. The association of camping with enjoying the dirt of the outdoors was clear, as each of them talked about how much they enjoyed splashing around the puddles in their four-wheelers and not caring about what they looked like.

Trish, Molly, and the group of crafty campers all emphasize the shifts in gendered behavior and sense of self that correspond with distinct times and spaces: they may be one of the guys while at work, but on their days off away from the mine they can act like girly girls or tomboys. These shifts can also take place over the course of a few moments at the mine. One day when I was riding around with Laura in her haul truck, we started talking about how she and her boyfriend ended up in Gillette. "I'm not a girly girl," she said, "but I never imagined I'd be doing this for money." After we did the safety inspection and climbed up the haul truck, Laura attempted to retract the ladder but found that it was not functioning correctly. When she was finally able to insert herself into the busy radio communication and report the problem, she took care to use the correct procedure and specific terminology that the miners associate with expertise. When the mechanics arrived to investigate the problem, she braved the cold and windy winter morning to join them in their inspection. She told me that doing so was key in order to avoid being labeled a lady. Unable to find a quick fix, the mechanics muscled the ladder back into position so we could drive off and told her to use the completely vertical embedded ladder instead. In her opinion, that was not a real solution because the slipperiness of the embedded ladder made it dangerous. Instead of cursing and becoming aggressive as I had seen some of her coworkers do in similar situations, she tried a different tactic that she later described to me as involving "girl power." She began joking with the mechanic she knew the best, making allusions to her own "wussiness" and begging him to fix the ladder as a personal favor to her because she was too afraid of climbing down off of the steeper ladder. He did, and when we returned triumphantly to the cab, she explained the importance of what she called girl power: "Sometimes it's easier to get stuff done. But you have to be careful, because sometimes it can hurt more than it can help."

In the course of a few minutes, Laura modified her usual approach to interacting with her coworkers and the machinery in order to strategically invoke a more markedly feminine persona. Strategies and experiences such as these are far more typical than any static categorization of women would suggest. Unpacking what it means when a person calls herself or someone else a tomboy or lady reveals strategic shifts in gender performance. The cultural category of tomboy refers less to a specific group of women or stable identity than a tactic for managing the extent to which gender differences become salient in specific social and technological engagements. When women act like tomboys, they consciously downplay gender difference—but without erasing it completely—in order to craft camaraderie with their coworkers. On the other hand, women draw out stereotypically feminine characteristics when they feel that they are at risk of becoming too much like one of the guys. The next section delves further into what is at stake in taking on the "wrong" conventionally masculine characteristics.

Bitches

Bitch encompasses a wide array of insults at the mine, the majority of which are directed at women (see Paap 2006 on the term's use by American construction workers).[9] Whereas ladies or girly girls were criticized for being too feminine, the uniting thread of the bitch insult is an accusation that women have pushed the boundary too far in departing from conventional notions of femininity. This may seem surprising given the value placed on gender neutrality in the mines and the praise given to women who "act like the one the guys" by pulling their own weight and not getting offended by swearing or jokes. Delving into the specifics of the insults reveals that accusing a woman of being a bitch is not simply a critique of her departing from conventional expectations of femininity, but of her acting in too masculine a manner as well.

One cardinal sin is swearing too often or in a too vulgar manner. Although Nicole wanted to be accepted as one of the guys rather than be viewed as a lady, she said, "At the same time, I do make a very strong point to be careful." She elaborated that being careful meant not crossing the line of acting and speaking too much "like a man" while still being accepted as a friend with whom the guys feel comfortable making jokes. Finding the right balance can be difficult. Laura said she started off at the mines "throwing swear words around" in an attempt to be accepted by the guys, but found that she could not keep up with the one-upmanship and had backed herself into a corner. "If I kept it up, they would have thought I was too crude," she said, and that would mean that they would lose respect for her. Mary remembered a woman who was upset with a guy on their crew who "had a potty mouth worse than a sailor, even worse than a miner." After work one night they were washing their hands around the large communal sink in the women's locker room, and she "had a hissy fit" complaining about how he was always saying f-ing this and f-ing that. She announced, "I'm not gonna tolerate it, I'm gonna complain," and tried recruiting others to go along with her. Mary and most of the other women refused, partly because they felt that she also used language inappropriately. "She says shit all the time and tells off-color jokes without anyone getting upset," Mary said, insinuating that the woman gave up her right to be upset about off-color language when she used it herself.

Mary then shifted our conversation to talk about a rumor that two people from another crew were caught having sex at the fuel station. The guy got fired, she said, because the woman claimed that he was raping her. He said it was consensual, but the mine took her side because they wanted to avoid a potential lawsuit. Although Mary said that no one but the two of them would ever know what really happened, she also leaned toward his side because the woman was "loose and had a reputation." Mary shook her head, knowing that it sounded awful to call out a woman for having a sexual history; logically she knew that even if the woman had a sexual history with that guy or others, it did not give the man under question a free pass to have sex with her then. But she maintained that women had a responsibility to manage their own reputation. "It's bad if you have no credibility," she explained. "It's a catch-22, how to champion women if they don't care enough to take care of themselves."

Mary's segue between swearing and sexuality is telling because women who swear aggressively are also often accused of using their sexuality aggressively. Candace, for instance, told me that she hated the dispatcher on their crew because "she wears tight jeans and low-cut shirts. She has bitch written all over her." Daisy also viewed clothing as a sign of a woman's intentions on the job. Describing herself, she said, "I've always been a tomboy I guess. I get along with men." She generously included me in the category, saying, "You seem laid back." She then distinguished us from women who caused trouble at the mine because of their bitchy attitude: "Some women don't want you to be in their territory with the guys. Some women dress provocatively and you know they're sleeping around. And if you act that way, that's the way guys are going to look at you."

At another mine, Wanda and many of her coworkers ostracized a woman who used vulgar language and openly propositioned men while at work. "She's a slut and is always talking about guys' dicks," Wanda complained. Drawing a distinction between hardworking tomboys like herself and women who used the mines as a dating service, she said, "There are women who want to do the job and there are women who want to grab guys' dicks. This bitch, she was always asking them, 'You got a hard-on today?' That makes it hard for me to do my job. They're trying to make it so they don't have to work, but I pull my own weight. I don't expect to be treated different. For example, I fill my own damn truck [with gas]. Women like her ruin it for the rest of us." Wanda then explained that some guys on their crew were just as frustrated as she was: "There are some guys who feel the same way, that it's not okay for women to act like that. They'll call her a slut and a whore." She recalled a story about one of the guys eventually threatening to report her for sexual harassment and then concluded with another telling insult to her unbecoming behavior: "She's a drunk." Excessive drinking, after all, is associated with aggressive masculinity even though women equally enjoy tipping a few drinks back with their coworkers at the end of a rough rotation. These ethnographic materials suggest that bitches are criticized not simply for not being feminine enough but also for being too masculine.

In part, Wanda recognized the double standard that disadvantaged the woman under debate. "At another mine where I worked there were women screwing guys on the job, too," she said. "But guys do it, too! They'll point to women doing acts, but it takes two. But the guys are studly and the females are sluts. I feel like if they are two consenting adults, they know what they are doing." Wanda and her coworkers were equally offended by one of the guys on the crew who bragged about his sexual conquests, as the next section demonstrates, but women still bear the heavier burden for discouraging sexual activity on the crew.

Machos

Popular accounts of the mining industry portray it as a cult of hypermasculinity in which the manliest of men battle the elements, management, and sometimes each other to wrest a living from the earth. Scholarly accounts all too often follow suit, relegating miners to one of two ultramasculine ideal types: the mischievous and irresponsible man prone to reckless drinking, gambling, and fighting, on the one hand, and the respectable and highly politicized proletarian warrior, on the other (Metcalfe 1988). Though writers glorify these forms of aggressive masculinity (even as some ostensibly critique them), in the Powder River Basin men and women miners alike criticize their coworkers who emulate these macho stereotypes too closely.

The shovel operator Candace was frustrated when she and the other women on her crew have to "face a macho deal out here." Rather than ascribing this offensive form of masculinity to all of the men or all of the time, she picked out a few instances of "bad apples who don't believe that women should be out here and that they can never be as good as men." Recalling her first years at the mine as a truck driver, she remembered a shovel operator who treated her poorly. "He beat the crap out of me," she said, explaining that he always loaded her truck in a way that caused the entire thing to shake and hurt her back and neck. She confronted him and lodged a complaint with their supervisor, but he refused to change his behavior. "He's not going to change and there's nothing you can do about it," she told me, because it is "a macho ego thing." This attitude offended her sense that "you have to keep your ego and your temper at home. You're here to work, that's it. And of course keep each other safe while you're doing it." She was careful to distinguish the surly shovel operator and his few cronies from the majority of guys on the crew. A few were instrumental in mentoring her and taking the time to explain all of the different angles on the shovel, for instance. Others were in the same position she initially was and suffered because they refused to buy into their "good old boys club." She observed that such men, especially when they are new hires, "get dogged up here too." But she was ultimately hopeful because "the bad people are less and less, and more and more men are receptive to women being out here."

Jo's biggest frustrations at the mine also stemmed from having to deal with what she called "male egos." She contrasted her attitude about work with the one she saw in most of the twenty-year-old guys who were just hiring on to replace people of her generation. To explain the difference, she said that she chose to operate the blade instead of the rubber tire dozer because she is a "safe person, not wild" and hated the tipping feeling that accompanies dozer work. Pointing at her brain, she said, "I'm way smarter than that." On the other hand, according to her, younger men "have an ego thing, and think they are ten foot tall and bulletproof. You see that when they drive too fast . . . they think they're invincible." In her recent attempt to train a guy like that on the blade, she discovered a trick: "let him show his stuff and let him be the boy he wanted to be." After he got that out of his system, she said, he was loosened up and more willing to listen to her advice. "The young ones have egos that won't stop," she summarized, "so you have to learn to work around it, and hopefully they come around."

Candace and Jo both enjoy the relative luxury of being recognized as competent, experienced operators, which helps them deal with the machos of all ages by defending themselves and attempting to change their behavior. Women who are just starting at the mine face more difficulties in coping with or standing up to aggressive masculine coworkers. Laura, for instance, found herself speechless after one coworker was particularly rude to her. On their way out to the pit, she remembered him telling her, "Wait till you get a look at that ramp, then you'll be scared." She turned away and ignored him, angry that he was insinuating that she could not do her job as well as he could but unable to quickly come up with a clever response to defend herself. In telling the story to me later, she made a larger argument about the cavalier attitude guys like that took toward safety, and wished that she would have told him that "macho guys like him treat this like a racetrack instead of a workplace and make it dangerous for all of us." Although Laura was upset that she remained silent in the face of criticism, other women routinely use this kind of avoidance strategy. "It's just work, you have to get along with everyone," Melissa said. "Just like any job, there are some egotistical male assholes and you avoid them if possible." In the weeks that followed, I noticed that when one of the guys known for being macho called her on the radio to tell her she was doing something incorrectly, she answered by simply clicking her radio key rather than responding to the comment verbally—a time-honored technique for acknowledging but not directly engaging whatever has been said.

Others took a more forceful approach to dealing with the guys who were viewed as overly masculine. Molly, for instance, was incensed when some of the "older generation" guys told her that it was bad that her husband was at home cooking and cleaning while she was at work. She retorted, "I am working my ass off and I'm perfectly capable of doing a great job at whatever job a man can do, and how dare you say I should be at home raising kids, cooking, and cleaning!" To combat the perception of the "macho assholes" had of young women like her, she purposefully acts like one of the guys: "When the mechanics work on my truck, I go outside and stand with them when it's cold instead of staying in my truck and staying warm." Diane also directly engages guys who tried to boss her around. She and one of the macho guys used to get into tiffs over his aggressive driving: "We'd tell each other's side and come to an agreement or not about what happened, like if he'd pulled out in front of me, but we'd always talk and then move on. You have to confront them because it's a life-or-death issue."[10] Fay, another new hire, took an even more emboldened approach to "getting even" with one of the "macho ego guys" on her crew. Noting one night shift that he was sleeping in the dozer instead of monitoring the progress of the dump, she dumped each load short until she had left more than a dozen piles of dirt on top, rather than where they should have been placed below. She relished the punch line: everyone who drove by the dump realized he was slacking off, and he would have to push each one over himself when he eventually awoke or risk being disciplined by their supervisor.

Men are also quick to critique other men who act too aggressively. A dispatch operator named Wade, for instance, complained to me about an equipment operator who was always trying to engage him in a "pissing contest"—a specifically masculine way of characterizing a power struggle over the radio.

The driver routinely refused to follow Wade's instructions about where to park and when to refuel his truck, and he attempted to pass off his insubordination on technical problems with the communications equipment. Wade rolled his eyes at me during one of these exchanges and tried to diffuse the situation by calmly repeating his instructions.

Example 3:

1   Wade: Dispatch to 175 [pause].
2   Dispatch to 175 Trent.
3   Trent: Go ahead.
4   Wade: Did ya get my message?
5   Trent: Nope, must be a problem with the equipment.
6   Wade: Time for a fill up if that works for you [to me: fake smile, rolls eyes].
7   Trent: Pretty tied up preppin' this west pit.
8   Wade: Sure but the fuel truck is right there.
9   Would take him a while to get back to your area
10 And you're gonna need fuel in the next few hours, right?
11 Trent: Well we gotta get this coal face cleaned.
12 Wade: Shot's a long ways out [the blasting won't occur for a while].
13 Should give you plenty of time.
14 Trent: Where else does the fuel truck gotta go?
15 Would be a lot more convenient for me if we could do it later.
16 Wade: He's on his way.
17 You can meet him at the entrance to the shot pattern.
18 Appreciate you helpin' us out.
19 Trent: 10–4 [audible sighing].
20 But you better put this dozer on the list to be checked out.
21 Wade: 10–4.

Turning to me, he said, "It's just not worth it to get into it with him. He tries to turn everything into a fight to show what a tough guy he is, but he doesn't realize that he just ends up looking like an asshole. I try not to let it get me riled up." Trent attempts to dominate the conversation and the planned course of action at multiple points, for instance, by not responding to Wade's call until he uses his proper name (line 2). Even more significantly, he repeatedly portrays the timing of his task as more important than the smooth functioning of the entire operation (lines 7, 11, 14–15). Wade attempts to flatter Trent's sense of importance to smooth over his directions (lines 6 and 18). Backed into a corner, Trent eventually relents, but not without registering his discontent with a sigh and ending the conversation with a command of his own to Wade (lines 19–20), thus reestablishing himself as a giver rather than receiver of directions.

The incident in which a group of guys turned in Rick for sexually harassing their coworker Daisy—the opening vignette of the next chapter—also provided fertile ground for men to publicly critique exceptionally macho attitudes. Josh was the harshest in his criticism and viewed the clash as a larger lesson about the appropriate way to treat coworkers. "In my opinion," he told me as we were driving around the mine the day after the episode, "Rick is a male chauvinist pig. If he was our supervisor, I would have hammered him for what he did." He was proud that he and the rest of the crew took the initiative to turn him in and send him a message that his behavior was not acceptable to men or women. "He's always talking about his conquests: who, what, when, and how. He treats women like stupid bitches. I'm just like, 'Do you mind? I don't want to hear this.'" In contrast, he viewed himself as a model of enlightened behavior. "Rick is immature. That's not the way I was raised. I got a lot of respect for women. I've been around good operators who are women." He thought that creating a positive atmosphere was essential for their success as well as his own, explaining, "We're like kids—if you encourage us, we'll work our butts off to do better."

Other guys on the crew were on the same page. Earlier that year Bill heard Rick call one of the office clerks "the most offensive female insult you can imagine" because she would not give him the overtime he requested. "We all stopped that right away," he said, explaining that they did not tolerate hateful speech because it ruined everyone's morale. Bill, Josh, and their friends all delighted in Rick's eventual apology to the crew, in which he promised to try and "tone it down a notch" and be "more respectful" to everyone, not just Daisy. Men as well as women miners, therefore, critique displays of what they view to be excessive, aggressive masculinity because it not only offends their sense of propriety but also threatens the smooth functioning and cohesion of the entire crew.

Softies

Men and women alike reserve their highest praise and affection for men who are what they call "softies." Carrie favorably described her supervisor as being "a big, burly guy who is really a teddy bear at heart." She illustrated her point by first pointing to his tall stature, broad shoulders, and sturdy legs, and then telling a story about how she found a mention of his illustrious local boxing career in a community history book about the town's "bad boys." Adding another layer of intrigue to the picture of his personality she was painting, she reported hearing a rumor that he pushed his crew at a different mine so hard that he refused to go out to any bars after work for fear that they would beat him up.

She paused to let the full effect of his intimidating presence sink in, before tearing that image apart. "But he and his wife are religious and just really nice people," she continued, explaining that they took a week this year to go to a poor country and help build orphanages, and they always help their kids out a lot financially, and with their houses. Content in her effort to prove to me that you can't judge a miner by his exterior, she concluded that part of our conversation by saying, "A lot of these tough guys are really just softies when you get to know them."

As in the tale that Carrie told, religion was a common thread in many of the stories about such softies. In fact, at each of the mines I visited men and women alike made an effort to point out men whose generous philanthropy and kind spirit were grounded in their deep religious faith: a man who travels to the Cuba every year with his wife to do humanitarian work with their church; a man who helped found a new church and supports their young members' mission trips and leadership training events; a "Secret Santa" who buys Christmas presents every year for needy children in the community; and an ordained minister who is "the nicest guy but can even tell jokes with shock value," according to one of his coworkers. These observations would hearten the sociologist Robert Moore, whose 1974 book *Pit-Men, Preachers, and Politics* attempted to replace the glorified macho image of miners with attention to their deep-seated religious convictions and family values (Lahiri-Dutt and Macintyre 2006: 6).

Others took a more secular approach to patrolling the borders between right and wrong behavior, grounding their philosophy in the principle that crews are families with moral obligations to one another. On my first day at one of the mines, Donna gave me the lowdown on all of the crewmembers while we spent the day driving between the coal shovel and the crushers. She told me that Ron was "just like a dad" to the summer students because he always looked after their safety and made sure that they did not get into any tricky situations. I raised my eyebrows since I had just overheard him telling dirty jokes to one of the women on the crew during the morning meeting. She laughed and assured me that it was just a show, that "deep down he's just a big softie." Later that summer, we had a chance to revisit our conversation. Don had just turned in Ron for a safety violation that most people viewed as inconsequential, but management considered technically grave enough to warrant firing. On the way back to the office at the end of the shift, the bus was abuzz with people sharing what they knew of the story. Everyone took Ron's side, partly because Ron had used his own good sense and skill with the equipment to help each one out of a sticky situation at some point in their decades together, and partly because they hated Don for attempting to step on people to become a manager. People made jokes about Don not dallying in the parking lot after work, for fear of being beaten to a pulp by Ron, who also had a reputation for being a tough guy who did not shy away from fights in the biker bars he frequented.

Later in the women's locker room, we lingered to talk about the day's events. Brenda kept insisting that Ron was "rough around the edges, but he'd do anything for you. He has a heart of gold." Lisa agreed, recounting how he once told her that "if he ever killed someone, he'd slit their wrists and throat and feed them to the pigs so there wouldn't be any evidence." Lest I take this observation as evidence of excessive or psychotic aggression, she qualified this by revealing what had prompted the comment: he was upset when he real-ized that one of the temporaries on their crew had been hitting on her, and he viewed it as his responsibility to protect her from unwanted sexual advances. Brenda nodded in approval and looked at me, reminding me of her comment months earlier that he took on a father role with the crew, especially for the younger employees.

A part of what makes people like Scott and Ron so endearing to their coworkers is the mismatch between their tough-guy external demeanors and the sensitive, thoughtful personalities that shine through in key moments and conversations. The mines are filled with countless more examples, such as the steely shovel operator who demanded constant precision from truck driv-ers, but whose hard edges melted whenever he had the opportunity to boast about his grandkids. Or the dispatch operator who was so gruff on the radio that people avoided calling him unless it was absolutely necessary, but was also unfailingly kind to the summer students that he gave them easier and gentler driving assignments whenever they called him privately on the phone in his office. Or the utility guy (a jack-of-all-trades position that requires expertise in a variety of tasks) who perpetually spit chew as well as curses from between his thin lips, but took an hour each morning to mentor a new shovel operator, sitting down in the dirt with him to draw out the angles of hypothetical equip-ment arrangements and brainstorm solutions to them.

Other men let down their tough exterior almost completely and posi-tion themselves as caretakers for the crews and their own families. Henry, for instance, is known for being one of the best mechanics at the large mine where he works. He is also known for being one of the nicest guys on-site. One of his coworkers vividly described him as "the guy who's always happy, even when it's four A.M. and his car has been totaled by a deer. When he calls he's always very nice. That's just how he is, he's sweet, the epitome of a grandpa." Henry enjoys this reputation, even if he occasionally gets frustrated when people call in rela-tively simple issues that they should be able to fix themselves. At another mine, it is an equipment operator who holds the position of being the nicest, most easygoing person on-site. His coworkers chalk up his noticeable care and con-cern for others to the multiple years he spent as a teacher in the school district, patiently working with even the most trying students.

On an everyday basis, the vast majority of men also position themselves as family men when they discuss their kids at work by sharing their accomplishments, telling a funny story, seeking advice about a parenting conundrum, or complaining about their misbehavior. They insert these moments into the myriad spaces between their official responsibilities: a supervisor who shared his son's career aspirations with me while he was driving me around the pit; a plant technician who bragged about his daughter's college scholarships while we were all waiting for the coffeepot to fill; a pair of equipment operators who took advantage of a downed shovel to climb out of their trucks, light their cigarettes, and share their strategies for making sure their kids did their homework; or a plant technician who carefully drew out a photo from his daughter's recent wedding from his flannel shirt pocket to show his coworkers as they waited for the start-up meeting to begin, and then admitted with a smile, when they teased him about his sentimental side, that he had cried when walking her down the aisle.. In fact, these conversations are so common that summer students show up to their first shifts at the mine to find out that their new coworkers already know them intimately, having followed their ups and downs over the years of working with their parents.

Just as the women discussed above, men also shift between differently gendered social positions over the course of a conversation, a shift, a month, or a lifetime. In one-on-one conversations, Scott was as caring and understanding as anyone could hope for in a supervisor. With a wink, he feigned innocence when people on his crew publicly accused him of really being a softie underneath his tough exterior, though we had all observed it in action. For me, the lesson was driven home one unforgettable afternoon when the wheels of the truck I was riding in along with another operator caught on fire. Our eyes wide, we made the decision to bail and immediately began throwing all of our things we had strewn out around the cab into our backpacks. Once the truck pulled to a stop on the side of the road, we shimmied down the ladder as quickly as we could after throwing on the parking brake and setting off the fire suppression system. Scott was there in a matter of moments to make sure that we, along with the errant truck, were okay. Seeming to breathe a bit easier when he saw us standing nearby with pale faces but no visible injuries, he gave us a strong one-armed hug and then took off his hard hat with one hand and ran his other through his hair. He bashfully admitted how worried he had been—and how powerless he felt—when he heard our distress call on the radio. "I think I hit ninety on the coal road I was driving here so fast," he said with a good attempt at a chuckle. "I kept thinking, what could have I done? What did I miss to not see this happening? You guys mean the world to me, and damn, that is terrifying when something like that happens." Concerned that we were shaken up from our misadventure, he suggested that we spend the remaining hours in the shift having a cup of coffee in the office instead of returning to work.

While Scott displayed remarkable empathy, care, and vulnerability during our near-mishap, he also took on a decidedly more macho persona in other moments, such as when he argued with one of the women on the crew on the radio. She had called him to report that one of the ramps seemed steep.

Example 4:

1 Brenda: 923 to Scott [pause]
2 923 to Scott.
3 Scott: Go ahead 923.
4 Brenda: Scott I'm here in the north pit
5 and it seems like one of these ramps is too steep.
6 Scott: I don't think so.
7 Brenda: 'Kay
8 But have you been out here lately?
9 Just thought you'd want to know.
10 Scott: Yeah, it's fine like it is.
11 Brenda: I don't know, it just seems steep
12 Worry that somebody might tip over
13 If they're heavy on the way out.
14 Scott: I don't think so.
15 Looked fine to me.

This exchange happened while I was sitting with one of the youngest women on the crew. She made a face and described Scott as intimidating and sometimes rude. In this exchange, she viewed his initial ignoring of Brenda's call (lines 1–2) and quick dismissal of her legitimate concerns (lines 6, 10, 14–15) as evidence of his macho attitude. Her most troubling concern was that he sets a poor example for the few guys who also ignore this same woman. "He disrespects her when he does that," she said, so she just tries to stay out of his way.

Other men do an abrupt about-face when they realize they have offended their coworkers. On a night shift with Laura, for instance, we noticed that the loader operator flashed two sets of four lights to signal her to switch over to the line-of-sight channel that was not broadcast around the entire mine. She announced her presence on the channel, and he immediately yelled at her, "Don't you ever, ever get behind a loader when he's trying to clean face. Do you see this tiny window? I can't see jack shit out of it and I've got my eyes on the floor here that I'm not looking to see what's behind me because nothing should be there." She told him that it looked like everyone else was doing the same thing, so she did not realize it was an issue. With an overly nasal voice, he mimicked her whining and made fun of her for not thinking for herself. Stunned, she apologized and said she would do her best to not commit the error again. Curtly, he said, "Good. Because if you do, I might back into you and then you'd be in a world of hurt." She pressed her lips together and then said, "What a jerk."

Later that shift, Laura saw the same loader operator parked on the line where everyone was eating lunch. She groaned and said that she dreaded getting another lecture from him. The other drivers had all started parking illegally by starting at the opposite end, which meant that they had to pull up to each other's blind side. Defiant, she did it the safe way, and when we climbed down we found him waiting for us at the bottom of our truck. The first thing he did was apologize, which shocked her. "I'm sorry, I didn't realize you all were being taught that way," he said. "I feel bad for chewing you out on the radio for something everyone else was doing." She thanked him for the apology, and with an embarrassed grin he said, "Yeah, sometimes we get too big of egos. We need somebody to remind us we're not the king out here." Relieved, we ate our lunch in peace. When we returned to the privacy of the truck, Laura explained how impressed she was with him for apologizing, since it means that he had to "give up his macho act." In fact, when we got back out to the pit, he talked her through the tricky new position they were in. After her first attempt, he said, "That's perfect, just one thing," and then gave her another pointer. Laura nodded and waved at him through her window, and then turned to me to explain how happy she was that he was no longer acting like a "bossy know-it-all guy."

Finally, men also shift between different notions of masculinity over the course of a lifetime. Even the biggest aficionados of the stereotypically macho pastimes of drinking, roughhousing, and womanizing gradually abandon their vices as they age and become progressively less able to pursue those interests while working the exhausting rotating twelve-hour shift schedule.[11] Men with children feel these changing pressures the most acutely. Greg reflected on how having children had changed the tenor of the crew by saying, "Look at us now, a bunch of old farts. We used to go out and tip back a few [beers] and ride our motorcycles and just have a good time. And now everybody gets all starry eyed wanting to brag on their grandkids, me included." Laughing, he speculated about a possible reconciliation of his previous and current joys: "Well, maybe my daughter-in-law will let me take their kid out on the bike in a couple of years. That wouldn't be so bad." With the main cohort of miners solidly ensconced in middle age, many have comfortably settled into their new roles as grandfathers—a social position with very different expectations than a single twenty-something or even a young husband. Moreover, being a good husband, father, or grandfather at home shares many of the qualities that miners value in members of workplace families: empathy, understanding, care, and safekeeping.

Sissy

The crews' kinship ethic encourages men to develop and share their softer sides, all the while avoiding the most egregious displays of macho self-centeredness. But men who depart too far from conventional notions of masculinity find themselves under criticism, most often by being labeled a sissy or any one of its closely related categories. Talk about the much-maligned Don, for instance, frequently hinged on complaints about him being too macho: stubborn, prone to damaging the equipment, and unwilling to follow directions or take advice. But hefty insults to his masculinity also circulated around the crew. His record of equipment damage was rumored to stem from his own incapability with machines, which was particularly insulting given the larger cultural association between technical competence and masculinity (Rolston 2010a). His perpetual status as a single man also invited speculation about his inability to attract, please, or keep a woman as men are expected to do. In regard to the safety debacle described above, people referred to him as a "little bitch" that needed management to fight his fights because he could not handle them on his own, and they accused him of being a "sissy" since he avoided Ron after turning him in for the debatable safety violation.

This genre of insults is also used to disparage men who consistently avoid work. They cluster around the men's excessive dedication to their personal appearance, in cases that are reminiscent of the accusations leveled at women who care too much about maintaining painted nails and makeup. One man had the dubious honor of earning not just one or two but three nicknames for this behavior: Fonz, because he walks around with a comb in his back pocket and is particular about his hair; Muffy, because he considers himself a stud muffin; and Walking Eagle, because "he's so full of shit he can't fly." His crewmembers were incredulous that he actually answered to all three of those names, making them suspect he was even stupider than they believed since he obviously did not understand their critical intent. The combination of names is revealing. The care he took to maintain his personal appearance was not unusual on the crew, but it became devious and a marker of sissyhood in the larger context of his inflated sense of self-importance and lackadaisical approach to his job.

The link between this social category, self-importance, and slacking is especially clear in the story Al loved telling about a practical joke that was intended to teach a lesson. One guy at the mine was late to the bus nearly every day because he always wanted to take an extended shower, dry off, and comb his hair before leaving work. The people waiting for him were upset because they did not want to extend what was already a fifteen-hour day. One of his coworkers decided to play a joke on him using Never Seize, a lubricant that miners use to keep nuts and bolts from getting rusty and help get equipment pieces apart. One little drop of the stuff, Al noted, ends up everywhere like an ink spot. For the prank, someone put a few drops of Never Seize on the perpetually late coworker's towel. They were imperceptible, but when he dried off, the silver paste spread all over the meticulously clean man's body and through his hair. "He came on the bus and he was spitting nails because he was so mad!" remembered Al. "If he would have known who'd done it, he would have whipped them!" Al chuckled and concluded, "Every time I see Never Seize, I think about that guy and laugh." Together, these instances in which men are accused of sissy-like behavior gesture to the boundaries of acceptable deviations from conventionally masculine behavior, especially as it concerns hard work and crew solidarity: the miners disparage men who are too macho or too feminine.

Gestures to Gender Neutrality

When considering the categories as a whole in relation to one another, the similar qualities ascribed to tomboys and softies, ladies and machos, and bitches and sissies are striking. People labeled as tomboys and softies share similar orientations to work and social relationships that contribute to the overall smooth functioning of the crew. Crucially, these categories signal a departure from dominant notions of masculinity and femininity alike. Women identified as tomboys eschew the conventionally feminine distaste for dirt and muscle in their love of the outdoors and willingness to give their all in a muddy, dusty, greasy, and otherwise filthy work environment. Men identified as softies set aside cultural expectations for their emotional distance, competitiveness, and invincible swagger to make themselves vulnerable and treat their coworkers with conspicuous care.

People labeled ladies and machos, on the other hand, come under criticism for following dominant gendered scripts too closely—the ladies for letting their prissiness get in the way of hard work and crew friendships, and the machos for letting their inflated self-confidence and competitive approach to their jobs and relationships diminish their empathy for fellow crewmembers. In both cases, the exaggerated forms of femininity and masculinity are deemed troubling because they hinder the smooth functioning of the crew's daily responsibilities and social ties. Yet at the same time as the crews value and reward their members for moving away from dominant notions of masculinity and femininity, accusations of being a bitch or sissy clearly show the limits of the social acceptance of this practice. Both refer to men and women who act too much like the opposite sex: women who are linguistically and sexually aggressive or crude, like stereotypical men, and men who openly avoid hard work in favor of preserving their physical attractiveness, like stereotypical women.

People considered tomboys and softies are also distinguished by their enjoyment of working with people of the opposite sex. The mechanic Anne matter-of-factly informed me that she actually prefers working with men because of what she called the "dynamics of the way men and women are. If guys get mad, they might cuss you or yell at you or throw things, but ten minutes later they're over it. With girls, they hold grudges, so when you get all women together, that makes for a volatile workplace." She thought that having a "good mix" of men and women was important because they "temper each other, so that the overmacho or oversexed guys can get their testosterone toned down a smidge to complement each other." Rolling into a story about the "nightmare" of working in an all-female environment characterized by gossiping and backstabbing that she has yet to see in the mines, an operator shared a similar horror story from her job at a law office. She only worked with other women and left as soon as she could because she found the women there to be "manipulative and mean."

Women who share a tomboy orientation are also careful to point out that they would rather hang out with the softies on their crew than the bitches. Molly, for instance, initially hated her job at the mine because a few of the other women on her crew tripped her, causing her to lose balance and fall, on the bus each time she got on or off. "They were stuck in their ways, and they didn't want anything to change," she thought. But she eventually made friends on her crew with the "easygoing guys" and other women like her, and she made sure that her negative experience was not replicated: "It's tough at first, you know, so I always try to talk to new people." Smiling with satisfaction, she said that she is now to a point where she loves her job, even if it can get boring being alone in the equipment for twelve hours. Monica was also happy that she eventually earned the respect and friendship of her crew. Her success, she thought, was directly attributable to her "working as hard as the men. I finally proved myself, and they'd say that I ran as hard as the guys and they'd apologize for their bad language and ask if it's okay and if I needed anything else." She confided that she actually preferred spending time with the guys because "women can be catty. So can some men, obviously, but there are more women into drama. With the guys, it's easier to know where you stand, which is refreshing."

For their part, men known for being softies appreciate working with women. Returning to the conversation that opened up this chapter, the group of guys I was joking with came to the consensus that they actually enjoyed working with women because they were often more receptive to taking advice and more likely to "bust their ass" than guys because they wanted to prove the nagging stereotypes about women in blue-collar fields wrong. Although they were willing to admit that some of the "ladies" did a good job because they also sought to be respected on-site, their compliments ended abruptly when it came to the women they labeled bitches. Those women, according to them, were no good because they upset the crew dynamic. Curious, I asked them what they meant, and they explained that in order for a crew to function cohesively as a unit, people have to respect and at least tolerate each other even if they would not otherwise be friendly off-site. The women under discussion were problematic because they were rude to their coworkers and introduced what they called a "sexual element" into the workplace by openly hitting on men. They held men up to the same standards, explaining that those same issues animated their distrust of the overly macho guys on-site.

This discussion highlights another point of commonality between tomboys and softies: they enjoy intimate friendships with crewmembers, but they downplay any potential sexual overtones to them.[12] In fact, I heard the same philosophy from women as well as men: don't date or otherwise screw around with crewmembers because if it doesn't work out—and most likely it will not—you will have to see them every single day at work or transfer to another crew and sacrifice the years of friendships you have developed with them [your crew family]."[13] In fact, the pressure against crew romances is so strong that couples go to great lengths to keep their relationships secret by avoiding carpooling together, sitting near each other during meetings or social events, or the appearance of special treatment or extra joking. I did not learn that two of my closest friends on one crew had been dating for more than a year until my last day at the mine, when they figured it was safe to finally tell me. At another, an operator confided in me that she had dated one of her coworkers for almost a decade without it becoming public knowledge. Even husbands and wives bend over backward to avoid the appearance of any kind of special relationship between them. An extreme case comes from a husband's refusal to stand up to another guy on the crew who made a raunchy comment about women in front of everyone, including his wife. When explaining his lack of action, he said, "Hey, my wife is a big girl. When we're out here, we're not married. She's just like any other operator."

Although both men and women held each other to this standard, women faced harsher criticism for disregarding it. The mechanic Anne's assessment of such women was typical: "Most women aren't out here to mess around. They're here for the job, to make some money, support their kids, whatever. But some girls come out here to look for a husband, they find him, and they're gone in a year. But they don't realize that he left his wife for you and he'll just do it again." She then recalled an instance in which she was stepping up (or formally serving as the crew supervisor while their boss was on vacation) and had to talk with a woman about the midriff she was wearing because it was not appropriate for work at a coal mine: "Women like her are just trolling, and they sure as hell don't last out here very long."

People assigned to the categories of tomboy and softie therefore are considered to share a few key qualities: they enjoy physically demanding outdoor labor and leisure, and they nurture intimate but platonic relationships with their coworkers of both genders. To return to Bucholtz and Hall, this analysis suggests an adequation of categories. Although not completely identical, they are "sufficiently similar" to prompt miners to liken them to one another. In fact, the people most often recognized as good hands are those labeled tomboys and softies in other moments and contexts. This evidence suggests that even though the miners maintain separate social categories for men and women—evident in the distinctions between softies, machos, and sissies on the one hand, and tomboys, ladies, and bitches on the other—the drawing together of the most highly valued ones points to an emergent gender-neutral notion of personhood in the basin that persists in the face of social processes that otherwise draw out difference.

Conclusion

When gender difference loses its hold as an explanatory framework for everyday life, the miners and their families find themselves in what literary scholar Teresa de Lauretis calls the "space-off" or "chinks and cracks" in dominant representations of what it means to be a man or a woman (1987: 25).[14] Building on this work, anthropologist Kath Weston proposes what she calls a zero concept of sex and gender to draw attention to the "hiatus in which gender momentarily slips away" (2002: 41, 33). For her, zero gender represents ephemeral movement rather than an enduring social position, given the power of gender dichotomies: "Ambiguity resolves back into certainty, doubt into gendered absolutes" (Weston 2002: 28).

My use of undoing gender in this chapter and the next shares Weston's careful focus on time for seeing gender along with its "temporary lapse" (Weston 2002: 41). But while Weston emphasizes the fleeting nature of these moments, in this book I show that they have built into more durable dispositions in the Wyoming mines by virtue of particular historical, cultural, and institutional contexts. That is to say that to varying degrees and lengths of time, people can comfortably position themselves, their relationships, and the issues at stake in them outside of dominant norms of masculinity and femininity. Though this gender-neutral positioning is common, it does not represent a simple transcendence of gender, since dominant notions of gender difference remain present in the background, waiting to be activated. Nor has it solidified into a recognizable type, identity, or strategy akin to third gender categories. In fact, the miners and families grasped for language to capture this movement between and outside of dominant notions of masculinity and femininity; the best they could do was to position themselves in opposition to dominant ideas about men and women and compare themselves favorably to the local categories such as tomboy or softie. This lack of terminology underscores the extent to which their everyday practices are located in the "space-off" of dominant and legible representations of gender. This ethnography thus builds on the work done by Deutsch, Risman, de Lauretis, and Weston to offer a fine-grained ethnographic account of how the ties of accountability to dominant norms of gender difference can become loosened in the everyday lives of one group of working families in the United States.[15]

Language is a key site for tracking the push and pull of gender similarity and difference, or adequation and distinction in Bucholtz and Hall's more precise terminology. In this chapter I have traced the linguistic moves through which people position themselves and others as particular types of people in interviews, remembered speech, conversation, and radio talk. The primary cultural categories of tomboy, lady, bitch, softie, macho, and sissy circulate around the worksite and become meaningful as people reference them explicitly and gesture to them indirectly.

Observing language in action resolutely shows that the static typologies of femininities and masculinities that are found in accounts of the mining industry (e.g., Yount 1991) as well as the increasingly popular literature on hegemonic masculinity obscure the actual complexity and creativity with which people make sense of their own lives and interpret the everyday practices of their associates.[16] In their everyday talk and practice, miners in the basin move between categories over both fleeting moments and entire lifetimes. If their practices routinely cluster around one ideal type, they may develop a reputation for exemplifying that category. But even the most predictable people maintain a clear view of gender as something that shifts and is emergent through everyday practice, such as when the diehard tomboy Molly delighted in going out to bars with full makeup and girly girl gear.

Of particular significance in this analysis are the multiple points of similarity between tomboys and softies, the two most highly valued cultural categories for women and men. This convergence of qualities and characteristics gestures to an emergent gender-neutral form of personhood in the basin, though not without its limits. Acting like a tomboy or softie requires distancing oneself from normative ideas about masculinity and femininity. But those adjustments are different, and it is here that we see the greatest struggle and pull of gender difference, such as the instances documented in this chapter in which men snapped back into aggressive macho forms of interaction to deal with workplace conflict or women called on notions of superior feminine respectability to justify their place at the mines.

The genres of criticism analyzed here also point to a tension between gender difference and similarity. The criticism leveled against people who act like ladies and machos shows the undoing of gender difference in action, since at their base they are accusations that men can be *too masculine* and women can be *too feminine* for the good of the crew. The cutting remarks directed at people accused of being bitches and sissies are more ambiguous. On the one hand, they can be interpreted to show that people can take their departure from gender ideals too far or in the wrong direction by performing exaggerated versions of masculinity or femininity. They may value women who can turn a wrench and laugh at a dirty joke, but they taunt those who venture to swear as mightily as their male coworkers. They may value men who can provide a soft shoulder to cry on, but they question the masculinity of those who do more emotional, rather than physical, labor on the worksite. On the other hand, these insults can be interpreted also as warnings to avoid embodying the opposite gender ideal too closely. The complaints about bitches closely resemble those about machos, for instance, and the complaints about sissies closely resemble those about ladies. According to this logic, women and men alike should avoid acting either too feminine or too masculine.

In the next chapter I further develop the constant tension between social processes that emphasize gender neutrality and those that highlight difference as the miners create workplace relatedness with one another. In examining the ways in which the Powder River Basin miners evaluate each other's work ethic and good humor, I analyze the different social pressures at play in men and women's efforts to be recognized as a "good hand"—one of the highest compliments and ostensibly gender-neutral designations in the basin.

6

Hard Work, Humor, and Harassment

————————————————————◄o►————

Accusations of sexual harassment in the Powder River Basin coal mines are rare but unforgettable occasions for everyone involved. At only two points during my employment and research at six different mines did the crew I was working with or observing label an action sexual harassment. One of them involved a thirty-something equipment operator named Rick, whose high regard for his own abilities operating equipment outstripped his experience actually doing so in a mine. The more experienced members of his crew grumbled that he was a "fine construction worker": he could make the machinery do exactly what he wanted it to do, but lacked the wisdom to appreciate the larger context of how quick-fix decisions would adversely affect their activities months down the road when it would take extra effort to build ramps, establish the correct grade for a shovel, or begin a new pit. One morning while the crew was informally socializing before the start of shift, he announced, "Women should mind their men." His closest friend guffawed loudly, while coworkers spread out among the tables conspicuously ignored him, either by continuing their conversations or reading their newspapers. Daisy, the only woman present, found herself at a loss for words, interpreting his comment as a statement that she did not belong in the mine. "It was pretty much an insult to my own skills as an operator," she explained to me later that day when we were alone in the haul truck she normally drove. The comment was particularly hurtful to her because she took pride in her work ethic and the positive relationships she had formed with her coworkers. In fact, Rick's comment surprised her; she thought they were on good terms since they were comfortable joking with one another. In defending himself to those who approached him over the next few hours, Rick claimed that he was simply referring to a sermon given by his church's preacher the previous Sunday and that he did not intend to direct his comment at Daisy.

Daisy did not report the incident to their supervisor primarily because she wanted to handle her own business without involving management. Later that day a group of her male coworkers took matters into their own hands and reported it to the supervisor, who had been in his own office when the incident occurred. As they discussed their reasoning with other people around the mine and me over the shift and next few days, they said that they did so to support Daisy, but also to teach Rick a lesson. "He's always running his mouth," explained Lance. "He's either bragging about picking up women at the bar, using them, and then dumping them, or he's trash talking somebody out here. It's disgusting." People on his crew were frustrated because their own attempts to encourage Rick to modify his behavior had been unsuccessful. Because his history of offensive comments did not violate company policy, but rather trampled the crew's expectations for the treatment of coworkers, they had few options to force him to change his habits. The miners quickly and astutely noted, however, that his comment about women minding their men fell under the company's sexual harassment policy, giving them an opportunity to subject him to formal sanction. Rick received a lecture from the supervisor that afternoon. At their meeting the next morning, Rick stood in front of the room, shoved his hands into the pockets of his Wrangler jeans, and offered what most interpreted to be a heartfelt apology to Daisy and the entire crew for both the specific comment and his longer history of being inconsiderate. When he raised his eyes to meet the gaze of the people he had offended, they gave him a quick nod and he returned to his regular seat. Over the next month, Daisy and Rick gradually returned to their normal joking routine, which typically included bodily humor and sexual banter.

Incidents such as these raise a number of intriguing questions. Under what circumstances do men and women label interactions as sexual harassment rather than as entertaining teasing or mere annoyance? What is the significance of men turning in reports of harassment on the behalf of women who do not request or especially desire for them to do so? In this chapter I approach these questions by embedding accusations of sexual harassment—a crucial arena in which potential differences and hierarchies between men and women are constructed and debated in the workplace—within larger social networks of workplace relatedness and power. In so doing, I build on anthropologist Krista Van Vleet's rethinking of gendered violence. Her ethnography of an Andean village shows that domestic violence, normally viewed as a product of power asymmetries between men and women, cannot be solely explained by gender differences and hierarchy (2008: 181). Expanding her analysis beyond married couples to encompass larger kin networks and obligations shows that while violence is "not outside a system of gender," it is "laminated on relationships and discourses of kinship" that create the conditions in which conflict can emerge (2008: 164). The ethnographic materials from the Wyoming mines similarly suggest that what is at stake in situations labeled as sexual harassment is not a simple matter of men dominating women but rather the politics of crew families grounded in a distinctive blue-collar work ethic. Recall that Daisy's hurt centered around the injury to her work reputation, and that, in the decision to report his behavior, the history of Rick's hostile treatment of other men was equally as important as the sexist comment under fire.

Evaluating the work ethics of coworkers is the primary mode through which miners distinguish the quality and depth of relationships among crewmembers. The crew families do not rest on all-or-nothing notions of relatedness—you are either family or you are not, as is common in dominant Euro-American ideas of kinship—but rather distance is created by a type of gradual fading away that is similar to what Carsten notes for Malays (1997: 104). Although crews as a whole identify themselves as a large family, people within those families consider themselves to be more and less closely related to particular crewmembers. This fading of relatedness takes place as people interpret and judge how gracefully coworkers embody the stresses of shiftwork described in chapter 3, while safeguarding the well-being of their coworkers. Evaluations of crewmembers' work ethic simultaneously bind particular people together while pushing others to the margins. These judgments involve a complex calibration of effort and competence. To be deemed good hands, miners must be skilled and care enough about their work to do a good job and avoid creating extra toil for their coworkers. At the same time, they must temper those efforts so that they do not push those same coworkers to perform outside their skill or comfort zone. Humor is a key component of this balancing act, since it cautions miners to not care about their work more than they care for other people.

Taking a closer look at the blue-collar work ethic under construction and contestation reveals a key arena in which gender differences are undone as well as reproduced. The expectations to which crewmembers hold each other in their everyday working lives are potentially and partially gender neutral. In other words, many of the key qualities believed to make someone a good hand and valued member of the crew family are not locally associated with either masculine or feminine characteristics. This constitutes a partial undoing of gender, rather than a simple redoing of gender, since social space exists in which men and women are not held accountable to specifically gendered norms (West and Zimmerman 2009: 118). The chapter therefore builds on the larger purpose of the book by showing that even in a context in which gender differences would be expected to play a leading role in the way people interact and interpret each other's talk and behavior, the miners mitigate their potential significance by placing them within more gender-neutral notions of a strong work ethic and workplace relatedness.

Like the rest of the book, however, in this chapter I probe the limits of that gender neutrality by also examining the moments in which gender differences are reproduced and reinforced, especially as purportedly gender-neutral ideals of a strong work ethic are put into practice and under evaluation. For example, while most accusations of sexual harassment enforce the crew families' notions of a proper work ethic, others are indubitably troubling cases of gendered persecution. I document and analyze these outliers, but for two reasons I place them within the much larger framework of the more mundane patterns and practices of social relationships in the mines. First, cases of harassment are already vividly represented in the existing academic literature and in popular films.[1] Second, people in the Powder River Basin believe—and I agree—that the emphasis on isolated cases of sexual harassment at the expense of the everyday camaraderie among men and women creates offensive and exaggeratedly gendered caricatures of miners that have little to do with the challenges and joys that dominate the majority of their working lives.[2]

This chapter therefore situates sexual harassment and gender hierarchy within the larger field of workplace relatedness by investigating the contested construction and evaluation of a proper work ethic in the mines. This analysis is crucial to understanding the politics of gender in the mines because failing to meet those supposedly gender-neutral expectations unravels the workplace kinship ties that make the miners' work meaningful, erodes one's position in the crew families and authority at work, and dissuades people from maintaining their employment in the long term. This analysis is critical because attention to historical, cultural, and institutional structures shows that undoing (or consolidating) gender difference is not a simple expression of free will or desire. This chapter follows Risman (1998) and Salzinger (2003) in analyzing people's everyday actions with an eye to larger institutional pressures and the cultural context. This background is key for understanding the ability of the Wyoming miners to diminish the significance of potential gender differences.

The Gender Neutrality of Hard Work?

The cultural background of the women who went to work in the Powder River Basin miners is a key element of their overall positive experience. With few exceptions, these women had grown up on or near family ranches and farms, where girls and women were expected to work alongside their brothers, fathers, uncles, and cousins to do the gritty work necessary to preserve their agricultural way of life. Mining seemed like a natural extension of the work and relationships they had engaged in while growing up, likely because the specific habitus of mining is constructed out of and shares many qualities in common with the habitus of agricultural ways of life (see also Desmond 2007).

Men and women miners alike describe their specific form of work ethic as gender neutral largely by linking it to popular ideas and personal experiences with farming and ranching, the region's primary industry before oil and mineral extraction began in the 1960s. In so doing, they draw on common if romanticized ideas about the American West as a place where grit would liberate women.[3] Patty attributed her success in mastering the social relationships and technical challenges of the pit to her agricultural background in the Midwest: "I grew up on a farm, so I was very used to physical labor. Getting dirty didn't matter to me. You did what needed to be done. You didn't wuss out, wimp out, or worry about your fingernails." She remembered that when she first hired on, there were four women in production. Three of them had rural backgrounds, and she thought the fourth's lack of that experience was noticeable and made her integration onto the crew more difficult. Similarly, Peg, who eventually became a shovel operator, argued that a career in mining "seemed natural" because she had been doing "nontraditional" things all her life on the family ranch. Not only did growing up around equipment and driving horse trailers make it easier for her to learn how to operate the mine equipment, it also prepared her to work with men without asking for special treatment: "It was easier for people to come out of an agriculture culture, at least in this part of the world. It's egalitarian; you just grow up doing everything. You're just another one of the hands!" The terms "good hand" or just "hand" is likely popular in the Powder River Basin because it is gender neutral when compared to other terms such as manpower.[4]

Ranching metaphors also frame the ways in which nonproduction personnel think about their work. Marie, who now works as a land permitting and management consultant for many mines in the basin, grew up on ranch adjacent to a coal mine. She remembers being raised to do "whatever needed to be done" irrespective of gender, "just like that Nike commercial: Just do it. I grew up in a family where whatever needed done, whoever was available did it. Whoever was there pulled the calf [to help a cow give birth] with the equipment, whoever was at hand was expected to do it. That benefited me later on." In explaining the success that many of the ranch kids had working in the industry, she pointed to their understanding of "twelve-hour shifts, running the heavy equipment and working until a job is done. The product doesn't magically appear." She also drew similarities between mining and ranching, in that both involve "preparing the land for the harvest, harvesting the product, and then getting the land ready for its next step."

Even women without personal experience on farms or ranches found inspiration from popular ideals about ranch work, especially for women. One human relations manager who grew up in an eastern city had integrated these notions into her own understanding of the industry. In discussing the mine's affirmative action plan, she compared her experiences in Wyoming favorably with those in eastern underground operations: "It was harder to get those [Appalachian] women to apply. Here mining is more traditional work for women . . . it's just like putting a daughter to work on the farm out here." Jenny, an equipment operator who moved to Gillette from a more urban area, found that she took on these ideas in her own life: "I'm a lot more like these women out here. They've always been independent, and they do what they want to do. They have the freedom to do that. I love it. That's why I stayed here." Sally loves working as a driller and blaster in the pit, though she sometimes gets tired of dealing with other people's incompetence. Wearing a hard hat emblazoned with a sticker reading, "They don't pay me enough to be nice to you," she traced her success in the industry back to her great-great-aunt: "She homesteaded around Gillette and taught in a one-room schoolhouse in the middle of nowhere." Smiling, she drew out the similarities in their personalities by saying, "She was a tough lady."

Men, too, drew on their understandings of women ranchers and homesteaders when talking about the success of their women coworkers. Jerry explained, "Women out here are different. I think that's why they've been able to do so well in this industry. They stand on their own two feet and they don't need anybody to take care of them." His coworker Greg agreed, saying, "There's a history of that here, with those old ranching families. Those women had to be tough to make it, and these women here have to be tough to make it, too." Tom, who worked at a different mine, expressed a common sentiment in the area. "The women who make it out here are the ones who pull their own weight," he said. "It doesn't matter if you're male or female. You have to get the job done. I think people from an agricultural background understand that. And if you don't understand that, then you'd better learn real quick."

The attitude that everyone pulls his or her own weight irrespective of gender plays a large role in women's integration into the industry and to the diminishing of potential gender differences. People frequently told me, as did an equipment operator named Randy: "It doesn't matter if it's a man or a woman out here, as long as they do their job." A former truck driver named Katie agreed with this sentiment. "Being an equipment operator is an excellent opportunity for a female since it doesn't matter if you're female or male," she said. "It's very open. Men don't care as long as you can get back to the berm square." Here she is referring to the ability of talented truck drivers to align themselves with the berm at the edge of the dump so perfectly that all the material in their dump beds falls completely over the edge of the dump, making the job of the dozer operator much easier—a key goal of most people's work practices, as described below. Each of the women pit supervisors I came to know shared these opinions and pointed to their work ethic as the main factor in their positive relationships with their crews. "If you cared about your work, then people like and respect you," explained Monica.

Although assertions of the gender neutrality of hard work are no doubt idealistic, they do form a part of the social fabric of the mines. They ostensibly welcome particular kinds of women into the workforce, and they serve as an ideological resource for miners of both genders seeking to support women in a nontraditional occupation. Analyzing concrete situations in which miners evaluate each other's work ethic, however, reveals a considerably more complex situation in which gender differences are consolidated as well as partially undone.

The Politics of Giving a Damn

The pillars of the miners' work ethic are caring and expertise. Caring encompasses the multiple senses of the word teased out by anthropologist Michael Lambek in a discussion of kinship: "to care for and to care about; but also to take care of someone; to take care, as in to be careful; to have cares, as to be full of care; and to be vulnerable, to care what others say and do" (2007: 220). Miners express fondness for each other and the equipment they operate, and they seek to treat the beneficiaries of their affection well so as to safeguard their welfare. Being cautious and alert for hazards is a crucial component of this commitment. With few exceptions, they also monitor their own performance to be sure that their coworkers will also look upon them favorably.

In some ways, care is the basis of expertise since skills are honed through constantly trying to improve oneself so as to lighten the load of one's coworkers. A shovel operator made this point succinctly to me in comparing the truck drivers who were cycling through his shovel. As I watched Gus load trucks, he showed me how he could tell some of them were recalibrating their approach in an effort to position themselves better in relation to the shovel. One driver positioned too far to the right on his first approach, too far to the left on the second, but gradually straightened out each subsequent turn. "See, that takes some effort. He's figuring out what he got wrong the first time and adjusts each time after that," he said and then compared him favorably to another driver whose front end of the truck was consistently off-kilter, which meant that he was not making any changes in his approach even though it created extra effort for Gus to load. I nodded, all too familiar with the process from my own two summers driving truck, when I would gauge my position and then make small changes until my position was as square as possible. I would try to swing a bit closer to the shovel or crank the steering wheel a second earlier to create more or less distance between my truck and the shovel, or I would straighten out once I saw more or less of the shovel tracks in my side mirror to achieve a better angle in the approach. I vividly remembered the struggles that plagued one of my first night shifts, when it seemed like I was never quite perfect. Worried that I had created extra work for the shovel operator, I apologized to him on the bus ride home. He waved his hand, minimizing my concern, and said, "I'd rather you try and figure out how to put everything together than come in there crooked every time." Gus brought my mind back to his shovel when he made a similar comment about the people on his crew. "You just try better next time, that's the important thing," he said. "It takes some experimenting to get the feel for it, but some people just can't be bothered to give a damn."

Assessing someone's competence and caring—or the extent to which they give a damn—is less an objective measure than a subjective judgment that is established and contested in everyday interactions (S. Carr 2010). These assessments color and are colored by longer histories of interactions, friendships, and betrayals. People recognized for their work ethic may hold particular characteristics in common, such as regularly volunteering to help a coworker out of a sticky situation, cleaning up their own mess rather than leaving it for the next operator or crew, or driving back to the shovel for that last load rather than being the first person to park on the line at the end of the shift. But these same characteristics can be overlooked in someone who already has a reputation for being lazy, and people are more willing to turn a blind eye to well-respected crewmembers cutting corners.

People recognized for their work ethic are labeled good hands. According to miners, a good hand is not just dependably competent in meeting their everyday responsibilities but can also be counted on to skillfully address any of the myriad anomalies that appear on a daily basis. For instance, almost all pit trainees eventually master the spatial skills and hand-eye coordination required to navigate a haul truck down the road and correctly position it in relation to the shovel, dump, and plant hoppers. Good hands, however, can also decipher particular smells, sounds, and irregular jerks as signals of impending failures in the machine long before they are registered on the automated alarm system or the equipment breaks down. Catching these failures at an early stage prevents more major equipment damage and potential injury. It also enables the operator to easily bring the equipment to the shop for repairs, which avoids a time-consuming tow or a dangerous repair for the mechanic in the middle of pit traffic. The intimate knowledge of the machine required to make those assessments and interventions comes from actively learning about the machine through years of practical experience and experimentation coupled with asking questions of more knowledgeable hands.

As the shovel operators were quick to point out, a mark of a good hand is continuously trying to improve one's performance. I watched as Daisy, for instance, carefully trained her eyes on the blade operator and the road rather than staring off into the distance as she drove her truck from the shovel to the hoppers, where the coal entered the plant, and back again. I asked her what she was looking at, and she said that she constantly watches other people to "learn and try the things that they're doing." Hoping to be trained on the blade, she was observing her coworker's strategy for smoothing out the road: how long were the stretches of road he worked on at one time, which projects of rough road he prioritized, and which soft spots he ripped up and which ones he just smoothed over. "I'm a very visual learner," she said, "and when you have more experience you understand what's going on." When it would come time for her turn to be trained on the blade, she would begin with more perspective and better questions than if she were starting from scratch, which would speed her transition to being considered a good blade hand.

Road quality also features largely in how crews as a whole distinguish themselves in relation to other crews, likely because it is an area that can take resources away from production but is necessary for it to happen smoothly: assigning people to run blades means that they are not directly participating in the extraction or transportation of overburden or coal, but without blades to repair the roads trucks have to slow down and become more prone to damage. One crew, for instance, boasted about their reputation at the mine for excelling at special projects, such as building ramps, creating new roads, and maintaining the existing ones. One of their long-term members cast her crew's de-emphasis on making production the top priority as evidence of their care not simply for each other, but for the entire mine, by saying, "We take care of the roads. There are restrictions on how fast you can go, but some people turn off the auto-retarder and go way too fast, which means that they can make more rounds but they also abuse the machines and the roads." The other crews, she said, have an attitude that "if it ain't my truck I don't care," but hers does not share that attitude because "we respect people and the equipment."

As much as crew families are quick to praise one another for their work ethic, they also critique those who do not appear to care about their performance and thus the smooth operation of the entire crew. Daisy's coworker Josh, for instance, frowned each time we drove past a particular blade operator. Examining the roads, he critiqued the other operator for "not really blading or cutting, he's just pushing some rocks around." He compared what he saw with his own practice, saying that he shortened the length of the sections he was working when he came across a bad spot; that way he could cut the entire hole out. "I'd call the scrapers, and they would take really good care of me," he added. "They'd follow with loads of gravel to heal the road." Here Josh succinctly uses multiple senses of the word care: he is personally invested in his own performance, the scraper operators show their respect and affection for him by going out of their way to help him do his job well, and they all care enough about the mine to make sure that the roads are in good condition.

When we drove past the blade the next time and nothing had changed, Josh grinned and said, "I'm gonna call him Pebbles. Let's see if he gets it." Calling him Pebbles was meant to call attention to Josh's observation that he was push-ing rocks around rather than improving the quality of the road. He keyed the radio and said, "90 Pebbles we'll be coming around on your right." The blade operator did not engage the joke, but the next truck driver we passed gave us a thumbs-up, which Josh returned with a laugh and a wave. Turning to me, he said, "Blade operators should think of truck drivers, especially since they used to be one." As we pulled up to the hoppers, he drew my attention to the pile of spilled coal that was slowly creating a ramp and said, "They should come up here and scrape the hopper off." The ramp was potentially dangerous because it would enable a truck to back up into the hoppers, instead of being stopped by the tires hitting the lip. Josh continued, "I can see getting sick of it, espe-cially today with someone leaving a mess, but usually it's not that big of a deal." In his assessment of his coworker, Josh tried empathizing with his coworker's frustration—admitting it was tiring and annoying to constantly clean up after other people's mistakes—but asserted that a good hand who cared about his coworkers and own integrity would do it anyway.

Later that month, a deluge of curses streamed from Wanda's mouth when she realized that the person who had operated the haul truck the shift before her had let the engine oil reach hazardously low levels. We had been doing the requisite safety walk-around the equipment at the beginning of the shift when she realized that she would have to take the truck immediately to the shop or risk breaking down later in the shift. Resigned to the delay, she called the shop to report the problem and then turned to me to use the incident to prove her larger point about her idea of a proper work ethic: "I'm gonna take this into the shop because that's what you're supposed to do, even if it means I get behind in my load count." She then contrasted her willingness to sacrifice for the rest of the mine by painting the other operator as selfish: "See, whoever did this didn't think about who was going to come after them. There's no pride there. No thinking about the other guy, just yourself. That attitude is danger-ous out here." For Wanda, watching out for other people is the mark of not just a good hand but of a person with an upstanding moral character.

People labeled as being selfish or just plain slackers reject the cultural fram-ing their coworkers use to critique them, but not the criticism itself. I met Randy standing in the hallway at a large mine where it was easy for people to "get lost," as they said, because there were simply too many people on each crew. He was normally quiet on the radio and sometimes found himself the target of complaints from his crew for one offense or the other, such as driving so fast around corners that he spilled coal that the blades had to clean up. Skeptically eyeing the aerial photographs of the pits, calendars of shift schedules, and lists of production statistics, he said that he had lost the fire he had when he first started there a few years earlier. "Now I'm just out here to put in my twelve hours and go home." I asked him what happened and he explained, "I learned one person can't really make a difference. It doesn't matter if you bust your ass because there are five other guys right there who don't give a shit." Later that afternoon when a check-engine oil light came on in the haul truck we were in, Randy sighed and continued driving. "I could call that in to the shop, but they'll just tell me to keep running since they don't have the people or time to fix it, so I don't even bother anymore. Their policies are always changing anyway, so even if we're supposed to call it in today we probably won't have to next month." He only called in equipment failures if they were major because he thought it took too much effort to contact the shop and switch out equipment, especially since it was likely that the next piece of equipment would also have problems since the shop was so short-staffed.

Randy attributed his lackluster work ethic not to his own moral shortcomings—as his coworkers insinuated when they called him lazy—but to the conditions under which he worked. In his opinion, he took a more realistic and sustainable approach to work since he acknowledged the features of the mine that could "suck the life out of you if you let it": shifting management policies, too many people on a crew, too many problems, and limited resources to fix them. Even the most conscientious members of his crew acknowledged the truth behind his assessment of the limitations of the mine, but cast their continued efforts as indicative of their character, specifically the pride they took in their work despite the difficult conditions. Greg said, "You have to have pride in what you're doing, and take ownership over it." He gestured out of the truck window to the new ramp that one of his coworkers was building: "You have to be able to look at what you're doing, like building that ramp, and be proud of putting your name on it even if you're not going to get an atta-boy from your boss or a thank you from the next crew that has to finish it or [from] the rest of them that are going to drive on it."

Asserting the importance of a work ethic signals one's dignity in a potentially demeaning environment (Lucas 2011). Yet the process of evaluating that ethic also naturalizes a specific approach to and investment in one's labor and marginalizes people who do not share it. Linking "caring" with continuous improvement asks workers to invest their moral worth and sense of self in activities over which they sometimes have very little control. Randy, for instance, realized that his chances of advancing in the pit hierarchy were slim since the most established miners kept their positions operating the most prestigious equipment. He also recognized that because his crew was so large, his own efforts to perform well were overshadowed by other people's incompetence and mistakes. By disassociating himself from his work performance and from gossip at the mine, he limited the extent to which his self-worth would be insulted by complaints from coworkers or what he called "shit jobs" that took lots of energy but reaped little appreciation. Daisy and Josh, on the other hand, were much more likely to advance in the equipment hierarchy because they worked on a small crew. People on small crews have more opportunities to train on new equipment and frequently have to fill in for one another. Moreover, because their crew was so small, they developed much closer relationships with the people who would benefit from their efforts at improvement, and a few of their older coworkers had taken her under their wings in a mentoring relationship. Aligning with the crew's expectations could feasibly lead to promotions and closer relationships in a way that it would not for Randy.

The most significant pattern that emerges in tracing how miners evaluate each other's work ethic in general is related to mine size. Accusations of specific people being lazy and more general complaints about people "not caring" about their work appeared in almost every single interview with employees of large mines, some of which were characterized by crews with upwards of one hundred members each. These comments decrease dramatically for the smaller mines, where crews average less than twenty-five people each. At both large and small mines, men and women were represented in these categories in equal rates according to their percentage of total workers, suggesting that the qualities of caring and laziness did not take on strongly masculine or feminine associations. In other words, women overall were not more likely to be labeled either a good hand or slacker. This pattern also supports the women's self-reports that they generally did not feel less invested in their work or more pessimistic about their opportunities to advance compared to men, since so-called laziness is indicative of detachment from one's work and coworkers.

Gendered Evaluations of Caring and Expertise

Women and men are equally represented and comfortable filling the category of good hands. Finding subtle gender differences in evaluations of a proper work ethic requires breaking down the category of a good hand into its two main components: caring and competence. Although Gus and many others linked the two by saying that the former led to the latter—that caring about one's work and coworkers led to expertise—these two characteristics can be differentiated with distinct consequences for women and men.

At all of the mines where I worked and conducted research, miners were quick to point out women as well as men who stood out for being particularly skilled or exceptionally hard working. During my first day with his crew, the pit supervisor Scott pulled his pickup truck alongside the one I was riding in so that we could chat through our rolled-down windows. Although a representative from human relations had introduced my project to him and the crew at that morning's meeting, he wanted to hear more details about what I was interested in studying and why. I started explaining that not many people had written about women miners, and he jumped in, saying, "Women do a great job out here. You know, they actually make better operators because they're more safety conscious. They don't try to muscle it." I nodded and took notes as he went through all of the women on his crew and their accomplishments. He listed all of the women who were well known for being excellent shovel, dozer, and haul truck operators, and then argued that women better manage the dump (where truck drivers haul and deposit the overburden) because "they don't scream like the other ones. That means that people are more willing to work with them."

In private conversations, women did feel that the majority of their crew currently recognized their skills and dedication, though all begrudgingly remembered that they first had to "prove" their worth. For example, a pit supervisor cautioned, "You can't have it both ways, equality and preferential treatment. . . . With the guys I had to work harder, make sure my skills were better. I worked my way up, so no one will bad-mouth me now." A woman mechanic agreed: "You have to be tough to keep your status, especially on the mechanical end, because people think it's a man's job." In talking about their first years in the industry, the women's resentment came not from simply having to demonstrate their technical expertise in order to be recognized as a hard worker. It seemed logical for them to do so given the highly technical and interdependent nature of the mine jobs. Their frustration stemmed from observing that new men did not go through the same testing period; rather, they seemed to arrive on-site with technical credentials that were questioned only after a mistake. These gender-specific struggles dovetail with insights from the field of feminist technology studies that document the ways in which "in the contemporary world . . . technology is firmly coded male. Men are viewed as having a natural affinity with technology, whereas women supposedly fear or dislike it" (Bray 2007: 38).

The interpretation of mine radio talk further draws out gender differences by (perhaps unintentionally) undermining perceptions of women's technical expertise. A linguistic analysis of conversations in which miners reported mechanical failures to their supervisors and the shop (Rolston 2010a) reveals that when more novice women use indirect language such as hedges (um, uh, or maybe), tag questions at the end of a phrase (you think?), or vague terminology ("that thing" instead of "the braking system"), these are viewed as being evidence of their technical incompetence. As one experienced male miner complained about a woman who was perceived as both "speaking in circles" and lacking expertise, "Her talk on the radio is just as jumbled and confused as she is." As they gain more experience with the equipment and with workplace social relations, most women shift to using more direct language valued by experienced crewmembers for being clear and concise. At the same time as they shift their linguistic practices, they find more respect for their technical abilities. The crux of the issue is that this correlation between language and perceived expertise does not hold true for men. Whereas novice women frequently come under fire for using imprecise language, men use the same indirect language but without comment or judgment. This disparity in the interpretation of radio talk points to an arena in which perceived gender differences are being shored up to the detriment of women despite frequent appeals to the gender neutrality of hard work.

The miners' awareness of this dominant equation of masculinity and technology, coupled with their desire to dislodge it, may animate their frequent statements that women are either equal or superior equipment operators to men. In my conversation with the supervisor described above, he demonstrated his own support for women on his crew and in the industry by appealing to a notion that he believed was gender blind: women can be equally good operators as men. Yet the way in which he and others did so subtly reinforced gender difference. When men like Scott talked about the best equipment operators on their crews, they emphasized the technical competence of the men they mentioned, such as in their abilities to consistently load high numbers of trucks using the shovel or to create perfectly graded roads on the dozer. When discussing the best women equipment operators, however, they listed women with technical prowess along with those with a reputation for being exceptionally safe or caring. Brian, another pit supervisor, echoed Scott's assessment, telling me that the women on his crew were better truck drivers. When I asked him why, he explained, "They're more conscientious. They don't get careless. They don't get macho, trying to go around the corners. And they'll call a mechanic when something's wrong." The association between women and safety consciousness appears throughout the industry (e.g., Fortson 2007; Lahiri-Dutt 2006).

The mine radio, the main form of communication for workers separated by distance as well as the metal of heavy equipment, is one of the key arenas in which people's reputation for safety is constructed, reinforced, and debated.[5] For example, the policies of most mines require drivers to first call on the mine radio and ask permission from the vehicles they wish to pass. These situations typically involve haul trucks passing the slower moving blades as they grade the roads, or light duty vehicles such as pickups passing any kind of the slower heavy equipment. Verbal warnings are vital because the blade operators are often focused on the ground below, and many pieces of equipment have large blind spots that can completely obstruct views of the smaller trucks. Very few operators routinely follow these policies, either because they are confident they can pass safely or because they assume the other driver has already seen them. Besides high-level managers under more pressure to follow official company rules, the only other people who consistently call other vehicles before passing them are women operators. During one winter day shift in which I transcribed the pit radio, women operators called and asked permission to pass over twenty times, whereas their male peers did so only twice. These patterns are noticed by miners—who spend shifts transfixed by the radio as a form of entertainment in an otherwise repetitive environment—and build up notions of women's supposed inherent commitment to caring and safety.

Men, of course, also develop reputations for being safe. The man who first trained me to drive a haul truck took advantage of our time together to make sure that I could not just identify, but anticipate, potential hazards. As we were driving down the road or sitting parked at the shovel, he walked me through his thought process as he surveyed potential hazards in our surroundings. People on my crew said it was good that I had been assigned to him because he was one of the safest operators on-site. They also assured me that everyone would all look out for me, but one of the shovel operators in particular would make sure that I never got into a dangerous situation since he made the safety of the summer students his primary concern. "He'll be just like a dad to you," one of the women said approvingly. During my later fieldwork the importance crews placed on safety for both men and women was driven home perhaps the most strongly when one of the crews lost a member. He had died at home unexpectedly the night before, and when his crew gathered at work the next morning the first thing they talked about was his dedication to making sure that everyone felt safe.

Developing a reputation for safety and caretaking is not problematic on its own. What is concerning is when expressions of care overshadow expertise. My crew described an especially safe and caring equipment operator as a father, and another crew gave another equipment operator the nickname Mama Love because she took care of her coworkers. "I think of myself as a caregiver. If people are sick or having problems, they just get on the radio and call me," she said. If people need to talk or vent, they pull over to the fuel station and she meets them there. She also always carries a medical kit to take care of whatever situation might arise. In fact, she frames her medical training and expertise in terms of caregiving. She is a member of the mine's emergency rescue team, a certified CPR instructor, and a frequent teacher of safety trainings at the mine.

Mama Love's caretaking activities, however, sometimes overshadowed her substantial technical competence. She is not just her crew's go-to person for medical assistance and emotional support; she is also the only person on her crew selected to regularly operate the mine's biggest brand-new haul truck. Management decided to have the same people operate the truck rather than inserting it into the regular rotation because they hoped that the chosen operators would be more invested in keeping it in excellent condition if they had to run it all the time. In explaining why she was selected from her large crew, she initially pointed to her work ethic and reputation for being a safe driver. She never missed work unexpectedly, and she was diligent in running through the end of the shift instead of parking early like some of her coworkers. Still, she also attributed her selection to her technical skills in operating equipment. Her knowledge of the machine and the angles associated with being loaded by the shovel makes her one of the most efficient truck drivers in the pit—a fact that was not lost on her supervisors. Whereas many of her coworkers often have to reposition themselves in order to be properly loaded by the shovel, she rarely does even though her truck bed is considerably larger and thus more difficult to position perfectly. Her expertise is also evident in her being selected by management to train new hires—a compliment since it means that her supervisors wish for the new employees to learn to drive like her.

Crafting themselves as safe and caring operators provides women with a well-accepted strategy to integrate themselves into the crew families, but it also predicates their integration into a male-dominated industry on markedly feminine terms. At stake in these practices is the potential erasure of women's other achievements. For at the same time as many women have found it both professionally empowering and personally meaningful to develop reputations for being safe and caring workers, they also seek to have their technical skills recognized. As described above, many women were frustrated that they originally had to "prove themselves" on-site to earn the respect of their coworkers (see also Rolston 2010a). Most leave those complaints in the past, saying that their skills are now equally respected. This reflects not an idealistic relegation of problems to the past as researchers have found elsewhere in the mining industry (Mayes and Pini 2010), but years of effort on the part of the women and a willingness on the part of the men to revise deeply held cultural assumptions. Although the association between masculinity and technical expertise may be strong, it is not immutable.

Although I have focused on the difficulties women face in having their technical skills recognized in order to be considered a hard worker, notions of expertise do present challenges for men, albeit different ones. Because men are viewed as naturally skilled in operating and fixing heavy equipment, they feel pressure to avoid asking for help or advice in front of others, especially on the radio. Instead, transcripts of these conversations are filled with men asking their peers and supervisors, "Where can I catch up with you?" The question is an indirect request for a face-to-face meeting. Even though I was not able to sit in on most of the discussions that followed these questions, participant-observation suggests that most are used to privately discuss and seek out help for equipment problems. These miners' efforts to avoid publicly speaking about mechanical problems point to the force of local ideological linkages between masculinity and technical competence. Novice men feel the most pressure to avoid public requests for help, almost certainly because their inexperience at the mine or in the entire industry means that their skills are less firmly established. This situation is problematic because seeking out more covert ways of learning requires effort and its own kind of skill. If miners do not take the time or energy to ask for help, they can develop habits that are dangerous to themselves and their coworkers. If there is hope in the situation, it is that as they age and gain more experience, this pressure relaxes; transcripts show that the most experienced miners frequently seek assistance more directly, most likely because their expertise is not subject to the same kind of scrutiny.

Miners therefore may be quicker to recognize women as caring and men as technically competent, but these associations do not exhaust the full range of either their everyday practice or the way in which it is evaluated socially. Crews recognize women's technical achievements and men's dedication to safety, even as they acknowledge the powerful gender ideologies (women are naturally caring and men are naturally technologically skilled) that contradict them. The miners may not be able to completely overcome these ideologies, but they do acknowledge and try to move past them. These efforts represent their attempts to loosen the hold of gender difference on their everyday working lives, which are noteworthy even if they are only partially successful.

Finding a Delicate Balance

At the same time as good hands take pride in working hard, they carefully distinguish their own work ethic from what they call overachieving. At one mine, I formed a close relationship with a group of plant technicians whose motto was "work smarter, not harder." We spent many night shifts listening to the classic rock station, laughing at the "after hours" extraterrestrial-themed call-in radio show, and experimenting with how far the pickup would go without pressing on the gas pedal. They shared their tricks for washing down the plant equipment and floors quickly but efficiently, tutored me in the best strategies for avoiding the supervisor, and showed me their secret places for taking naps. They also helped me play my first practical jokes, and the man who considered himself the most erudite of the bunch eventually lent me his favorite books so that I could improve my mind while parked on the outskirts of the train loop or sitting in the load-out facilities, where operators sat in front of control panels to open and close the chutes through which coal fell into the train cars. Near the end of my time there, the supervisor took me on a tour of the pit, perhaps to use the opportunity to share his thoughts about the crew. He was well aware of their techniques for avoiding extra work—and his watchful gaze—but claimed that it did not bother him. "They might have a reputation for slacking off sometimes," he said, "but when push comes to shove, they're good hands. If something big happens, like if the crushers go down or we have a coal spill, they are right there in the muck to help out and fix it. And I think that's the most important thing, so it doesn't matter to me if they're not 100 percent busy all of the time." Based on our discussions, I knew that the guys shared his attitude; they were proud of the work they did in keeping the plant running smoothly, but did not feel the need to run themselves ragged by going far above and beyond what was required of them. One of them explained the situation succinctly, saying, "If you're gonna make it twenty, twenty-five years out here, you've got to pace yourself. I pull my own weight so no one has to cover for me, but I'm not going to break my back for this company or make anybody feel bad about themselves." This sense of balance was key for them and the majority of miners I came to know through my work and research.

This group's approach to their work exemplifies the larger balance miners must forge between working hard enough to take pride in how they spend the majority of their waking hours, and not working so hard that they endanger their own well-being or put too much pressure on their coworkers. This local notion of a proper work ethic balances individual and collective concerns, emphasizing the value of work in relation to the perceived larger good of everyone's well-being, and to harmonious relationships with coworkers.[6] For the miners, working diligently is viewed as evidence of good character (Fricke 2008; Lucas 2011), but only insofar as it does not subject one's coworkers to undue stress or imply that they are a cog in the machine. This tension is especially evident in the breakdown of these expectations, as occurred while I was conducting research with an otherwise close-knit crew.

Candace is a wiry woman in her forties who chain-smoked cigarettes while showing me the ropes on the shovel. We spent one afternoon discussing a recent event that had unraveled an otherwise close relationship. On the bus ride at the end of the shift from the pit to the changing rooms, the shovel operator Cory criticized the way she had been operating the dozer. In front of the entire crew, he accused her of ruining the grade of the dirt and making his job more difficult. Her eyes stinging with tears, she told him, "Ever since you've been on that fancy shovel, all you care about are numbers instead of people or equipment. That's rude." She recalled that he "barked" at her pretty badly and added insult to injury by justifying his behavior, saying, "You're damn right it is," affirming that he privileges production numbers over other people's feelings. She responded by saying that she had always given him "150 percent" of her effort and that she would never do anything to mess him up.

In retelling this event, Candace contrasted two different work ethics. She interpreted Cory's drive to operate the most prestigious shovel as inappropriate and troubling because it had threatened her own personal integrity and violated the feelings and practices associated with kinship relationships on the crew. "We're supposed to support each other, not tear each other down," she explained. On the other hand, she cast her efforts to give 150 percent as serving the greater good of the crew rather than personal gain. Almost everyone on the crew shared her interpretation, and I observed as they ostracized Cory by not inviting him to crew social events and refusing to do favors for him unless he directly asked, in marked contrast from the otherwise prevalent practice of anticipating one another's needs. A few days after my conversation with Candace, in fact, I heard Cory ask a dozer operator when he might be available to clean up the shovel area, and without missing a beat, the operator replied, "About two months."

Now a shovel operator herself, Candace does her best to keep the emotional and physical well-being of the other equipment operators in mind. One new truck driver considers her as the best shovel operator partially because "she cares enough about the operators to feather out the first bucket on the beds." Feathering out is a particular style of dropping the shovel's bucket load into the truck beds. If the shovel operator drops the first load of dirt directly in one place in a truck bed, it can cause the entire truck, including the cab, to shudder violently and jar the driver. Alternatively, if they try to spread or "feather" it throughout the bed, the truck shakes much less and makes the entire shift more bearable for the driver. In feathering, shovel operators imagine what it is like to inhabit a different machine and act in ways that they believe will make that experience a little gentler.

People also appreciate shovel operators like Candace who are slow to "honk out" truck drivers. If the shovel operator honks twice after the truck has backed in to be loaded, it is a signal for the driver to pull out and back up again in order to reposition. Repositioning creates extra work for drivers and can be demoralizing since it critiques their ability. It is sometimes necessary because if the truck is positioned at an incorrect angle to the shovel, loading it is difficult and sometimes impossible because the shovel bucket and truck bed must be aligned for the dirt or coal to wind up in the bed rather than pile up on the floor. Misalignments cause delays in loading, which reflects poorly on the shovel operator's production statistics. Some therefore honk out drivers who are even slightly out of angle, hoping that it will push them to become more accurate. Others refrain, believing that constantly being honked out puts undue stress on equipment operators, who then perform even worse. This distinction is so important that when Christie, a high school classmate of mine who eventually went to work at the mines full-time, described her father to me in an interview, the first thing she said was that everyone thinks he is nice because "he doesn't say nothing, he just goes and operates his shovel. You can be in there so crooked and he would still load you, you know. He wouldn't say boo, and that's why everybody likes him." Her father's willingness to load even crooked trucks stands as evidence of his respect for his coworkers and desire for things to proceed smoothly in the pit.

For every man like Cory who feels the pressure to produce, there are more men like Christie's dad and the plant operators described at the beginning of this section who are careful to temper their own drive with the feelings and security of their coworkers. Josh and his good friend Taylor also exemplified this approach to work. They worked on the same crew, sometimes as a team of "rovers" who supported the shovel and did special projects around the pit, and worked out at the same gym after their shift and on their days off. Competitive in both realms, they frequently compared their achievements with each other and with the rest of the crew. One of the afternoons when I accompanied Josh in a haul truck, he critiqued the guys who were acting as rovers, showing me how their strategy for setting up the shovel cable would come back to haunt them in a few hours. "They weren't thinking ahead because they don't have enough cable for when that shovel has to turn when it gets to the end of that coal face," he said. "What we do is avoid that in the first place instead of having to take even more time and energy to fix it later." Tapping the side of his head, he repeated the same motto, "You gotta work smarter, not harder."

At the same time as Josh and Taylor took pride in their own performance, they strongly criticized people who took their work too seriously. One of their coworkers, they believed, was angling to step up to a supervisor position. Like many of the people I met, they thought the only people who wanted to be bosses were power hungry or had huge egos since there was scant financial incentive in the deal: more pay but more hours. They discussed the situation in the pickup as we drove to move a sump pump. "Vern just can't have any fun," Taylor said. "But you know what's worse? People who step over other people to get ahead. At least he doesn't do that." I asked them what stepping over people meant, and they listed a string of offenses that had one thing in common: critiquing a coworker in the presence of or directly to management in an effort to make oneself appear more responsible, more knowledgeable, or more skilled. "We've got to watch out for each other first," Josh summarized and Taylor nodded.

Hard work, therefore, consists of a fine balance. Everyone has to pull their own weight, as the miners say, so that no one has to pick up the slack from anyone else, and there is no shortage of insults for people who regularly create extra work for others. Yet hard work also requires tempering one's efforts to ensure that the drive to do a job well done does not alienate those same coworkers. Just the right amount of hard work is not simply evidence of personal character, therefore, but of the ability to attune one's actions to the rhythms and needs of the larger group.[7] People like Cory who violate this ideal are marginalized in the crew families, pushed out to positions where their ties of relatedness with others are weak but not completely severed.[8] After all, miners take a pragmatic attitude toward conflict at work, admitting that its presence stresses but does not negate workplace relatedness. As they say, you cannot choose crews any more than relatives, so why not make the most of it?

The people who struggle the most to balance the ideal of working hard enough but not too hard are men like Cory and the macho men described in the previous chapter. Candace and her crewmembers viewed his efforts to be as productive as possible on the prestigious shovel as an affront to the dignity of the truck drivers who were running off of his shovel. But talking with him one-on-one revealed a more complicated situation. He confessed that he felt a lot of pressure to "be the best out there." He identified this pressure as coming from both management and his own desire to be a stable breadwinner for his family. "Management, they pretty much so say that we set the pace of the pit and basically the whole mine's production, so they put more pressure on us," he explained. "They say that they ask more of us, like working through lunch, since we are in a position of leadership. But we take that on voluntarily." He paused and then qualified how voluntary his desire to be successful in the pit was, especially since the mine had undergone numerous changes in corporate ownership. "I just want some security, you know? I've got a wife and two little kids at home, so I'm gonna bust my ass while I'm out here." This ethnographic material suggests that men in the basin continue to wrestle with the breadwinner ideology that dominates cultural expectations of fatherhood in the United States (Townsend 2002). Men who feel the most pressure to produce at work in order to provide at home can produce tensions and gender difference in the mines.

Theorizing Humor and Harassment

Workplace humor is a primary mechanism for counterbalancing the drive to work hard and continuously improve. In this chapter, I show that miners value coworkers who are able to appreciate the myriad jokes, both verbal and practical, that they play on each other. With few exceptions, these jokes are not intended to be humiliating nor interpreted as cruel, but are a sign of care and a strategy to infuse some merriment into the otherwise humdrum ticking down of the shift clock. But to what extent can men and women equally and comfortably participate in these highly valued joking rituals? In what ways do they reinscribe gender difference and power asymmetries, and in what ways might they challenge them? How do differently positioned people draw the line between humor and harassment? These questions return the analysis back to the questions of gender hierarchy that opened the chapter.

Both ethnographic and historical studies of humor, gender, and workplaces document the role masculinized joking plays in maintaining gendered hierarchies.[9] Scholars of mining industries in particular have suggested that these joking behaviors systematically marginalize women in the industry. In these studies, sexualized joking served as a form of sexual harassment or discrimination. Sociologist Suzanne Tallichet's research is representative. She suggests that the men at the mine where she studied engaged in both verbal and practical jokes as a form of male bonding and argues that these practices simultaneously "'otherize' and 'sexualize' women so as to reaffirm men's dominance" (2006: 47; see also Vaught and Smith 1980; Yount 1991, 2005). Although acknowledging that harassment lies in the "eye of the beholder," she also suggests that the women who profess to enjoying the "sexist" jokes or at least accept them as a part of their initiation into the workplace suffer from double consciousness in which they identify with their oppressors in order to get by (Tallichet 2006: 46–47).

Sociologist Kristen Yount's research in western underground mines also leaves little room for enjoyable workplace joking relationships. Like Tallichet, she concludes that harassment is a means of expressing male domination and managing the stresses engendered by working conditions (Yount 1991: 405; 2005: 66). Her work is notable for theorizing both the overlaps and distinctions between harassment and what the miners term "razzing." Some women like being razzed and consider it one of the highlights of their days, not a form of harassment (Yount 1991: 415; 2005: 68). Yet razzing can hold multiple and contradictory meanings for different people, and even the most enjoyable razzing can escalate into harassment (Yount 1991: 400; 2005: 66–68). To account for this ambiguity, Yount eventually collapses the two into a term she calls "harazzment": a hybrid category of harassment and razzing that includes everything from playful and humorous jokes to hostile behavior (2005: 66). This term is helpful in identifying a range of practices whose interpretation varies according to specific individuals and contexts. Collapsing the two terms is problematic, however, since they refer to different sets of intentions, contexts, and interpretations. This difference is key for the Powder River Basin mines and potentially other workplaces.

The concern held by both Tallichet and Yount that harassment disadvantages women in the workplace corresponds with Catherine MacKinnon's (1979) foundational argument that sexual harassment is illegal because it constitutes sex discrimination under Title VII of the 1964 Civil Rights Act. Yet MacKinnon established a model of sexual harassment in which "the harassers are always male, their victims always female, and their mode of harassment always sexual" (Anderson 2006: 307). This formulation raises complications for thinking about practices that fall outside of this paradigm, such as the treatment of gays, lesbians, and transsexuals, or aggressive horseplay among men and nonsexual harassment of women (Anderson 2006: 288–289). Especially pertinent to the present discussion of the Wyoming mines is the question of sexual banter in the workplace. Philosopher Elizabeth Anderson identifies the difficulty in labeling such behavior harassment because it is not clear that it constitutes discrimination, and she cautions that regulating expressions of sexuality could threaten sexual autonomy and impose heterosexist norms on people with queer sex/gender identities (2006: 289, 291).

In this vein, scholars have called for more nuanced theories of the "unwelcomeness" standard and consensual sexual activities and sexualized verbal interactions at work (Anderson 2006: 300).[10] As sociologist Christine

Williams and her colleagues argue, "Sexual harassment and sexual consent are not polar opposites, in contrast to the assumption of much legal theory. Instead, they are interrelated and overlapping moments in a complex and context specific process" (Williams, Guiffre, and Dillinger 1999: 77). This insight is pertinent to the Powder River Basin mines, where women and men carefully and clearly distinguish joking from harassment. Tracing the ways in which they do so requires a closer look at how the frame of workplace relatedness influences the way in which miners interpret each other's joking practices and responses to them. This analysis points to the significance of regional context. Tallichet reconciles the presence of sexual harassment with her observation that crews come to think of themselves as family by arguing that the family is the place where Appalachian gender dominance is learned (2006: 30, 136–138). The dominant—if romanticized—ideologies about the gender neutrality of hard ranching work in Wyoming provide an alternate vision of the mutual imbrication of kinship, gender, and questions of sexual harassment.

Blue-Collar Comedy

Mine equipment and the jargon used to talk about it present seemingly endless opportunities for statements and interactions that could readily be interpreted as sexual harassment: shovel operators put their sticks into truck boxes, truck drivers worry if they are heavy on top, dozer operators instruct trucks on exactly how to back it up, and almost everything needs to be greased or lubed. From the perspective of miners, however, specific circumstances and interpretive frames dictate whether a gesture, joke, or action will be considered a hostile attack or a welcomed and entertaining distraction from the routine. Humor, after all, turns on multiple and sometimes competing layers of meaning (Holmes 2000, 2006; Seizer 2005). When Josh nicknamed the blade operator Pebbles, for instance, he intended to correct his coworker's behavior in a way that was potentially humorous but still critical, serving as a reminder that comedy often mixes pleasure and pain (Seizer 2005: 232).

Unambiguous Cases of Harassment

For miners a few behaviors are unambiguous forms of sexual harassment: unwanted touching and coerced exchanges of sexual favors Connie, who worked in billing during the early years of the industry in the 1970s, found that when she would venture into the plant, a few men would push her petite frame up against a wall or purposefully bump into her. "I literally used my hard hat as a weapon," she remembered. Similarly, the fiery longtime equipment operator Wanda explained, "I can deal with anything a guy could say to me. But if he reaches up and grabs me while in the working place, that's different." The defining moment of harassment in her career also took place during her early years in the industry when she was a temporary worker cleaning shovels. "A guy I was working with grabbed my ass, so I kicked him down the stairs and quit." She felt vindicated about her judgment of his character when she later learned that he was in charge of hiring and would force the new girls to give him oral sex in his office. In our conversations, Wanda was careful to note that women could also be perpetrators. She and others were disgusted with a woman on a different crew at the mine that would perpetually "grab guys' dicks" while people were hanging out before shift or during lunch. "That makes it hard for me to do my job. But I pull my own weight and I don't expect to be treated different. Those women ruin it for the rest of us." She and some other people from the mine eventually convinced her to stop by threatening to turn her in for sexual harassment.

Connie and Wanda, like women miners in general, also consider the lack of what they called "equal opportunity" to be a form of sexual harassment since it is directed at women and harms their emotional and mental well-being. Connie encountered discrimination in the office in the 1970s.[11] When she decided to leave her job in billing for a better paying position in the pit, she was delighted to learn that her boss had to hire two men to replace her. Her excitement was tempered when she learned that each of them was paid double her wage, plus benefits. She complained to her boss and he justified his decision by saying that the men had to provide for their families, whereas she did not since she was a woman.

The pit presents its own barriers to equal opportunity, especially as some women find it difficult to advance because they the lack the opportunity to train on more prestigious pieces of equipment. Wanda thought that her daughter was advancing well in the pit because her supervisor "was like a dad to her" and made sure she learned new equipment. Another equipment operator named Darlene thought that the situation was worse during the 1970s and early 1980s. According to her, women on her crew did not receive the same promotions that men did, and they were not encouraged by management to train to be shovel operators. Echoing Connie, she described the era as one in which "it didn't matter how good the woman did at her job, they were not considered the bread providers. . . . A woman had to prove herself and work really hard or be somebody's girlfriend." In fact, Peg found herself in that very situation during the early 1980s when she sought to become an oiler, the position that is a stepping-stone to becoming a shovel operator. To attempt to deter her, some men invented seemingly impossible tasks, such as carrying heavy material straight up the shovel ladder, which she had to accomplish before being considered for the job. With the help of the shovel operator who had encouraged her to bid on the position, she successfully met their requirements and became one of the first women shovel operators in the basin. Despite the initial hurdles and resistance, she went on to become one of her crew's best performing and most well-liked shovel operators.

All these cases are clear examples of sexual harassment and discrimination. They are also, however, outliers to the majority of everyday interactions that require careful interpretation of the context to debate and establish meaning.

Joking as Caring

The primary frame of reference used for this interpretive work is whether the people involved are close members of the crew family. This is likely because jokes are one of the most valued means for crafting and nurturing close relationships. On the one hand, some jokes create solidarity among coworkers in critiques of management.[12] The best example from my fieldwork involves a story deemed to be so funny that every single member of the crew recounted it to me. One of the managers decided that the pit operators should not have a microwave in their break room because it could encourage them to return late from lunch. The crew was upset because they felt professionally and personally insulted: they were not usually late and every other area of the mine had a microwave to make hot lunches. After the manager took the pit's microwave up to the office, the crew's unofficial leader promptly drove to the on-site warehouse, got another one, and took it back to the room. During a pit tour a week later, the same manager found the new microwave and threatened the entire crew with locking up the break room (which also had their coffee machine and water cooler) and making them eat lunch by themselves on their equipment if he found one there again. The next day, an as yet unnamed person showed up to work early and posted a sign that said "When microwaves are outlawed, only outlaws will have microwaves"—a clever play on the National Rifle Association slogan well known by the miners, many of whom were avid hunters.

Needless to say, the manager interpreted the joke as an issue of insubordination and bad attitudes rather than a legitimate critique of unfair workplace policies. The manager threatened to put the person who posted the sign on "step," a disciplinary measure. But after the pit crews expressed their frustration by intentionally following every safety rule to the letter, thereby slowing down production for two weeks, the manager quietly let it be known that he would no longer be stopping by the break room during his rounds in the pit.[13] The microwave was just as quietly replaced, and the crews returned to their normal levels of production and microwaved lunches.

On the other hand, most joking practices in the basin do not rely on nor invoke labor and management divisions.[14] Rather, they animate relationships among miners who consider themselves to be part of the same crew family. In speaking about why she loved her crew family, Daisy equated practical jokes with expressions of care, saying, "They make fun of me. I like it. It cheers me up, gets my day going. Otherwise this place could be pretty bleak." Mary felt the same way, explaining that her favorite part of her work was the camaraderie she crafted with her crew by sharing jokes. "It reminds you that there's a person sitting in that truck with their own unique personality," she explained. "It's not just a machine."

Like many other summer students who put on their hard hats only to discover that their coworkers had surreptitiously filled them with ice, water, or butter, I enjoyed my fair share of jokes first as an employee and later as a researcher. On my first day as a truck driver, my trainer and I talked politics. He learned that I tended to lean more to the Left than to the Right, a position that was rare in Gillette and even more so in the mines. With a straight face, he told me that the only Democrat on-site was the shovel operator I had just met. Excited, I approached him the next day before the start of shift. As our coworkers were chatting and settling into their chairs for the preshift meeting, I said to him, "So I hear you're the only other Democrat out here." Eyes wide and face red, he composed himself enough to correct me as the entire room burst out laughing, cueing me to realize that I had been tricked. I quickly learned that he was the staunchest Republican and biggest fan of radio pundit Rush Limbaugh on the already conservative minesite. The shovel operator turned our interaction into a joke that would be repeated throughout the summer when he started calling me "Leftie" on the radio and requesting that I reposition—not simply my truck but my political philosophy, he implied—to the right.[15]

Other jokes continued during the next two summers, as I returned to my truck after a break to find that the much-needed air conditioning had been turned off in favor of full-blast heat; when other drivers honked their horns in an attempt to get me to leave the shovel early; or when the water truck operator sprayed my newly washed windshield just in time for it to be covered with coal dust from the hoppers. Like the majority of my coworkers, I interpreted these acts as gestures of belonging and trust, especially since the people who first played jokes on me were the ones who had originally "adopted" me onto the crew by engaging me in conversation and introducing me to others. To return to Handelman (1990), discussed in chapter 3, these caretaking activities provided the integrative frame that helped us interpret these actions as jokes rather than attacks.

Nicole, who has been operating equipment in the mines since the 1990s, similarly considers her closest family at the mine to be those who she can "joke around with." Her memory of her last day of work before transferring to a new mine highlights the importance of jokes in these relationships. One of her favorite things about her old crew was something they called "Sing and String." Whereas truck drivers are expected to back up completely to the berm so that their loads of overburden fall over the side, "stringing" refers to the practice of leaving the dirt in long strips on the top of the dump. Because this causes extra work for the dump's dozer operator, the act can be either malicious or funny depending on the strength of the relationship between the dozer and truck operators. Nicole's crew had turned stringing almost completely into a joke. The twist was that they also composed songs that could be silly or tell a story about the dozer operator, and then they sang it over the radio while stringing dirt everywhere. "It was fun," she said. "I would just laugh so hard when someone did that to me." On her last day with the crew, she knew that she had to Sing and String. "So I made a nice little song and everybody was in tears and then all I could do was say 'Okay' and then string out a little smiley face on the dump. And it was just fun. It was just a good time." Just like the crew who shared a hot meal on their last night together before being scattered into new crews, Nicole intended for her joke to leave her coworkers with a sense of close ties.

Nicole suggested that distinguishing well-intended jokes from those that were more malicious depended both on the intention of the person and on the closeness of the friendship they shared. Christie, who was originally hired as a summer student, learned this distinction quickly. She became an aficionado of practical jokes as she stayed on at the mine as a full-time employee and loves recounting stories of good jokes that she played on others or that others had played on her. Laughing, she explained how she turned a somewhat distant coworker into a friend:

> Wherever I work I try and make people have fun. I'm always laughing, I'm never down or anything. So there's this one time this guy on my crew is wearing these coveralls, and they have big pockets in the back. He always wears coveralls. So I got a cup of water—and see with coveralls, you can't really tell anything until it soaks through or you sit down—so I took a cup of water and poured it in its back pocket. And he was walking around and you could kind of see the water jiggling. And then he sat down for our preshift meeting and he's like, "Christie!"

In this case, the joke provided an opportunity for the two of them to become closer.[16] Christie was clear in explaining that she only played jokes on her friends. "I like to make people have a smile on their face for the rest of the shift, you know?"

Practical jokes are rarely used to punish or alienate coworkers since jokes evoke closeness and the preferred method for dealing with people one does not like is to ignore or disengage them. Lenny, a longtime equipment operator who was hurriedly counting down the days to his retirement, told his crewmembers and me a story of one of the only instances of revenge. After being drenched when someone hid a bowl of water under coveralls and paper towels in his locker, he watched the person he suspected of the prank every morning on the bus to work until he noticed him take a nap with his work boots off. Stealthily, he emptied two packets of Kool-Aid into the boots without the person noticing. After sweating in them all day, the man returned home and failed to notice that his socks were red. "His wife got pissed at him for staining the carpet!" celebrated Lenny, who gleefully explained that the guy's feet stayed red for two weeks and he ruined eight pairs of socks. Lenny laughed and asked the guys sitting with us, "You think he ever tried getting me back?" The rest of his coworkers were laughing along with him, and the story prompted one of the younger ones to tell one of his own. Explaining that he used to work at a sawmill, he said that one time he and his friends put green paint in everyone else's gloves because no one checks them before they put them on. "They had green hands for three weeks! Man, that was funny. I miss those guys." The younger coworker made no mention of his acts being inspired by ill feelings or revenge, so it seems that in telling his story, he subtly reframed the original one told by Lenny to emphasize the positive, relationship-building aspect of practical jokes.

For miners, the familial nature of their relationships precludes most sexual banter from being interpreted as harassment and the instigators of these interactions from being labeled harassers. Jenny, a woman my age who had worked in both the office and the pit by the time I came to know her, said that she did not consider herself harassed when engaging in joking relations because her coworkers "look at you as part of a family, not someone you'd date. They thought of me like a daughter." When I asked her how she would distinguish between joking and harassment, she said, "It depends on how you take it. The same joke can be offensive or not when told by different people. You have to think: Are they a part of your family or not?" She highlighted the importance of family by pointing to the men's expectations for how their own daughters would be treated: "These are nice guys, friendly guys. They have daughters, and they don't want to them to be treated like that."

Carrie agreed. In her nearly twenty-year career, she experienced only one incident of harassment that she took to a foreman. She explained, "Sometimes women don't know that the guys are just having fun with you. You have to look at intent. Is it vulgar, personal, or flat out gross? Do they keep it up if you tell them you don't like it?" She was frustrated that some women complained about the dirty jokes that frequently circulate at the mine. She thought that the women's reactions to the jokes, rather than their content, were demeaning: "That's degrading because it's stupid. Every guy has respect for women. They tell jokes to make you a part of the crew. And once you're family, they protect you." Mary took a similar approach. She enjoyed recalling tales of good practical jokes, including one in which a guy bumped into the back of her blade when she was first learning how to operate it and was still "thinking through every action." She was so taken aback that she immediately got on the radio and started "yammering" about how something was wrong until she looked in her rearview mirror, realized what had happened, and began laughing along with the coworker who had instigated the joke. A few years later, she had an opportunity to play the joke on someone else, which gave her great satisfaction. Whereas she technically could have interpreted her coworker's behavior as hostile sexual harassment, she viewed it as a joke because they had a close relationship. She aptly explained the differences between sexual harassment and joking: "Camaraderie. I love that word because of what it builds. It's more friendly, building a trust, because they know that I'm not going to go to HR [Human Relations]. . . . You have to know the person first, then you build [trust] and you can say whatever you want—body humor, sexual jokes, whatever—because you know each other. You're not going to run off to HR." Body humor plays a large role in the crew family relationships among men and women, perhaps because it is potentially incendiary and thus requires great trust to not take offense.[17] During one gruelingly hot summer day shift, Melinda's truck had lost its air conditioning and she was waiting for another truck that was in the shop to become available. She had worked at the mine for nearly three decades and that day was working with a younger loader operator named Derrick, who was well respected among the crew for his work ethic. When a mechanic called to tell her she could switch trucks, she said, "Good. Derrick is too young and would get scared if I take off any more clothes." His response was deadpan: "I was kind of enjoying the show." On the bus ride back to the locker room, everyone laughed about the exchange. It was hilarious, they said, because any hint of a sexual relationship or interest between the two was ludicrous.

At a different mine, a pair of friends was infamous for exchanging barbs about their appearance. She would make jokes about the size of his penis— "Stick it out, arch that baby!"—every time she saw him pulled over to the side of the road, presumably taking a bathroom break; he would counter with comments about her breasts being so old and low they fell into her boots— "Boobs in boots!" At still another mine, another pair of coworkers loved engaging in witty banter that included a hefty dose of sexual innuendo. During a discussion about where each of them would work in the pit, Sally said, "I'll go on top." Jim quickly replied, "I like it when you're on top." Not to be outdone, Sally raised an eyebrow and said, "I like being on top." Jim burst out laughing and said, "Be careful, I'll take advantage of you!" Sally and Jim had become devoted friends over the years they had worked together, and they viewed their teasing as evidence of that closeness. Separately, they both insisted that the banter was harmless fun, and they offered their spouse's observation and support for the behavior as evidence of its innocence. For them, like Melinda and Derrick and the other miners, their interactions were not about a possible sexual relationship between the two of them; instead, their ability to joke comfortably about sex proved its insignificance and the depth of their trust of each other. As Mary would say, sharing that kind of humor means that you know the other person is not going report it as harassment to management.

Perils of Parody

Sometimes the line between humor and hurt is fuzzy, as illustrated by two situations that appear similar on the surface but were interpreted in almost polar opposite ways. Before the start of a shift, Ron, who was well liked and well respected on the crew, began reading aloud from the local newspaper loud enough so everyone who was sipping coffee and organizing their lunch boxes could hear. The lead article chronicled the legal trouble a few strippers from the local club found themselves in after hitting male customers with paddles and belts. Parodying an exaggerated macho stance, Ron announced that the customers must not have been "man enough to handle it." He continued, "I can't believe that somebody or somebody's friends would pay for something nice like that and then complain about it." As the laughter in the room grew, he shared more details from the story, such as how one stripper was in trouble for putting a guy in a headlock between her legs. Emboldened by the escalating laughter from the crew, he embellished his performance, adding, "Why would you complain? That's the best part. Enjoy the view, man!" He then made a joke imagining a young crewmember named Lisa working at the club, and she retorted that she'd make more money out there than at the mine. Ron and the rest of the crew burst out laughing, and he slapped his knee with his hand and acknowledged that he had been one-upped, saying "Good one, kid. Good one."

Not a month later, the same crew found themselves once again talking about men, women, and sexuality in the context of the newspaper. A middle-aged man named Don started reading the personals aloud to the rest of the crew, and he asked Lisa what voluptuous meant. She said curvy, and Ron made a joke about liking women who had meat on their bones. Don then rhetorically asked what passionate meant and then quickly answered his own question by saying "horny." He continued reading the personals and editorializing with his own comments about penises and cocks. But rather than inspiring laughter, the room became quiet, and the rest of crew became visibly uncomfortable and started shifting in their seats. They seemed relieved when their supervisor began the preshift meeting. During their lunch break, Lenny pulled Lisa off to the side and encouraged her to report Don for sexual harassment.

Lenny's reasoning for considering Don's behaviors to be sexual harassment points to the crucial difference between that day's incident and the one about strippers the month prior. Lisa recalled that he explained, "What Don said in your presence was inappropriate. You would make a lot of people very happy if you turned him in. I wasn't there because I was getting my timecard, but four or five other guys said they'd support you. Then we could get Bill back." Bill was a well-loved shovel operator who had been transferred from this crew to a different one when the mine was reorganized. Don had taken his place in the shovels, but the crew generally ostracized him. He had a reputation in the basin for being what they called a "problem child"; he had moved, partially of his own volition and partially due to management pressure, among mines and crews because of the frequent fights and conflicts he caused. People who worked with him complained that his big ego got in the way of his being a good operator since he refused to follow advice. Even though he bent safety rules himself, he regularly turned in coworkers for safety infractions that departed from the letter but not the spirit of company regulations—a major violation of crew camaraderie—likely because he viewed it as a springboard to a management position. What made his behavior even more infuriating was that he felt entitled to boss other people around even though he was not an excellent operator and was frequently caught slacking off. In discussing the issue, Melinda commented wryly, "We didn't realize that stepping up required so much stepping on people." In the end, Lisa chose to not report Don. She did not want to develop a reputation for turning people in to management, and she knew his behavior would otherwise be acceptable if only other men had been present and did not want to "play the difference card." And while he was an annoyance, she did not want to feel responsible if he actually lost his job over the incident.

In both situations, men with relative power and authority introduced highly sexualized and sexist topics into collective conversations. Both men also compelled the participation of a young woman whose position on the worksite was comparatively vulnerable given her age and lack of experience at the mine. Yet while crewmembers were quick to label Don's actions as harassment, no one considered accusing Ron of the same, even though their actions could seem similar on the surface. The reasoning returns to Daisy's experience described in the introduction to this chapter. Like Rick, Don had a long history of acrimonious relationships with this crew and others, and his coworkers viewed the incident as a rare opportunity to punish him formally. They could not report him for routinely violating their sense of camaraderie, but they could report him for saying aggressively sexual things to a woman. Ron, on the other hand, was one of the crew's best operators and their informal leader. He was known for mentoring people without making them feel stupid, and he always lent a hand to help when there was trouble. Another woman on the crew described him by saying, "He may act rough on the outside, but he's got a heart of gold."[18]

The longer histories of the relationships among Ron, Don, Lisa, and their coworkers shaped their strikingly different interpretation. The crew laughed at Ron because they recognized his performance as parody: he was playing up the stereotype of the sexist male to poke fun at it. They considered it parody because they identified the mismatch or social distance between his position as a conscientious, supportive member of the crew family and the role he was playing. In distancing himself from the stereotype, Ron subtly downplayed its power to explain people and relationships at the mine. The miners, like the actors and audiences in Susan Seizer's ethnography of Tamil special drama artists, see each other "simultaneously as themselves and as roles they play and are constantly making judgments about the fit" (2005: 362). This insight undergirds her argument that social distancing is the basis of humor. On the other hand, the crew did not interpret the incident with Don as parody because the fit between his performance and personality was too close since he was already viewed as antisocial, rude, and flippant in regards to his coworkers' feelings. Their discomfort stemmed from his performance reinscribing a particularly aggressive form of masculinity that the rest of his crew generally condemned. Comparing these interactions confirms a long-standing insight of linguistic anthropology: content alone is not enough to determine meaning, which depends upon the context of when it is said and by whom.

At first glance, these two events could appear to have very different implications for understanding the waxing and waning of the social significance of gender difference. Ron, after all, critiqued an exaggerated form of masculinity and power and suggested that he was not held accountable to it, whereas Don reinscribed its significance and aligned himself with it. But Seizer cogently reminds us of the danger inherent in parody, including the type in which Ron engaged, since it "is itself often implicated in the same regimes of power it parodies" (2005: 194; see also Butler 1993: 125). To be successful, parody "must be cut from the same cloth as that which it parodies" (Mannheim 1995; quoted in Seizer 2005: 194). Seemingly ridiculous joking displays like Ron's reference harassment even as they criticize it, and the threat remains that they could slip out of a joking frame.

This double-bind resonates with anthropological research that points to the ambivalence of humor for creating social change. Donna Goldstein's ethnography of women living in a Rio shantytown elegantly shows that black humor is a "fugitive form of insubordination" since it reveals "both the cracks in the system and the masked or more subtle ways that power is challenged" (2003: 5). Because black humor is a site in which the women critique dominant ideologies and structures of power without revolting against them, it offers a window to see how people perceive the hierarchies that shape their everyday lives (2003: 35, 37). Seizer affirms those insights by showing the potential for social commentary in humor along with its limitations for subverting dominant norms and ideologies: "One becomes only free enough, that is, to see the trap in which one is caught" (2005: 199). Following this logic would suggest that the miners are not entirely subverting gender norms so much as criticizing its hold on their everyday lives. There are elements of this at play in the mines, such as when women joke about the hallowed connection between masculinity and technical competence. But it is also true that when women regularly engage and go so far as to instigate bawdy joking, and their coworkers recognize their behavior as not being particularly out of the ordinary, they gradually dissociate that kind of humor from masculinity.

Although the radical potential of humor is ambiguous, what a textured analysis of joking practices does clearly show is that harassment is not a static category that can be analyzed outside of context. Moreover, the incidents involving Daisy and Rick as well as Don, Ron, and Lisa suggest that outside of rare egregious cases of discrimination, unwanted sexual touching, or coerced sexual favors, sexual harassment in the mines is not a simple matter of men dominating women. Rather, accusations of harassment are a complex interpretive practice in which miners evaluate each other's intentions based on longer histories of interactions within the crew families. This observation confirms an earlier insight by Guiffre and Williams, who argued that because workers in their study did not consistently label the same behavior as harassment if it was undertaken by different people (coworkers versus management, for example), "it is not the sexual behavior per se that some workers find objectionable, but rather, characteristics of the individual who engages in the behavior" (1994: 76–77).

In Wyoming this interpretive work often happens quickly and below the level of consciousness, but questionable statements and actions bring such evaluations into sharp relief and can spark heated debate. The intertwined notions of work ethic and crew family dominate miners' efforts to understand these gray-area situations. How loyal are the people to the crew family? Do they pull their own weight? Do they support the rest of their coworkers? The cases they choose to mark as harassment are part of much longer histories of hostile (and largely nonsexual) social relationships that momentarily take on a gendered form by virtue of the people involved. As such, accusations of harassment often can be strategies for formally disciplining workers who fail to conform to their crew's expectations for hard work and harmonious relations. It is in this sense that I suggest that sexual harassment—perhaps the primary arena in which gender differences and hierarchy would be expected to be paramount—can be principally but not exclusively an issue of an employee's work ethic.

One nagging question remains. Might these women miners avoid accusing their coworkers of sexual harassment because they fear the repercussions of involving management, or feel pressured to just play along? All of the women I got to know rejected this possibility. Women did turn in their coworkers to management when they felt it was the appropriate strategy. They rarely did so, however, for two main reasons. First, they preferred to handle it themselves. At one mine, the name of a conflict resolution program stayed with its employees for many years. "Adult to adult," explained Kelly. "That means we handle our own business." The sentiment was shared throughout the basin and resonates with the ideals of the independent rancher that many find meaningful in narrating their own life experiences.

Second, women did not want to "play the gender card," in the words of Mary and many others. Outside of unwanted touching or sexual exchange, accusations of sexual harassment are tricky because they emphasize gender difference whereas most women just want to blend in. Labeling a joke or statement in this way takes a practice that would be unremarkable if occurring among men and singles them out for disciplinary scrutiny simply because people with different reproductive organs are involved.[19] By refusing to claim sexual harassment, women are attempting to minimize the significance of being female. "I don't want people to look at me as a woman miner, but just a miner, period," Jenny explained. "Raising the sexual harassment flag means that you're saying you're different, that you want to be treated different, and that's not what I want or what most of us want. We want to be treated the same." In their logic, therefore, if gender is ideally irrelevant, dirty jokes can be fun or annoying, but they are rarely sexualized hostility.

Conclusion

Miners appeal to popular myths about gender-neutral agricultural labor to explain the success of women miners in the basin. This chapter shows both the truth and limitations of such statements. Women and men are held to the same expectations for good hands and are recognized as such at equal rates, thus partially loosening the miners' notion of work ethic from gender difference. Where the lingering strength of dominant ideologies of gender difference surfaces is in the evaluations coworkers make of one another. Although miners note the technical achievements of women, they also invoke more stereotypical notions of femininity in praising their safe performance. While miners note men's commitment to safety, they also point to those who overperform and place their own egos ahead of the literal and emotional security of their coworkers. The troubling issue is that these difficulties are differentially valued and rewarded in the workplace. The erasure of women's technical expertise can negatively affect their standing in the crew hierarchies at the same time as their perceived dedication to safety aligns them with management and potential promotions as safety officers. The Herculean efforts of some men to demonstrate their abilities, on the other hand, position them for promotions within production itself. Gender difference diminishes when women and men are equally expected to competently execute their job tasks and balance their own efforts with the well-being of their coworkers, but they are brought partly—though not entirely—back into focus when those ideals are put into practice.

Examining humor as a valued counterbalance to hard work also reveals moments and situations in which gender difference is both reproduced and undone. Joking practices in the mines frequently take on sexualized overtones. In other eras and regions of the industry, such practices constitute sexual harassment and discrimination because they shore up mines as masculinized places and push women out of well-paying blue-collar jobs. The ethnographic material from Wyoming draws attention to an overlooked dimension of these issues, as women there participate in this style of humor as a valuable method for crafting camaraderie with their coworkers and maintaining a balance between caring about one's performance and one's fellow coworkers. This insight supports sociolinguist Janet Holmes's finding that, in New Zealand, supportive and collaborative humor was more frequent in workplaces that included women as well as men, whereas what she calls contestive and competitive humor was more prevalent in those where only men were present (2006: 41). Holmes's research also sheds light on why joking more likely (though not exclusively) constitutes harassment in the coal mines studied by Tallichet and Yount: those underground mines had far fewer women than did the surface mines in Wyoming.

Moreover, being part of a crew family provides an alternate framework for miners to interpret joking practices that might otherwise be considered harassment. Viewing one another as family largely desexualizes relationships among miners, and because the thought of dating or hooking up with each other is ludicrous, bawdy jokes are understood as fodder for building trust rather than as come-ons or attacks.[20] When miners do accuse one another of sexual harassment—outside of the clear instances of unwanted bodily touching or discrimination—they are trying to uphold a work ethic that is ideally gender neutral, even if it is imperfectly realized in practice. The key factor uniting these accusations is a longer history of antisocial behavior that only sometimes takes on gendered dimensions. Recall that Rick and Don's crews thought they treated everyone disrespectfully, but were unable to sanction them formally until each one of them targeted a woman. Censuring Rick and Don was an attempt to push them away from macho behavior into the more gender-neutral ideal they held for all miners. In other words, they were temporarily drawing attention to the salience of gender difference (by labeling an action or event sexual harassment) so that it could ideally be ignored in the larger scheme—a twist on McElhinny's insight that some women "perform gender so that gender can be ignored" (1995: 220). In this case, the women are not performing masculinity so that their femininity will be ignored, but the crews are asserting gender difference in hopes that it would eventually diminish.

Sexual harassment can constitute troubling instances of gendered aggression. But understanding why particular events or statements are labeled harassment while similar ones are not reveals that their meaning derives from larger debates about a proper work ethic and longer histories of social interactions. In this way, these incidents are not simply about men dominating women but about crews drawing the boundaries of their families and punishing people who violate the overarching expectations of the work ethic. This insight demonstrates the benefit of combining studies of sexual harassment with fine-grained ethnographic research into local conceptions of workplace relationships, much like Clifford Geertz (1973: 16) famously calls for cultural analysts to distinguish winks from twitches. To understand the frames that help participants interpret practices and differentiate joking and harassment, perspective is crucial because even though many scholars have identified the sense of family felt by mining crews, none have used this framework to critically retheorize sexual harassment.

7

Conclusion

————————————————————————◄o►—

Theories and ethnographic accounts of kinship and gender are rightly intertwined. Both are cultural concepts that Euro-Americans naturalize in biology, and kinship is one of the primary social forces behind the enculturation of masculine and feminine persons (Rubin 1975; Yanagisako and Collier 1987). In fact, the foundational text for the feminist analysis of kinship and gender pushed for anthropologists to examine "what specific social and cultural processes cause men and women to appear different from each other" (Yanagisako and Collier 1987: 15)—in other words, to analyze the cultural construction of gender difference. After all, the production of sex/gender systems through kinship and marriage is based on the "suppression of natural similarities" (Rubin 1975: 180). Unmooring relatedness from the Euro-American focus on marriage, procreation, blood, and genes to encompass families created through shared space and time opens up space from which to theorize less restrictive understandings of gender as it relates to the practice of kinship.

Studying the contested construction of workplace kin-ties alongside those nurtured in the home sheds light on the processes through which gender difference is reproduced as well as undone. While the Wyoming miners have partially decoupled their understanding of crew kinship from dominant gender ideologies, the salience of gender difference lingers for women miners in a few social arenas. Adjusting to the demanding shiftwork schedule creates similar temporal beings out of sync with their families and larger community, drawing out similarities between men and women miners. But the demands of pregnancy, sleep, and bodily functions foreground gender differences to women's detriment. The social categories of tomboys and softies celebrate men and women who embody less gendered approaches to work and workplace relationships: they enjoy physically demanding outdoor labor and leisure, and they nurture intimate but platonic relationships with their coworkers of both genders. But while men and women alike are criticized for conforming to gender stereotypes too closely, women bear the heavier burden for desexualizing workplace relations. Finally, accusations of sexual harassment are rarely simple instances of gendered aggression, but opportunities to discipline coworkers who violate expectations for the partially gender-neutral work ethic of crew family members. But while women are included in the prized category of good hands, they are also signaled out for "caring" for coworkers and equipment more than men, which distracts from their technical expertise.

The undoing of gender in mining families is more limited, revolving around the cultivation of gender-neutral characteristics in children through shared labor at home and eventually at the mines during the summer student program. These efforts focus on daughters, perhaps because they would have the most to lose by pursuing careers in fields dominated by women. These parenting practices run up against a stricter gender division of labor between parents, though some flexibility exists for the dual-earner couples who share household responsibilities in order to cope with the shiftwork schedule. To keep a household running, these men use their time off during the week to shop for groceries, do laundry, clean the house, and shuttle children while their wives are working. The most gender-neutral divisions of labor were found among childless couples in which the women worked in the mining industry. The tenacious gendered division of labor in the home highlights the importance of structural constraints—in this case, rotating shiftwork—for undoing gender.

Get an Education

The shiftwork schedule also comes under fire for the bodily and social stresses it places on miners. The miners continued to surrender themselves to it partially because it seemed inevitable and partially because they came to love their crews. But perhaps even more important, they saw minework as a rare opportunity to support their families and ensure that their children were not placed in the same predicament in which they found themselves: attempting to find meaningful, well-paying work without a college degree. This desire was crystallized in the pervasive injunction that children pursue higher education. In fact, the value of the summer student program stemmed not just from the shared time, space, and empathy it encouraged between miners and their children. The miners interpreted the program as an opportunity to teach their children and their coworkers' children the importance of getting an education so as to avoid working in the mines as adults.[1] In a sense, miners asked their children to learn to respect them and their work, but not engage it in themselves. This apparent paradox is traceable to specific critiques of the industry.

When discussing what stood out from their mine summers, the students I interviewed all pointed to the same thing: their crews' insistence that they stay in college and not end up as coal miners like them.[2] During the three summers she worked at the same mine as her father, Chloe found that new coworkers tended to start off conversations with her in the same way. "They'd see your name on your hard hat and ask if you were so-and-so's daughter, and you'd say yes or no. And then they'd ask if you were his kid who was going to school here or there." She was amazed not only by how much people already knew about her before stepping on the minesite but also by how interested they were in hearing about her college plans:

> It was so strange because the [pit] bus would stop and people would get off and get to their equipment. I told people about my college plans that first summer hundreds of times. I was asked hundreds of times by different people. And almost all of the time, they would end that conversation by saying, "Well, stick with it." That's always how it was. "You'll do well, I wish I had done it." A lot of the younger ones who had asked, they'd say, "Well, I had two semesters left at Laramie [at the University of Wyoming] and I decided to come to work out here. I wish I hadn't done it." They'd always bring up some element of their own education experiences or encourage you to stick with it. I mean, I had more encouragement from my crew at the coal mine than my academic advisor at college! It was constant. And when you get to know them more, they would always bring up the students who had come back, who had quit school and come back, and they would always get teased. "Don't do that, we don't want you come back here, we really want you to do well."

Callie, Al and Sandy's daughter, had a similar experience during her summer at the mine. "People out there all told me to stay in school. 'You don't want to end up like me.' That's how they felt." Callie was careful to explain that this advice did not mean that the miners thought they had a bad life. "It's not that they failed," she explained. "I think they like working out there but they think the other world is a lot easier than their world, with the sacrifices they've made and the physical work that they put in. And I think they see the other world as much easier and much kinder and they want their children to be in that world."

Endowing children with the desire to pursue higher education and providing them the financial support to do so permeated miners' parenting practices on the job (in the summer student program) as well as at home. Miners and their spouses may hold hopes about what career path their children will eventually pursue—for example, Josh would love to see his snowboarding daughter become a veterinarian because he thinks she shares his understanding of animals—but above all, they view any kind of higher education as a ticket to opportunity. Stan, who grew up in a multigenerational mining family in Montana, was frank about his desire to see the family tradition stop. "My biggest goal for my kids is to go to college," he said. "That's the only way out of what I'm doing." Having experienced his fair share of "idiot ideas" from engineers, he explained that "education is not the most important thing, but it allows for opportunities. I'm not saying they learned everything there is to life in the classroom, but they've been given opportunities with those degrees." At the time of our interview, both of his kids were employed full-time in white-collar jobs.

An injury that forced Donna to quit her job as an equipment operator reinforced her conviction that kids her son's age need to go to college: "Stay in college. Get your degree. Have something to fall back on just in case coal mining doesn't work out for you, or it's not what you want. I don't have any computer training. I started in school a long time ago, and I wish I would've finished it because I was doing well in it. I enjoyed it. I would have had a career to fall back on now. So no matter what, get a career to fall back on." Because of her own experience, Donna did everything she could to get her kids to go to college and made sure that she supported them financially. As she suggests, the main motivation for earning that money was providing a secure future for themselves, their spouses, and their children.

Al felt similarly. While explaining his major accomplishments, he initially emphasized home ownership, the 401(k) retirement account he has built up, the pension he plans on receiving from the company, and the good health insurance he has been able to provide his family. His eyes lit up, however, when he talked about his ability to facilitate his children's educational accomplishments: "I've watched my kids go through school, from kindergarten all the way to high school. I've been able to put both of my daughters through college, good colleges. If I hadn't moved here, I don't know that I could have afforded the education that I've been able to provide." For both Al and his wife Sandy, higher education was an essential part of raising their daughters to be independent. Sandy worked full-time while raising their children, and took pride in both her financial contribution to their education and her everyday support as they were growing up. She remembers driving them to and from their extracurricular activities, meeting with teachers during parent conferences, and attending school events. Along with her husband, Sandy wanted their girls to be able to take care of themselves and "not depend on anybody. We felt that a college education would be essential in that." Both she and her husband frowned on some of their friends who believed that their children should be wholly responsible for funding their college education. "You have to help them out when they're just starting out," Al was convinced.

Educational support was not limited to paying the bills. Loren, a longtime equipment operator, took an early interest in his son Brad's distinguished running career. He ran with him, attended every race he could, and helped him start selecting colleges to visit and consider attending. Along with his wife, he wanted to be sure that the school had an excellent academic reputation as well as a strong racing team because even though running was a good way to get college scholarships, it probably was not going to be a stable, sustainable career. As such, they helped him think through possible majors and careers based on his interests and abilities. Brad was also an excellent student, especially in his math and science classes, and Loren and his wife also took an active interest in his education. Over pizza one night, they enjoyed recounting stories about funny essays or insightful papers he had written, and how his classmates would give him a hard time if he ever got something wrong on a math test. When I asked Loren what goals he had for Brad, he chuckled and said, "A lot more than I had for myself." He then told a story about his son helping him put up a fence at their new house. "I was cussing because something wasn't going right, and I said to him, 'See, this is why you get an education, so you don't have to do this yourself.'"

Ray, a longtime equipment operator, specifically got a job at the mine to provide financial stability for the children he and his fiancée hoped to have. When we sat down to have a cup of coffee on his day off, he said that his biggest goal now was to get his youngest daughter through college. She was a gifted student who also was successful in many extracurricular activities and sports. In talking about her work ethic, he made an analogy to his own: "That little girl puts in ten, twelve hours a day and still carries an A+ average." He and his wife have encouraged all of their kids to do well in school. "I just tell them that they need to get good grades because opportunities will open there. ... My wife, she pushes them, especially this young one. She makes sure she has all her grades in, and she pretty much handles that all at home." He appreciated that his mining job provided financial stability to send his kids to college, and he also appreciated that royalties the industry paid to the county and state made the educational system superb.[3] "I think we have more opportunity in Gillette here too because we have better teachers and opportunity there to do all these recreational things for the kids are just abundant."

Even though most parents hope for their children to attend college of some sort, they understand that such a path might not be appealing to them, especially given their own uninspiring experiences with higher education. Cindy encouraged her sons to attend college, but she also supported their decisions not to attend: "I think it's really hard when you're asking eighteen-year-olds what you want to do with your life when a lot of us are making major changes even in our forties and fifties." In talking about her life, she was the proudest of raising happy, healthy kids. She was happy that one of her sons had tried living in Denver, as she had dreamed of doing when she was growing up Gillette. But she was even happier when he decided to move back home. "I'm glad that he's realized that the city life isn't necessarily all that it's cracked up to be and that you can have a little bit more of family—I don't know if normalcy or whatever is the right word—but an ability to meet somebody in a smaller community like this," she explained.

Linda approached raising her four boys in a similar manner. "I just want them to be happy and have good jobs and have whatever education they can have. I mean, I'm not going to scream and yell at them because they're not going to the University of Wyoming. I mean, I didn't. I just want them to be able to make a good living. If they don't like school, then don't go to school. Try to find a trade of some sort." She is proud that each of her sons is able to manage money and support himself, and she points to the allowance she and her husband gave them while they were growing up: "My husband would make them put it in a bank account. That was money they had to put away." She thinks that the role of a parent is to "be there for them and help them with their decisions." Roger agreed. He approached raising a family and supervising a mine crew in similar ways. Just as he involved his sons in multiple home improvement projects to give them a chance to explore future career options, he took great care to rotate each of the mechanics around the shop so that they developed a variety of skills. He smiled, "It's just kind of fun to watch their growth. See what they're going to end up being good at."

In fact, many of the miners drew on their work experiences of being mentored to explain how they approached raising children, underlining the strong connection between work and home. Across the basin, the most respected mentors and supervisors are those who first worked their way up from the bottom to positions of leadership and then avoided micromanaging their employees, preferring instead to give them the tools to learn and succeed on their own. Al said that one supervisor in particular was the best because his long work experience fostered a brilliant understanding of the machines. However, he used his position to cultivate the skills of the novices. Rather than telling them what was wrong and how to fix it, Al said, "If you went up to talk to him, he would ask you the right questions that you were able to figure out where you needed to go." Al and his peers believed that children should pursue their own unique passions and interests, but that it is the parents' responsibility to make that possible through providing their sons and daughters with both formal and informal learning opportunities. Framing those expectations in terms of workplace relationships and responsibilities underscores the moral significance of work for the mining families (Fricke 2008); hard work was not a burdensome activity cordoned off from the home, but a valued way of life that infused it.

Limiting Occupational Relatedness

The mining families' insistence that their children pursue higher education is bound up in three critiques of their own career paths. In this way, the desire to endow educational success was not simply a product of the larger American ideal of education being a ticket to upward mobility but a specific critique of working conditions, industry instability, and labor market trends. Miners and their spouses viewed education not as a path to greater financial success or upward mobility—few of their children pursuing white-collar careers will make as much as they do, and the miners already consider themselves to be members of the working middle class—but to provide them with more opportunities to control the contours of both their everyday working lives and longer careers.

The children like Chloe and Callie quoted above aptly picked up on the criticisms underlying the miners' advice to stay in school. The first major concern of most miners is that their children and their coworkers' children avoid what they see as the most detrimental development in local labor conditions: the twelve-hour shiftwork that has made it difficult for them to participate in everyday family and community life. Anne, a mechanic who raised her son while working shifts, succinctly critiqued the schedule: "I don't think humans were made for these hours." Donna, whose injury amplified her regret about not going to college, explained that twelve-hour shifts "brought out the worst in everybody. I was just like a grizzly. 'Don't you come near me! Don't even look at me, I'll rip your head off.' Oh, it was terrible. I've heard so many people say that. It not only affects your body, it affects your thinking, your mind."

Miners and their spouses hoped that their children will not have to work rotating shifts throughout their life. Callie had been assigned a job at the mine that did not require shiftwork, which made her dad happy. Some parents such as Jerry consciously discouraged their kids from seeking work in the mining industry precisely due to the shiftwork requirements: "I've steered them away from these coal mines. I mean, they can do whatever they want, but I've steered them away from shiftwork if they'll listen. So far they've taken that to heart. There's a lot of stuff out there that you can do where you don't have to work this shiftwork. Maybe somebody would like it, and some people probably do. I've heard people tell me they'd rather work nights than days, but I think they're lying." Jerry was happy that his son who is a truck driver has not yet applied at a mine, even though "he would probably be the greatest equipment operator in the whole world because he likes to do it. There's just a lot of other opportunities, even in Gillette." Miners like him found that the shiftwork became tiring and trying for them both physically and emotionally as they aged. Those who could often moved into "straight days" jobs, finding that they had been unaware of the full extent of their fatigue over the previous years. As a case in point, after Al took a regular Monday through Friday job at the mine, he and his wife agreed that his whole personality changed for the better. Those middle-aged miners who did not wish to switch positions or had not been able to move into straight days struggled through the night shifts in order to protect their future retirement and to help their children avoid finding themselves in a similar situation.

The miners' second major criticism of the industry was the endemic instability they associated with mining's legendary boom-and-bust cycles. As much as they remember the excitement of booms, they also remember the stresses of busts. The Powder River Basin became home to miners from Arizona and Nevada to Minnesota and Colorado who moved to Gillette seeking work when other mines closed (Rolston 2013b). Al and Sandy, for example, were thankful they left a central Wyoming uranium mining town before the bust in the early 1980s. Al said, "I wasn't there when the mine shut down, but friends of mine that were said guys were literally crying because they were financed. Everything they owned—all those fast cars and toys—was financed, and they knew that they were never going get a job that paid the money they were making." Looking back, he remembered, "They told me that I could always come back, but by the time I graduated from diesel school, it was all over. There was never any chance to go back. It never has come back. I think everybody's given up hope now." Sandy was also happy they had avoided the uranium bust: "All of our friends, they had a shock. They just went to work, and they told them to pick up their tools and go home because they didn't want to give them any foreknowledge of it because they were afraid that they'd trash the mines. And then that whole area just became abandoned. There was a school out there and everything, and the whole community then was displaced. So yeah, it's kind of sad in a way. And all those people had to go someplace else." Sandy believed that the ever-present threat that her husband could lose his job has played a large role in their marriage. "Starting out very early, we realized that at any moment, Al could be out of work. Some people chuckhole every penny they can or else they live life like there's no tomorrow, because with mining, you never know. We hadn't even been married a year, and we saw all our friends get totally wiped out."

The third major criticism bound up in the miners' insistence that their children pursue higher education was the dwindling possibility they see for people without college degrees to "get ahead." Sitting around the lunchroom one day, a group of middle-aged men were discussing their efforts to convince their kids to go to either the University of Wyoming or the local community college after they graduated. When one of them reasoned, "We were the last ones who could make a decent living without having to go to school," the entire room nodded in agreement.

Except for those like mechanics or electricians with skills that transfer easily to other industries, miners were aware that they would face difficulties
finding well-paying work requiring their skills (see also Dudley 1994). Melissa
appreciated the uniqueness of her job as an equipment operator: "I'm making damn good money out here for doing what? For driving giant Tonka
trucks around? It's fun playing in the dirt all day. Not many people can say
that." Another equipment operator wryly asked me rhetorical questions as he
was showing me how to run one of the giant loaders: "How many places do
you know where the majority of your workforce drives multimillion-dollar,
giant trucks for a living? Where else, besides a mine, can I make this kind of
money?" The safer bet, according to all of these workers, was to get a college or
vocational education.

Al felt similarly. Even though he sent both of his daughters to college, he
realized that it is not right for every kid, but "you still need to send them to a
trade school or something. The days of people making my kind of wages right
now are limited. I don't think in the future that people with a high school
education are going to be able to make that kind of wages. I think as time goes
on, you're going to find that even a bachelor's degree is run of the mill. I think
it's going to be pretty hard for them to succeed with a high school education."
In his own experience, he found that when the uranium industry crashed in
his hometown, those jobs were not replaced by other well-paying industrial
jobs but by minimum-wage service ones. Grimly, he assessed the situation:
"They're Wal-Mart kind of jobs, fast food jobs."

The assessment of the blue-collar labor market made by Al and his peers
is apt. Real blue-collar wages were stagnant during the 1980s and actually fell
during the 1990s, recovering their 1981 levels only in 1997. After a brief period
of moderate increase from 1998 to 2002, they then remained flat and eventually plummeted in the recent recession, so much so that "high-school educated
young men today may be the first generation in memory to earn less than their
fathers did" (Cherlin 2009: 163). Powder River Basin miners have experienced
these economic trends firsthand, seeing their originally very high wages and
benefits fail to keep up with rising costs of living and wages in similar jobs
in the coalbed methane industry. Along with other blue-collar workers, they
also realize that if the mines were to close, it would be nearly impossible to
find those kinds of wages in other industries. As factories increasingly out-
source previously well-paying and often unionized assembly jobs, American
workers—even autoworkers, one of the most strongly unionized and highly
compensated groups—have difficulties finding comparably skilled, well-
paying work with which to support their families and maintain their middle-
class consumption patterns (Dudley 1994). As a matter of fact, during my
fieldwork Gillette officials were actively recruiting under- and unemployed
Michigan autoworkers to move to the area and work in the rapidly expanding

energy and construction industries. Walking around the break room before the start of the shift, I was often taken aback by the number of people who were wearing hats and shirts from the University of Michigan, where I was then attending graduate school.[4]

These three primary criticisms of local working conditions and the larger labor market animated the miners' insistence that their own children—and their coworkers' children whom they come to know through working with them in the summer—attend and complete college or trade school. The paradox of this situation is that the older generation socialized the younger one to understand, appreciate, and temporarily carry out the minework that the students are in the process of leaving behind by pursuing a college education, the primary requirement for participation in the program. The miners explicitly encouraged this leaving behind, repeatedly telling the temporary miners that "we work here so that you don't have to." This attitude prompted deeply felt, conflicting emotions for members of the younger generation, who were told to love their parents but not follow in their footsteps. Chloe, for example, struggled to reconcile her appreciation for her father and her dislike of her job at the mine: "By the time I started college, he'd been working at the mine for eighteen years. So for me to just buck up and work there for four months, I figured it was the least I could do. He had been paying for everything. You feel a certain sense of guilt knowing he'd been working nights and doing difficult but mind-numbing work, so for me to just buck up and work there for four months, I figured it was the least I could do to help pay for my expensive private college." Like Chloe, very few children of miners anticipated following in their parents' occupational footsteps, in no small part due to years of advice from their parents and their parents' coworkers. These explicit instructions to avoid work in the industry is striking given their own family histories of mining and the more general history of the U.S. coal mining industry, which was once characterized by familial apprenticeship systems in which a job was one of the things handed down from father to son (Long 1989; Montgomery 1987). These attempts to break familial occupational ties are not limited to the Powder River Basin. The American news media coverage of mine disasters, such as those at Sago and Upper Big Branch in West Virginia, included interviews in which miners and their family members explained that they no longer wished to see their children get mining jobs. Discouraging mine employment for their children in these cases, as well as in the basin, crystallized mining families' critiques of specific workplaces as well as the industry in general.

Uncertain Futures

Eyeing an increasingly hostile labor market and the mounting disadvantages of work in the mining industry, miners hoped for a kinder future for their children and actively sought to prepare them for it. These efforts took on heightened significance as I was putting the finishing touches on this book. The context in which I finalized the manuscript was strikingly different from that in which I originally conducted my research. In 2012 the coal market entered a tailspin. A relatively mild 2011–2012 winter season in the United States—including the warmest March on record—left coal-fired power plants with excessive stockpiles and mines with fewer contracts to fill. The sharp decrease in the number of mile-long trains entering and leaving the basin was palpable for residents. This surplus also dropped the price for coal, which was already falling due to decreasing prices for natural gas, coal's main competitor. Coal-fired power plants produce more than ninety times as much sulfur dioxide, five times as much nitrogen oxide, and twice as much carbon dioxide as those that run on natural gas (Government Accountability Office 2012). These factors encouraged federal and state legislation to favor the expansion of natural gas rather than coal plants to meet the country's increasing energy demands. By the summer of 2012, coal and natural gas reached equal shares of the country's electricity generation (approximately one-third each), which represented coal's lowest level since at least January 1973, when the Energy Information Agency began collecting data and the Powder River Basin mines began producing. In the wake of this downturn, the majority of companies slowed down production, and a few let temporary and even full-time employees go. Companies with multiple mines in the basin transferred contracts and employees from their smaller operations to their larger ones. By the fall of 2013, the coal industry appeared to be regaining ground, but many people in the basin remained uneasy. As national public support for coal dwindled, industry supporters advocated expanding exports to China through controversial expanded ports in the Pacific Northwest.

The majority of miners whose stories animate this book were on the cusp of retirement as the coal market deteriorated. They spoke of the eeriness of idled mine equipment and the decreasing frequency of trains to transport the coal to power plants. They feared job loss and dreamed of buyouts that would hasten their retirement plans of quiet fishing trips and visits with growing grandchildren. Unable to do much to change their increasingly precarious situation, they spent their time evaluating the veracity of the myriad rumors that circulated around the basin. They pinned their hopes on keeping their jobs long enough to pad their bank accounts—compromised by the Great Recession—and qualify for company retirement plans, and worried about their younger coworkers who still had decades of work ahead of them. The sudden downturn validated their long-held conviction that their children pursue other careers so as to avoid work in the industry.

The everyday experiences of rank-and-file miners rarely appear in national debates about energy futures, which turn primarily on environmental and security concerns.[5] But the reliance on coal-fired electricity in the United States has created both opportunities and challenges for workers in Wyoming. The coal industry's expansion to the Powder River Basin has provided miners there with at least four decades of geographic and financial stability, a rare achievement in an industry infamous for recurring booms and busts (see also Rolston 2013b).[6] Moreover, women were able to take advantage of the coal industry's westward expansion, seizing opportunities to earn excellent money, nurture meaningful workplace relationships, and earn respect in a historically masculine field. Yet as lucrative as these jobs are, they require the majority of miners to live with completely different rhythms of time than do their families, many businesses, and community organizations. Miners spend between thirteen and sixteen hours away from home, and the continual shiftwork rotation means that they can go a week without seeing their spouses or children, only to later find themselves with stretches of leisure time while everyone else is at work or school. Balancing work and family responsibilities is particularly demanding for single mothers, many of whom prefer to go without sleep rather than sacrifice time with their kids.

The women and men who work in the Wyoming coal industry have confronted these challenges with a great deal of courage, grace, and wit. In order to fully address pressing questions about future national energy policies, scholars and public intellectuals must engage in caring from a distance in order to, as my friend in Gillette put it, think beyond the wall and consider the entire chain of social relations implicated in a simple flip of a light switch.

Notes

Chapter 1: Putting Kinship to Work

1. The names of people and companies in the book are pseudonyms used to protect confidentiality.
2. This double role reflects the ambiguities in my own position in the mines, since I was there to learn from miners but could also be perceived as an office-like supervisor. At the mines where I conducted on-site research, human relations personnel or upper-level managers first introduced me to the crews. Because very few people were familiar with anthropology or ethnographic field methods, many initially viewed me as an office-type person who was there to monitor and evaluate their work practices. The supervisors of two crews even encouraged this association by offering me specific material items associated with management: one insisted that I carry a clipboard with me as I visited different areas of the minesite and the other offered me a company pickup truck—normally reserved for supervisors, managers, and the most experienced technicians—to drive around the property. As time went on, however, our interactions made it clear that I was there to learn from them, and people took up that frame each time they made jokes about me learning how to operate equipment or think like a miner.
3. This large White majority reflects the racial demographics of the surrounding area. According to the 2010 United States Census, 92.2 percent of the residents of Gillette were White. The state of Wyoming itself was 90.7 percent White in that year. Racial marking can occur in the mines, though individuals try to counter it. When a (perhaps well-intentioned) woman asked a new equipment operator if he preferred being called Black or African American, so that she could use the right term, the new hire responded by saying, "You can call me Sam."
4. Historian Thomas Andrews notes a similar phenomenon for underground coal miners in Colorado, interpreting their assertions of each other as family as indexing "relationships formed between relatively equal, autonomous, yet interdependent men and cemented together in the face of great peril" (2008: 173). He writes of the miners, "Every breath they took, after all, depended on the competence of other workmen, the capricious forces that their work underground unleashed, and the good faith of employers who passed up few chances to exploit them" (2008: 147).

5. The two female supervisors with whom I conducted research were both called "Mom" by their crews. The term had both positive and negative connotations. Their crews appreciated when the women rewarded them with homemade food when they met particular production goals or completed particularly onerous tasks. But in private conversations before the start of shift, during lunch breaks, or in casual conversations, both crews also used the term to signal that their supervisor was micromanaging them in a way that offended their own experience and expertise. Though the critique of micromanagement was common throughout the basin, the term "Dad" was not used in this manner, suggesting that leadership is one arena in which gender difference is made salient.

6. For a study showing that appeals to gender neutrality cloaked masculine work norms, see Mayes and Pini (2010).

7. Artisanal and small-scale mining (ASM) is varied, but generally refers to informal mining activities involving minimal machinery and a great deal of physical labor. The informal nature of the work makes it difficult to obtain precise numbers, but an estimated one-hundred million people, primarily in the developing world, rely on this work for income. The work is economically unstable and dangerous, given the lack of safety measures.

8. Comparatively fewer historical references to Wyoming women miners exist, perhaps because the state's coal mines opened late and industrialized quickly compared to states in other regions due to its isolation and the dominance of the railroad (Gardner and Flores 1989; Wolff 2003).

9. This difference is likely attributable to multiple factors, including the Wyoming miners' views of themselves as professionals with technical expertise (in contrast with miners viewed as superstitious or unscientific) and the general lack of a family history in mining that would pass down terminology. The fact that the mines are surface operations might also be significant, since the other cases of the symbolic opposition between female mines and male miners are drawn from underground operations.

10. See Beckwith (1998); Ferguson (1999); Ferry (2005); Finn (1998); Giesen (1995); Kingsolver (1989); Lahiri-Dutt (2011a); Mercier and Gier (2007); Merithew (2006); Nash (1993); and Reichart (2006).

11. This argument parallels the insights of feminist technology studies, which show that in the industrialized world that "[m]en are viewed as having a natural affinity with technology, whereas women supposedly fear or dislike it" (Bray 2007: 38).

12. This explaining away of women's abilities as exceptions to the rule contradicts the miners' simultaneous practice of assuming that individual women represent all women (Tallichet 2006: 56).

13. This research stretches across disciplinary boundaries. See Campbell (1984); Duke (2002); Gibson-Graham (2006); Lahiri-Dutt and Macintyre (2006); and Mercier and Gier (2006).

14. See Women in the Labor Force: A Databook (2010 edition), available online at http://www.bls.gov/cps/wlftable14–2010.htm.

15. Beginning in the 1970s, Appalachian women in search of well-paying jobs began protesting the coal companies' decisions to pass over their applications in favor of equally or less qualified men. The Coal Employment Project was founded in 1977 as an advocacy group for women coal miners. Drawing on the Equal Employment Opportunity Act's conception of affirmative action, in 1978 women represented by the organization won a settlement in their lawsuit against CONSOL, one of the

largest coal companies, for sex discrimination in hiring practices. The company was forced to institute hiring quotas, establish affirmative action practices, and pay back wages to the women, who were eventually hired along with many others (Baker 2007: 72). The Coal Employment Project also offered technical training sessions, held national conferences, and eventually turned its attention to understanding and combating workplace sexual harassment (Baker 2007; B. Hall 1990; Moore 1996).

16. See Disney (1987); B. Hall (1990); Hammond and Mahoney (1983); Moore (1996); Prieto (1983); and Tallichet (2006).

17. The way in which these myths nonetheless influenced everyday life illustrates historian Richard White's argument that "as people accept and assimilate myth, they act on the myths, and the myths become the basis for actions that shape history. . . . The mythic West imagined by Americans has shaped the West of history just as the West of history has helped create the West Americans have imagined. The two cannot be neatly severed" (1991: 616).

18. See N. Daly et al. (2004) for an analysis of expletives as signals of solidarity in blue-collar workplaces.

19. Federico Helfgott and I (Smith and Helfgott 2010) document a shift in the Peruvian Andes to "bus-in, bus-out" operations, in which the companies shut down mining camps that once housed entire families and instead bus in workers, who live in major cities, to the mine for a stretch of working days only. Company officials attributed this shift to a desire to lessen their "social load" by supporting workers and their families. This shedding of responsibility for mineworkers' families occurred at the same time as companies faced increased financial obligations to the communities nearest to production sites, where few workers actually lived. Their social load, in other words, remains substantial but is directed at "communities" instead of "workers" (Smith and Helfgott 2010).

20. These cycles, however, are not reminiscent of soundly critiqued static notions of unchanging, cyclical time (Munn 1992: 98–102). The miners are consistently working toward vacations, production goals, and holidays.

21. Communication in the pit by way of body language is not impossible, since a variety of messages can be sent by the wave of a hand, a slouchy posture, or facial expression, but the distance between equipment and the glare of windows make it difficult.

22. See Bunzl (2004), Narayan (1993), and Ryang (2005) for key critiques of native ethnography. I would argue that claiming the category does not require erasing many other salient axes of differentiation between scholar and community. In fact, some of the most persuasive work of people who engage the category specifically highlights and problematizes the differences among them and the people they study (Behar 1995; Finn 1998; Jacobs-Huey 2002; Limón 1994). This nuanced work is a far cry from fears that simplistic claims to "insider" status might create false confidence in scholarly authority.

23. Even the legendary June Nash, a tireless promoter of mineworkers' rights in Bolivia, was cajoled into conducting time studies for the company while she was underground.

24. Actually working in the mine—staying up for night shifts, hauling a heavy fire hose to wash down the plant equipment, returning home with sore muscles, and so forth—also provided a more visceral approach to understanding minework and the practical knowledge it requires (see also Desmond 2007).

25. For a critique of how Institutional Review Board structures reinforce power differentials within fieldwork research, see Smith (2009: 73–87). Many native

anthropologists appropriately signal education as a differentiating factor in their relationships with people at home (Behar 1995; Finn 1998; Limón 1994). In my case, this difference did not generally translate into any simple kind of authority. Not only did most of the miners already make more money than I ever would as a professor but years of pitting their practical experience against well-educated but inexperienced engineers had confirmed their belief that a college education was not a reliable marker of intelligence (cf. Dudley 1994: 109).

26. This call echoes throughout the history of mine labor, such as the United Mineworkers preamble that states: "There is no fact more generally known, nor more widely believed, that without coal there would not have been any such grand achievements, privileges and blessings as those which characterize the nineteenth century civilization. . . . Those whose lot it is to daily toil in the recesses of the earth, mining and putting out this coal which makes these blessings possible . . . are entitled to a fair and equitable share of the same" (Andrews 2008: 178).

Chapter 2: Labor Relations and Corporate Social Responsibility

1. The full text of this reference, which appears at the very end of the speech, reads that Marx "died beloved, revered and mourned by millions of revolutionary fellow workers—*from the mines of Siberia and California, in all parts of Europe and America*—and I make bold to say that though he may have had many opponents he had hardly one personal enemy. His name will endure through the ages, and so also will his work!" (Engels 1977 [1883]: 682; emphasis added).

2. Miners also clearly noted the importance of the union for curbing corporate exploitation in the earliest years of the industry. During the unsuccessful 1987 union drive, for example, one of the drive's most vocal opponents of unionization wrote: "Eighty years ago there was a great need for labor reform. . . . And nobody can deny that fact, we do owe a lot to the unions. But because they had their place in this country's past and play an important part in this present time doesn't mean we owe them our allegiance and whole-hearted support for its organization attempt here in the Basin." This attitude is emblematic of larger national shifts in public perceptions of unions as self-aggrandizing interest groups rather than levers for social change (Lichtenstein 2002: 141).

3. This gap is partially due to the fact that the work schedules of these miners make access difficult for researchers (McNeil 2011; Smith and Helfgott 2010).

4. Paradoxically, the growing environmental movement fueled pressure for the rapid industrial development of the region. The Clean Air Act made the basin's low-sulfur coal an attractive option for power plants that needed to meet new air quality standards but did not want to incur the expense of investing in new pollution reduction technology, such as scrubbers.

5. Union Pacific used a slumping coal market to justify hiring Chinese miners and firing whites affiliated with the Knights of Labor. On September 2 two white miners found a Chinese crew in a work area they claimed to have been assigned to work. The fight underground quickly turned into a race riot that spread throughout the streets of Rock Springs: "Throughout the town, whites unleashed their hatred of the Chinese—killing 28, chasing 600 others into the desert, and burning 100 homes to the ground" (Wolff 2003: 101; Gardner and Flores 1989: 46–48). Union Pacific called on federal troops to "restore order" under the guise of protecting the railroad against damage. Railroad conductors were instructed by officials to pick

up all fleeing Chinese, who were promised safe passage to Evanston and then San Francisco but were actually forcibly brought back to Rock Springs (Gardner and Flores 1989: 48). Under the watchful eye of federal troops, about a hundred of the original 331 Chinese workers returned to the mines along with only a few white surface workers and laborers, since the majority had been fired by the company for their participation in the riot (Wolff 2003: 101). No miners or community members were ever convicted for their role in the riot.

6. These developments correspond with larger neoliberal demands that entrepreneurial subjects prudently and independently navigate increasingly "flexible" and insecure domains as diverse as the market, workplaces, family life, and citizenship (Dunn 2004; Martin 1994; Ong 1999).

7. Thanks to Paul Durrenberger and Karaleah Reichart for bringing this point to my attention.

8. Historian Zeese Papanikolas writes that without his horse the cowboy was "but one more seasonal worker attached to the industrial world by railroads that led to Chicago stockyards and ranches owned as often as not by Eastern bankers or Scottish investors" (1995: 75). These cowboys sometimes organized formal protests against their working conditions, including an 1883 strike in Texas (McGuire and Reckner 2002: 49) and an 1885 strike in Wyoming's Sweetwater County (Papanikolas 1995: 75).

9. Randall McGuire and Paul Reckner (2002: 45) have argued that out of all the relationships comprising western history, class struggles are the "most inimical" to the notion of the romantic West. In her foundational work critiquing western historiography, Patricia Limerick (1987: 97) argues that the type of labor popularly associated with the West emphasizes nonexploitative independence, in which people "simply gathered what nature produced. The laborer was to be self-employed, and the status of laborer was to be temporary, left behind when the profits made escape possible."

10. See Richardson (2006) on union siblingship.

11. Workplace safety did not play a major role in this drive, in contrast with other union organizing activities, because employees felt safe at work, as described in the section below, "Responsibility for Safety, Safety for Responsibility."

12. This tension points to the importance of distinguishing blue-collar from working-class alignments and affiliations, since miners identify as the former but not the latter. Lucas (2011: 359–360) also captures these tensions in her research with coal miners in the Midwest, who earn large paychecks but recognize power differentials at work, enjoy leisure activities associated with working rather than professional people, and remain subject to boom-and-bust cycles.

13. The establishment of MSHA combined all federal health and safety regulations into one institution, strengthened and expanded the rights of miners, reinforced protection from retaliation against those who exercised such rights, and raised the fines associated with civil penalties for violations. This development contradicts theories of a continually retreating neoliberal state in favor of those that account for the state's contradictory impulses.

14. The incidence rate is calculated on the basis of 200,000 hours of employee exposure (equivalent to 100 employees working 2,000 hours per year), taking the number of cases times 200,000 and dividing that figure by hours of employee exposure. Thank you to Vanessa Stewart at MSHA for compiling this data.

15. At the same time, however, many temporaries considered the crew less as a loving family and more as a barrier to being hired. Mack sometimes felt alienated from the

crew because in order to be hired on full-time by the company, he had to prove both his loyalty to management and his ability to be productive. Sensing this, Tim and some of his peers were known for being opposed to hiring temporaries because they thought the practice threatened the integration of the crew.

16. In its ideal form, the program represents a reversal of Martin's (1997) characterization of corporate culture acting as an Other inside the self, since corporate culture should ideally be built out of the everyday habits of workers.

17. Keeping the observation interactions anonymous has proven to be difficult, especially at the smaller mines. Observers often have to use the public mine radio to initiate the observation, and their pickup trucks can be clearly noted by others in the vicinity of particular individuals and their work areas.

18. Conley and Williams (2005) argue that the language of trust evoked here indexes a debate over something that cannot be proven, but must be accepted on faith.

19. For a more in-depth analysis of continuing critiques and negotiations over mine safety in the basin, see Rolston (2013a).

20. Permanent Wyoming Mineral Trust Fund (PWMTF) FAQ, available online: http://www.wyotax.org/PMTF.aspx.

21. There appears to be no love lost on the part of Appalachians; a reviewer of an earlier version of the book remarked that Appalachian miners do not consider their Wyoming counterparts to be "real miners."

22. This support is strongest on the local level, with mine employees reserving their strongest criticism for corporate executives located elsewhere (chiefly in St. Louis, Missouri).

Chapter 3: Shiftwork as Kinwork

1. Such paternalism has been a corporate strategy to create stable, loyal, and productive workforces and to avoid intervention by governments and unions (L. Fine 1993; Lichtenstein 2002). Henry Ford's "five dollar day," which integrated workers into the "Ford family" on management's terms, exemplifies heavy-handed corporate paternalism in the United States (Meyer 1981). Workers received the full five dollars only if they were deemed to have performed efficiently and to have developed an appropriate family lifestyle that was evaluated by the company's "sociology department."

2. See Edwards and Strathern (2000), Franklin and McKinnon (2001), and Richardson (2006). Both Janet Carsten (1997) and Krista Van Vleet (2008) ground their analysis of relatedness in Malay and Andean communities, respectively, in nonindustrial labor, which draws attention to the coercive dynamics of kinship. Chapter 5 of this book also considers the more coercive elements of creating crew families.

3. A rich trajectory of labor history and shop-floor ethnography further shows that affective ties among employees can push against the alienating tendencies of contemporary work, as people laugh, tell jokes, create nicknames, and invent covert shop-floor games to entertain themselves and craft friendships with coworkers (e.g., Baron 2006: 150–151; Canning 1996; Dudley 1994; Halle 1984; Roy 1959).

4. See McKinnon (2000) and Munn (1992) for critiques of Evans-Pritchard's treatment of gender, space, and time.

5. The strict division between work and leisure or work and family is diminishing in some sectors, however, as companies seek out more "flexible" employees who can work from home, and technologies such as smart cell phones and computers make

telecommuting possible. Moe and Shandy (2010) illustrate the contradictions of the flexibility movement for middle-class American families: although employees criticize telecommuting for making more demands for constant accessibility and communication, they also value it for allowing them more freedom to schedule work around family responsibilities.

6. The main exception to this more general pattern is miners' keen attention to the precise date of their first day of work, since it plays a major role in determining when they can retire and with which benefits.

7. To address the increasing time it takes to transport coal from the pit to the plant, some mines have invested in large conveyor belt systems that reach from the plant to a central pit location.

8. Mines usually devote their best shovels to moving dirt because they need to move larger quantities of dirt than coal, especially as the easily recoverable coal is mined out. Many mines run a 2:1 ratio of dirt to coal, meaning that they have to move two tons of dirt to expose and extract just one ton of coal. Because of this ratio, one supervisor laughed and said that they were "actually in the business of hauling dirt, not coal."

9. Elana Shever (2008) signals the importance of workplace food sharing in translating the affective dimensions of work in the state-run Argentine oil industry to the privatized subcontracting microenterprises. The leaders of these firms viewed celebrations such as company barbeques and smaller dinners as a way to continue the tradition of "nourishing those who gave their labor" (2008: 709) and create a sense of kinship among workers. In his study of New Jersey chemical plant workers, David Halle (1984: 141–142) noted the importance of shared meals in bringing workers closer together, finding that the men had installed refrigerators, stoves, and hot plates in almost every section of the plant despite leisurely eating being unpleasant due to the proximity of chemical fumes. In the warehouse, workers "cook on a grand scale. Each day they prepare a large meal, the menu for which is enthusiastically debated the day before. About 11:00 AM they all sit down for lunch prepared by two workers who particularly enjoy cooking. Men invite friends from throughout the plant" (Halle 1984: 142).

10. At the smaller and medium-sized mines in the basin, this would require bringing in no more than two or three dozen doughnuts. At the largest, however, it would mean bringing in seven or eight dozen.

11. This comment is also interesting because it suggests that miners have feelings that can be hurt even if they are not perceived as being "sensitive."

12. This perspective might also help us to understand the practice of miners bringing in food for the entire group to celebrate a person's individual achievement. For example, during my research one of the newest loader operators reached a personal best that the experienced workers considered a benchmark of excellence. One of them brought in doughnuts for the entire crew to celebrate, perhaps not just to recognize that individual's achievement but also to emphasize that his accomplishment did not disrupt the overall harmony of the crew. This fits in to a larger tension between the competition among coworkers to do well and the value they all place on remaining a cohesive, generally egalitarian group.

13. Sociologist Leslie Salzinger (1997) made a similar argument in an initial analysis of Mexican maquiladora factories. At the one she labeled Androgymex, she found that the focus on production, coupled with androgynous uniforms and prohibitions against beards, jewelry, and makeup, caused gendered categories not to completely

disappear but to "subside into insignificance in daily interaction on the shop floor" (1997: 564). In a subsequent book, she revised her interpretation to argue that the plant remained masculinized because the more general categories of breadwinner and worker were implicitly masculinized (2003: 189n2). She therefore cautions that "ungendered shop floors are theoretically possible but difficult because of the historical relationship of masculinity and paid work" (2003: 189n1). The greater extent to which the Wyoming workers have decoupled their image of the "good miner" from masculine norms may be attributable to the longer history of women's productive work in the region, along with the widespread local acceptance of single moms as breadwinners.

14. It is not common for miners' children to end up working at the mines themselves, since the parents encourage their children to attend college to pursue other careers. Those who return to the mines usually do so because they were uninspired by school and enjoyed living in the Gillette area.

15. As I describe in Smith (2008), the large number of single moms at the mines is largely due to the high wages they offer.

16. The lack of affordable childcare that is accommodating to the shiftwork schedule is a common and key barrier for women maintaining employment in the mining industry (Lahiri-Dutt and Macintyre 2006; Lahiri-Dutt and Robinson 2008: 113; Smith 2008). See J. Williams (2010), Presser (2003), and Rudd and Root (2008) for descriptions of the "crazy quilts" of childcare assembled by shiftworkers.

17. See Lahiri-Dutt and Robinson (2008) for a more in-depth consideration of how menstruation in mines raises debates about gender equity and special protection for women in Indonesia.

Chapter 4: Interweaving Love and Labor

1. See Barnett, Gareis, and Brennan (2008); Deutsch (1999: 177); Garey (1999: 136); Perucci and MacDermid (2007); Presser (2003); C. Williams (2008).

2. See Rolston (2013a) for a summary.

3. See Deutsch (1999); Garey (1999); Perucci and MacDermid (2007); Presser (2003); C. Williams (2008).

4. Jerry uses the term "you kids" for two reasons. First, his kids were my age. Second, I had previously worked with him for two summers on small crews in which the people his age came to think about me and my peers as their adopted children.

5. This spatial or temporal distancing of close relatives such as parents, siblings, and spouses, also characterized work assignments for full-time employees who worked for the same company. I received multiple explanations of the practice, the most common being that it guarded against nepotism and that it ensured that multiple members of one family would not be injured if there were to be a serious accident at work.

6. His daughter's dressing in the same clothes and equipment as his might have been significant for Al because it created an iconic link between them.

7. Hochschild emphasizes that this development is a direct strategy of capital to reproduce itself: "If a family gives its members anything, we assume it is surely a sense of belonging to an ongoing community. In its engineered corporate cultures, capitalism has rediscovered communal ties and is using them to build its new version of capitalism. . . . In this new model of family and work life, a tired parent flees a world of unresolved quarrels and unwashed laundry for the reliable orderliness, harmony,

and managed cheer of work. The emotional magnets beneath home and workplace are in the process of being reversed" (1997: 44). Although it would be prudent not to romanticize family life, Hochschild does identify significant shifts in the ways in which people manage their time and create social relationships.

8. Max Horkheimer and Theodor Adorno argue that popular music has become subject to the "rhythm of the iron system" and to the repetitions, serializations, and standardizations characteristic of Fordism (2002: 120), suggesting that the parallel, repetitive rhythms of the community radio station and mine work tasks are no mere happenstance.

9. The grounding of kinship in shared time and labor represents another resonance between the many miners' agricultural backgrounds and their later work experiences at the mines, since farming and ranching families also spend many hours engaged in intense physical labor together to keep their operations running. The key differences between small-scale agricultural and mining labor are that family farmers and ranchers usually work for themselves (meaning that any profits accruing to their labor stay with the family, whereas miners are paid hourly by a company) and that the distinction between home and work is less pronounced in this kind of agricultural labor (since farmers and ranchers work where they live, whereas miners travel great distances to the worksite). Thank you to John Raymond for encouraging me to expand on this point.

Chapter 5: Tomboys and Softies

1. See Paap (2006: 79–80) for an alternative view of gender classifications made by U.S. construction workers. She argues that the "Bitch-Dyke-Whore" taxonomy explicitly asserted by one worker and implicitly constructed by others reproduces masculine dominance of the industry by explaining away successful women and justifying inequalities in the workforce. The mines are striking in applying gendered classificatory schemes to men and women alike, denaturalizing masculinity. The insults of calling someone a bitch or sissy do police gendered behavior in the workplace, but opening up women's positions to tomboys and ladies offers them a way to more successfully integrate themselves into crews and the industry.

2. McElhinny's (1995: 218) critique of West and Zimmerman's underlying binary view of gender anticipated their later resistance to the turn toward studying undoing gender. McElhinny shows that even though the theorists acknowledge that people's practices vary from gender norms and allow for diverse forms of femininity and masculinity, they nevertheless insist that people cannot opt out of being perceived as male or female by others. "By assuming that there is one 'commonsensical' view that allows people to organize their understandings of the world, the authors do not question the hegemonic understanding of gender. Their view occludes subversive perceptions of gender arrived at by subcultural groups, among them feminists and queer theorists, who might celebrate gender ambiguity or recognize a greater range of diversity" (McElhinny 1995: 218).

3. This orientation dovetails with poststructuralist theory, particularly the argument made by Judith Butler by way of Michel Foucault and Louis Althusser that subjects do not precede discourse, but are interpellated by it. See Bucholtz and Hall (2005) for a concise summary of this theoretical approach in linguistic anthropology.

4. For an introduction to this rich literature, see Eckert and McConnell-Ginet 2003; Hall and Bucholtz 1995; Ochs 1992.

5. These semiotic processes all point to indexicality as the "mechanism whereby identity is constituted" (Bucholtz and Hall 2005: 593; also see Lemon 2000: 26). Indexes point to things or relationships and take their meaning from contextualized interactions and ideologies (Peirce 1961). For instance, this chapter argues that for the miners, dirt is viewed as evidence of hard labor. In this sense, dirt indexes or points to hard labor. As such, indexes do the semiotic work of linking linguistic and material signs with meaning.

6. Noting the dearth of ethnographic research about tomboyhood, Kira Hall suggests that "the tomboy's unwritten nature . . . makes her ripe for all sorts of scholarly pickings" (2003: 368). Tracing a trajectory of research on "deviant" gender identities, Hall shows that tomboys have been theorized as exceptions that prove the rule of strict socialization of boys and girls into separate cultures; the social expressions of underlying biological differences; and simply one instance of a "complicated continuum of crossing" (Thorne 1993: 112). Central to my concern here is the variance in the extent to which scholars view tomboyhood as an expression of masculinity. Social psychologist Lynn Carr (1998) makes a popular if reductive argument that tomboyism represents a "choice" of masculinity and identification with men. Education scholar Carrie Paechter more carefully posits tomboyhood as "a way of being, performing, or understanding oneself as female that has significant elements that are stereotypically associated with masculinity" (2010: 223). Whereas Carr views tomboyhood wholly as a performance of masculinity, Paechter makes the link between masculinity and tomboyhood slightly less direct and leaves room in it for children to move in-between gendered social positions—a perspective that holds true for the Wyoming women discussed here.

7. A slight variation on this pattern is calling young women flirts if they emphasize gender difference (through provocative dress and speech) in order to convince their coworkers and bosses to do nice "extra" things for them, such as assign them to the most comfortable truck or fix a broken AM/FM radio. Even when sexual favors are not actually traded in such arrangements, the possibility that they could be remains an incentive for some miners to engage in such relationships. Most miners resent such women for "using their gender to their advantage" in order to unfairly get ahead of their coworkers, but rarely speak poorly of the men who enable such behavior.

8. Also note the prevalence of parallelism and repetition, in which Kelly and Mike make their utterances sound like each other's. This creation of similarity and gentle give-and-take is common among crewmembers who consider themselves to be close friends, suggesting that it might be a subtle linguistic strategy for nurturing such relationships, since it mimics the solidarity and gentle give-and-take of their relationships.

9. When the insult is leveled against men, usually in the form of calling someone a "little bitch," it is interpreted as an insult to their masculinity.

10. But Diane was willing to admit, "Nobody's perfect. Ever. So I have a hard time saying things to people because I'm not a great truck driver. You have to be humble because there's going to be one day when they'll tell me something. Somebody wrote something on the buddy sheet [a paper that technicians at one mine filled out to comment on a designated coworker's performance] once, 'Make your words soft and sweet because one day you'll have to eat them.' It's an adrenaline rush and you don't think sometimes." Her statement is compelling because she acknowledges that women can also act like machos but shows the efforts that can be made to make oneself vulnerable and create empathy with coworkers.

11. Wentzell (2013) observes a comparable phenomenon in Mexican men who forgo medical treatment for erectile dysfunction because they and their wives welcome their changed, less macho behavior as fitting for elderly men moving into the grandfathering stage of life.

12. This close-yet-platonic framing of relationships also contributes to the smooth running of the summer student program. As Chloe, one of the summer students profiled in chapter 4, said, "Having a father-daughter relationship with those guys is the only way the program works. Having a bunch of college-age women working with a bunch of middle-aged men could quickly become bad. But when they know your father and treat you like a daughter, it stays at a very platonic level."

13. It is beyond the scope of this chapter to fully explore homosexual relationships, but I note briefly that women tend to experience much less friction in coming out than do men, which is perhaps why so very few men ever publicly identify as gay. This pattern may be attributable to the desire for nonsexual relationships described here, since women who are not attracted to men would be even less threatening to crew harmony than straight women. Local interpretations of the treatment of lesbians vary widely. A few straight and lesbian women remembered graffiti and verbal harassment being directed at women who were out of the closet in the late 1970s when most of the mines first opened, while others adamantly insisted they had never experienced such harassment. Most currently pass without note. Molly's observation was typical: "I'm friends with 'em. People are just people."

14. By suggesting that it is in these margins that feminist scholars can find alternative notions of gender under construction, de Lauretis's work inspired a generation of feminist scholars to seek out what came to be called third gender categories—such as Indian hijras or Native North American Two-Spirits—and hail their subversive possibility. This research upset views of two-sex/two-gender systems as natural and universal, but sometimes obscured the practices through which people construct and rework these social positions and move in and out of them over time (Weston 2002: 46–47).

15. Treating gender difference as a potential frame that can be consciously or unconsciously put into play or deflected with a particular word, gesture, or image brings together contemporary social theory and neuroscience. Psychologist Cordelia Fine (2010) synthesizes current neuroscience research to show that gender can be primed, or made salient, according to the social context. For example, men and women behave, perform, and think of themselves differently if they are told they are being tested on conventionally masculine skills, if they take an exam in a room filled with more men than women, or if they have to check a box identifying themselves as male or female. When gender is pushed to the background, on the other hand, men and women's behavior aligns even in areas in which great differences would be expected (35, 51, 235). Studies attesting to the shifting salience of gender, however, rarely appear in academic journals or the popular press due to what Fine calls the file drawer phenomenon: researchers publish studies that find sex differences, but let those that do not "languish unpublished and unseen in a researcher's file drawer" (134). Her analysis confirms a long-standing insight of feminist anthropology: behaviors and even senses of self—normally viewed as constants—are actually in "continuous interaction with the social context" (236).

16. To be fair, R. W. Connell and James Messerschmidt (2005), two leaders of the field, recognize the problem in their recent appraisal of research being done under the banner of hegemonic masculinity and argue against the reified and essentialist models of gender that are based in rigid typologies.

Chapter 6: Hard Work, Humor, and Harassment

1. See Tallichet (2006); Vaught and Smith (2003); and Yount (1991, 2005). I also choose not to focus on harassment here to counter its problematic association with blue-collar more than white-collar workers. Joan Williams, for example, argues that the "hidden injuries of class" (2000: 78) prompt blue-collar male workers to assert their masculinity by harassing women. She describes blue-collar sexual harassment as "severe," "virulent," and "well documented" (2000: 78, 82, 84) while acknowledging that sexual harassment "sometimes" happens in white-collar work as well (2000: 84). Many of the Wyoming women involved in the mining industry deliberately left white-collar occupations because they found the harassment and discrimination to be far worse in those workplaces rather than the mines. Barbara Ehrenreich (1983) argues that working-class masculinity is not an issue of dysfunctional or immature men, but a strategy for generating power in confrontations with management. "'Working-class male chauvinism' might be an expression of class rather than gender antagonism" (Ehrenreich 1983: 135). See Baron (2006: 145–146) for a recent critique of the scholarly reliance on the "crisis of masculinity" to understand workplace gender dynamics.

2. It is significant that in talking about issues of sexual harassment, all of the Wyoming women miners carefully limited their criticisms to specific individuals rather than miners in general. Even today, women can easily pick out the few macho guys on some crews that sometimes give them a hard time, but they are careful not to argue that all men are sexist or discriminatory. Although some women did encounter discrimination and harassment in their attempts to seek better jobs at the mines, equal numbers found opportunities to advance quickly through the hierarchy of equipment assignments. Monica, for example, said that she was "hazed" when she first started, but she eventually proved herself to be a competent equipment operator and worked her way up to be a shovel operator and pit supervisor. Similarly, when Patty first started at the mine she found that "women were received well." She was the first woman to operate a shovel at her mine and found that even though she knew she would be "watched close," she was confident that she would do the job well. "People were also very supportive and very open minded, willing to give you the chance." In fact, she also later became a popular pit supervisor.

3. This idea partially stems from a broader association of the region with freedom and self-reinvention. A popular strand of scholarly literature replicates the same flaws of Turnerian-style western history by portraying the region as an escape from the gender confines of eastern society: "Any woman who wanted to escape Victorian restrictions or who yearned for a new life could get a fresh start in the West" (Sagstetter and Sagstetter 1998: 134). Although it is true that some western women could own property, vote, and stretch the limits of what was considered appropriate women's work before their eastern counterparts, it is crucial not to romanticize their experiences (Scharff 2003). At the same time, however, these myths of gender freedom do not have to be completely true to be influential in shaping everyday life (Garceau 1997: 9; Scharff 2003: 92).

4. This gender neutrality is also at play in the use of the term supervisor rather than foreman to refer to formal crew leaders.

5. To investigate the contested gendering of persons, practices, and jobs on the interactional level, I was given permission to transcribe radio conversations at each of the four mines where I conducted research. The analysis in this section focuses on

forty-eight hours (or four twelve-hour shifts) of transcribed radio conversations at two mines, with special attention to the practices of reporting mechanical problems and giving directions. The complete analysis can be found in Smith (2010a).

6. Notions of work ethics change over time and vary along with gender, ethnicity, and occupation. The one constructed by the mining families addresses the paradoxes of translating a middle-class idea to a blue-collar context: the models for dignified work were masters of their own working lives who profited from their own efforts (such as farmers, self-employed craftsman, and small businessmen), whereas diligent and disciplined wage labor increases rewards for capitalists (Rodgers 1978: 30). In fact, the influential historian Daniel Rodgers suggests that Taylorism, famously condemned for degrading factory work (Braverman 1998 [1974]), was in fact a logical outgrowth of the ideals associated with a work ethic: "Taylor, in short, gathered up all the obsessional energies of the work ethic and set them loose in the factories, turning the drive for order and output against the traditions of craft and independence" (1978:55). The miners in Wyoming temper the potentially alienating parts of the work ethic by casting it in collective rather than simply individual terms.

7. This collective and durable sense of work ethic is therefore distinct from the insincerity of profit-driven teamwork critiqued by Sennett (1988: 99).

8. This marginalization can happen through gossip, ostracizing at lunch breaks, and exclusion from off-site social events.

9. For an introduction to this literature, see Baron (2006: 152); Collinson (1988); Iacuone (2005); Willis (1977). Willis (1977: 53) influentially argues that the "intimidatory humor" of the masculine shop floor contributes to the reproduction of England's capitalist class society. He suggests that where the alienated labor has "emptied work of significance from the inside, a transformed patriarchy has filled it with significance from the outside. Discontent with work is hinged away from a political discontent and confused in its proper logic by a huge detour into the symbolic sexual realm" (1977: 150). Specifically, he argues that for the "lads"—the working-class young men who get factory jobs after disengaging from the bourgeois school system—sexism in the form of jokes, beliefs, and practices helps them give meaning to and maintain their work: "A division in which they take themselves to be favored (the sexual) overlies, becomes part of, and finally partially changes the valency of a division in which they are disadvantaged (mental/manual labor power)" (1977: 148). Compare Seizer (2005) for a consideration of Tamil humor performances that both subtly critique and reinscribe gender ideologies.

10. Psychologists Jennifer Berdahl and Karl Aquino (2009) add a note of caution to this research, showing that pleasurable sexualized relationships at work were associated with negative work outcomes and lessened psychological well-being for men and women, even for those who reported that they enjoyed such activities.

11. To return to the book's theme of time, it is also significant that the women here do not attribute such sexist behavior to all periods of the industry, but to its beginning in the basin.

12. See Baron (2006), Collinson (1988), and N. Daly et al. (2004). In relation to gender and sexual harassment, see Kanter's (1977) notion of a "loyalty test." As it was for Mary, one of the major distinctions men and women at the mine make when discussing their coworkers is whether they will turn you in to Employee Relations or Human Relations, the office at the mine that handles sexual harassment claims. Men and women miners alike acknowledge that sexual harassment does happen, but they speak bitterly about a few women who, they believe maliciously, have

turned in coworkers for sexual harassment to advance their own career or punish someone they didn't like. They spoke about these women as if they had "sided with management" over their peers. In this way, seemingly sexist jokes are not always used to heighten differences between men and women, but they can also serve to incorporate men and women into a single group opposed to management.

13. This work-to-rule strategy is a common theme in labor history, in which workers bring about the changes they seek by slowing down production while still preserving their jobs (since they are not technically doing anything against corporate policy).

14. For thoughts on why this division is less salient in the Powder River Basin mines, see Smith (2010) for an extended discussion of the role that cowboy imagery, particularly notions of independence and nonexploitative work, plays in shaping relationships between corporate officials and miners.

15. Our crew and the entire mine lost one of their best when he died unexpectedly from heart complications as this book was being finished. His obituary in the local newspaper tracked his career from graduating as high school salutatorian, to serving in the military in Vietnam, to working at a ranch and then at the mine, specifically stating that "[h]e enjoyed his job and was a hard worker." Especially moving were the statements about his adoption of his wife's children from a previous marriage, as well as his love for his motorcycle: "He loved riding his Harley. He fulfilled his lifelong dream of riding on the Firebird National Speedway the morning he died. . . . Those attending are encouraged to ride motorcycles to the funeral."

16. Telling this story reminded Christie of another one in which she tried putting soda in someone else's coverall pockets. That joke failed because it was not actually harmless: unlike the water, the soda was sticky and did not dissipate quickly.

17. It is sometimes difficult for new hires to successfully navigate the minefields of humor because they may not realize that explicit body humor is only appropriate for people who have worked together over many years. Those with the most astute observation skills realize that it is preferable to start off with safer, less incendiary jokes and build to the type of boisterous exchanges they witness among others.

18. The experiences of Don, Rick, Ron, Lisa, and Daisy are not unique. An excellent example comes from yet a third mine, where one supervisor had accumulated 112 write-ups for his mistreatment of employees but Human Relations refused to fire or discipline him. His crew was furious. Mama Love explained, "This guy was just an asshole to everyone. He degraded everyone on the radio. One time he even locked a guy in his pickup." Tellingly, he did not get fired until one of his misdeeds was labeled sexual harassment because it involved a woman truck driver.

19. Companies have developed larger categories of workplace hostility to capture some of these issues, but they remain closely associated with their original meaning. Even though mandatory annual Human Relations sessions cover a broad range of problematic workplace practices, most people still refer to them as "sexual harassment meetings."

20. A few crewmembers date and a few eventually marry one another, but these are rare exceptions.

Chapter 7: Conclusion

1. These injunctions are sometimes ineffective, as a few summer students choose to work at the mines full-time instead of returning to college.

2. As the labor historian Paul Willis eloquently writes: "Ironically, as the shopfloor becomes a prison, education is seen, retrospectively, and hopelessly, as the only escape" (1977: 107).

3. See also the description of the Wyoming's Permanent Mineral Tax Fund in chapter 2.

4. In fact, the sheer number of people who had moved from Michigan to Wyoming (primarily to Gillette and the mining area of Rock Springs in southern Wyoming) was evident in a poll taken by ESPN regarding the 2006 University of Michigan vs. Ohio State football game. According to their map, only two states in the entire country predicted a Michigan win: Michigan and Wyoming.

5. Labor concerns were also erased from U.S. debates about natural gas as a "bridge fuel" due to its cleaner burning properties, despite a rash of workplace fatalities that claimed the lives of eighty-nine people—the natural gas industry relies on a lot of subcontractors who are technically considered part of other industries (construction, transportation, and so on)—between 2000 and 2006 (Ring 2007).

6. The job security of the Wyoming miners came at the expense of workers in the eastern United States, as described in chapter 2.

Glossary of Mining Terms

Note: Many of these are terms for the mining process and for mining equipment whose use is described in more detail in the section "The Mines" in chapter 1.

berm. A ridge of material, usually overburden (dirt and rock) placed alongside roads and at the edges of dumps to block machinery from leaving roadways and working areas.

blade. A road grader with a long blade in the middle used to create a flat surface, such as to smooth out roads in the mine to minimize damage to equipment from potholes.

coal seam. A horizontal bed or layer of coal. In the Powder River Basin, coal seams stretch up to one hundred feet thick vertically, inviting efficient extraction with heavy equipment.

crew families. A group of coworkers who consider themselves to be related because they share time and space. People on the same crew develop a sense of relatedness through rotating between stretches of twelve-hour day- and night shifts. Members are only very rarely also related by blood or marriage.

crushers. Machinery in the processing plant that breaks coal into smaller pieces. Some haul truck operators say they are going to the crushers or hoppers when they drive to the upper opening of the plant and tip their truck bed, depositing coal into the plant to be processed and transported to the silos.

down. The ceasing of work when a machine needs repair. Equipment that is broken is "down." Downtime refers to the idling of work by multiple operators, especially when a broken machine is a requirement for their own work, such as when a broken power shovel means that haul trucks have to stop operating.

dozer. Short for bulldozer, a machine with a large blade on the front end used to clear and grade land. It may be mounted on tracks or wheels.

draglines. An extremely large excavation machine (the size of many suburban homes in the United States, and often costing tens of millions of dollars) used to remove the overburden covering a coal seam. The dragline uses a wire-rope-hung bucket to collect the overburden and then swings to dump the overburden into an already excavated pit to start the process of reclamation. Draglines are more efficient than shovels in loading overburden into haul trucks, but create pits with steeper highwalls.

dump. The location where truck drivers haul and deposit the overburden, usually to fill an excavated pit to start the process of reclamation. May also be used as a verb, as in to unload the overburden or coal.

equipment. Usually refers to heavy construction machinery (draglines, shovels, blades, trucks, scrapers, and so forth) rather than smaller tools.

equipment operator. The person at the controls of a piece of heavy machinery; someone who is assigned to work in the pit.

face. An active work area; the exposed area of overburden or a coal bed from which material is being extracted.

grade. The angle of a bench or road. As a verb, to grade is to use a blade to move material to achieve the correct angle of a bench or road.

haul trucks. Very large off-highway dump trucks used to transport coal to the plant and overburden to the dump. They can often hold up to three hundred tons of material. Haul trucks are the first piece of equipment novices learn to operate.

highwall. The unexcavated vertical face of exposed overburden and coal that forms the boundaries of a pit in surface mining.

hoppers. The upper opening of the processing plant. Some haul truck operators say they are going to the crushers or hoppers when they drive to the upper opening of the plant and tip their truck bed, depositing coal into the plant to be processed and transported to the silos.

load. To place overburden or coal into the bed of a haul truck using the bucket of a shovel or loader.

load count. The number of times a haul truck driver has taken coal to the plant or overburden to the dump.

loader. A piece of heavy equipment with a digging bucket mounted on the front end.

maintenance technician or mechanic. Workers who maintain and repair heavy equipment. Specific terms include oilers (a person who oils engines or machinery) and millwrights (a welder who works on draglines).

Mine Safety and Health Administration (MSHA). The federal agency that regulates coal mine health and safety and whose representatives conduct inspections on-site.

overburden. Layers of soil and rock covering a coal seam that, in surface mines, must be removed before the coal can be excavated. When mining has been completed, it is used to backfill the mined areas or can be hauled to other storage sites.

pit. In surface mines, the working area where overburden and coal are being extracted. Pits are technically below ground level, but the open sky is visible.

plant. The processing or preparation plant (collection of machinery and conveyor belts) that breaks coal into small chunks and transports it to silos to be loaded into train cars.

Powder River Basin. The region of northeastern Wyoming and southeastern Montana that has been the largest producer of coal in the United States since the mid-1980s. It supplies approximately 40 percent of all coal produced in the United States.

ramp. A slope that joins two different levels of roads or work areas.

reclamation. The restoration of mined land to its previous use and appearance, which includes filling excavated coal pits with overburden, contouring the land to its original dimensions, restoring topsoil, and planting native grasses and ground cover, such as sage brush. Reclamation is a continuous process in the Powder River Basin mines, as excavated pits begin being filled with the material dug from new pits.

rotating shiftwork. Shiftwork that switches between nights and days. The most common schedule in the basin is designed for four crews and consists of twenty-eight-day cycles of twelve-hour shifts: four nights on, three days off, three days on, one day off, three nights on, three days off, four days on, seven days off. The schedule then starts over at the beginning. Each group of shifts, such as the three days in a row, is called a block.

run. A cycle of driving a haul truck from a loading machine to either the plant or dump.

scraper. A self-loading excavation machine that scrapes soil into a large bowl; used to remove and replace topsoil and other soil materials during mining and reclamation. Moving material by scrapers requires less coordination among different kinds of machinery, since scrapers pick up material by lowering the bowl as they drive, whereas haul trucks require coordination between the truck drivers and shovel operators who put material in the truck bed.

seam. A bed or layer of coal. The term is usually applied to a large deposit of coal. See **coal seam.**

shop. The large area where mechanics repair and maintain equipment; usually adjacent to the warehouse and the administrative offices. The shop often functions as a place for a variety of workers to meet face to face from time to time during the workday.

shovel. A very large piece of equipment, sometimes called a power shovel or electric shovel, with a boom that supports a large bucket (which can hold material equal in size to several passenger cars) used for digging and loading overburden and coal into haul trucks. It is usually powered by electricity, requiring the proper management of large shovel cables, which must be kept away from roadways and work areas.

summer student program. The program in which mining companies hire the college-age children of employees to work at the mines during summer breaks from college. The college students are assigned to the same work as regular mine employees, usually as equipment operators, plant technicians, or maintenance technicians. They may work at the same mine as their parents, but are rarely assigned to work directly with them.

supervisor. The formal leader that directs crews, frequently called a foreman in other regions and other industries.

surface mine. A mine in which the coal lies near the surface and can be extracted by removing the covering layers of rock and soil. It is distinct from underground mining, in which the overlying material is left in place and coal is removed through shafts and tunnels. Surface mines are frequently called "strip mines" by their critics. Surface mines are also distinct from mountaintop removal mines, most often found in Appalachia, where entire mountaintops are leveled to access the underlying coal seam, which is mined using surface mining methods.

technician. An hourly worker in the mines, as distinct from salaried personnel. Companies originally began using the term *technician* when the mines were opened to signify the flexibility of their employees, in contrast with the rigid job structures of unionized operations.

References

Acker, Joan. 1990. "Hierarchies, Jobs, Bodies: A Theory of Gendered Organizations." *Gender and Society* 4:139–158.

Anderson, Elizabeth. 2006. "Recent Thinking about Sexual Harassment: A Review Essay." *Philosophy and Public Affairs* 34:284–311.

Andrews, Thomas G. 2008. *Killing for Coal: America's Deadliest Labor War*. Cambridge, MA: Harvard University Press.

Baker, Carrie. 2007. *The Women's Movement against Sexual Harassment*. Cambridge: Cambridge University Press.

Barab, Jordan. 2003. "Acts of God, Acts of Man." *WorkingUSA* 7 (2): 7–23.

Barnett, Rosalind, Karen Gareis, and Robert Brennan. 2008. "Wives' Shift Work Schedules and Husbands' and Wives' Well-Being in Dual-Earner Couples with Children: A Within-Couple Analysis." *Journal of Family Issues* 29 (3): 396–422.

Baron, Ava. 2006. "Masculinity, the Embodied Male Worker, and the Historian's Gaze." *International Labor and Working-Class History* 69:143–160.

Beckwith, Karen. 1998. "Collective Identities of Class and Gender: Working-Class Women in the Pittston Coal Strike." *Political Psychology* 19 (1): 147–167.

Behar, Ruth. 1995. "Writing in My Father's Name: A Diary of Translated Woman's First Year." In *Women Writing Culture*, edited by R. Behar and D. Gordon, 65–82. Berkeley: University of California Press.

Benson, Peter, and Stuart Kirsch. 2010. "Capitalism and the Politics of Resignation." *Current Anthropology* 51 (4): 459–486.

Berdahl, Jennifer, and Karl Aquino. 2009. "Sexual Behavior at Work: Fun or Folly?" *Journal of Applied Psychology* 94 (1): 34–47.

Bergvall, Victoria. 1996. "Constructing and Enacting Gender through Discourse: Negotiating Multiple Roles as Female Engineering Students." In *Rethinking Language and Gender Research: Theory and Practice*, edited by Victoria Bergvall, Janet Bing, and Alice Freed, 173–201. London: Longman.

Bureau of Labor Statistics. 2005. "Workers on Flexible and Shift Schedules in May 2004." Washington, DC: U.S. Department of Labor.

Bingham, Clara, and Laura Leedy Gansler. 2002. *Class Action*. New York: Anchor Books.

Bourdieu, Pierre. 1977. *Outline of a Theory of Practice*. Cambridge: Cambridge University Press.

Bowers, Carol. 1999. "'Chinese Warren' and the Rock Springs Massacre." In *The Equality State: Essays on Intolerance and Inequality in Wyoming*, edited by Mike Mackey. Powell, WY: Western History Publications.

Braverman, Harry. 1998 [1974]. *Labor and Monopoly Capital: The Degradation of Work in the Twentieth Century*. New York: Monthly Review Press.

Bray, Francesca. 2007. "Gender and Technology." *Annual Review of Anthropology* 36:37–53.

Britton, Dana. 2000. "The Epistemology of the Gendered Organization." *Gender and Society* 14 (3): 418–34.

Brown, Warren. 1981. "Powder River Basin Mines Try to Best Unions at Benefits Game." *Washington Post*, July 1, A2.

Bucholtz, Mary, and Kira Hall. 2005. "Identity and Interaction: A Sociocultural Linguistic Approach." *Discourse Studies* 7 (4–5): 585–614.

Bunzl, Matti. 2004. "Boas, Foucault, and the 'Native Anthropologist': Notes toward a Neo-Boasian Anthropology." *American Anthropologist* 104 (3): 435–442.

Butler, Judith. 1990. *Gender Trouble: Feminism and the Subversion of Identity*. New York: Routledge.

———. 1993. *Bodies That Matter: On the Discursive Limits of "Sex."* New York: Routledge.

———. 2002. "Is Kinship Always Already Heterosexual?" *differences: A Journal of Feminist Cultural Studies* 13 (1): 14–44.

Campbell, Bea. 1984. *Wigan Pier Revisited: Poverty and Politics in the Eighties*. London: Verso.

Canning, Kathleen. 1996. *Language of Labor and Gender: Female Factory Work in Germany, 1850–1914*. Ithaca, NY: Cornell University Press.

Carr, C. Lynn. 1998. "Tomboy Resistance and Conformity: Agency in Social Psychological Gender Theory." *Gender and Society* 12 (5): 528–53.

Carr, E. Summerson. 2010. "Enactments of Expertise." *Annual Review of Anthropology* 39 (1): 17–32.

Carrington, Christopher. 2002. *No Place Like Home: Relationships and Family Life among Lesbians and Gay Men*. Chicago: University of Chicago Press.

Carsten, Janet. 1995. "The Substance of Kinship and the Heat of the Hearth: Feeding, Personhood, and Relatedness among Malays in Pulau Langkawi." *American Ethnologist* 22:223–41.

———. 1997. *The Heat of the Hearth: The Process of Kinship in a Malay Fishing Community*. Oxford: Clarendon Press.

———. 2004. *After Kinship*. New York: Cambridge University Press.

Cherlin, Andrew. 2009. *The Marriage Go-Round: The State of Marriage and the Family in America Today*. New York: Alfred A. Knopf.

Cheshire, Lynda. 2010. "A Corporate Responsibility? The Constitution of Fly-in, Fly-out Mining Companies as Governance Partners in Remote, Mine-affected Localities." *Journal of Rural Studies* 26:12–20.

Collinson, David L. 1988. "'Engineering Humour': Masculinity, Joking and Shop-floor Relations." *Organization Studies* 9 (2): 181–200.

Conley, John M., and Cynthia A Williams. 2005. "Engage, Embed, and Embellish: Theory versus Practice in the Corporate Social Responsibility Movement." *Journal of Corporation Law* 31 (1): 1–38.

Connell, Robert W., and James W. Messerschmidt. 2005. "Hegemonic Masculinity: Rethinking the Concept." *Gender and Society* 19 (6): 829–859.

Daly, Dan. 1987. "Fight to Unionize in the Basin Continues." *Gillette News Record*, August 16, 1.

Daly, Nicola, Janet Holmes, Jonathan Newton, and Maria Stubbe. 2004. "Expletives as Solidarity Signals in FTAs on the Factory Floor." *Journal of Pragmatics* 36:945–964.

Damaske, Sarah. 2011. *For the Family? How Class and Gender Shape Women's Work*. New York: Oxford University Press.

Darling, Eliza Jane. 2009. "O Sister! Sarah Palin and the Parlous Politics of Poor White Trash." *Dialectical Anthropology* 33 (1): 15–27.

de Lauretis, Teresa. 1987. "The Technology of Gender." In *Technologies of Gender: Essays on Theory, Film, and Fiction*, by Teresa de Lauretis, 1–30. Bloomington: Indiana University Press.

Descartes, Lara, and Elizabeth Rudd. 2008. "Changing Landscapes of Work and Family." In *The Changing Landscape of Work and Family in the American Middle Class: Reports from the Field*, edited by Elizabeth Rudd and Lara Descartes, 1–16. New York: Lexington Books.

Desmond, Matthew. 2007. *On the Fire line: Living and Dying with Wildland Firefighters*. Chicago: University of Chicago Press.

Deutsch, Francine M. 1999. *Halving It All: How Equally Shared Parenting Works*. Cambridge, MA: Harvard University Press.

———. 2007. "Undoing Gender." *Gender & Society* 21 (1): 106–127.

di Leonardo, Micaela. 1987. "The Female World of Cards and Holidays: Women, Families, and the Work of Kinship." *Signs* 12 (3): 440–453.

———. 1998. *Exotics at Home: Anthropologies, Others, American Modernity*. Chicago: University of Chicago Press.

Disney, Anthea. 1981. "Where a Woman's Place Is Down in the Mines." *Observer Magazine*, July 27, 14–17.

Douglas, Mary. 2002 [1966]. *Purity and Danger: An Analysis of the Concepts of Pollution and Taboo*. New York: Routledge Classics.

Dudley, Kathryn. 1994. *The End of the Line: Lost Jobs, New Lives in Postindustrial America*. Chicago: University of Chicago Press.

———. 2000. *Debt and Dispossession: Farm Loss in America's Heartland*. Chicago: University of Chicago Press.

Duke, David C. 2002. *Writers and Miners: Activism and Imagery in America*. Lexington: University Press of Kentucky.

Dunn, Elizabeth. 2004. *Privatizing Poland: Baby Food, Big Business, and the Remaking of Labor*. Ithaca, NY: Cornell University Press.

Eckert, Penelope, and Sally McConnell-Ginet. 2003. *Language and Gender*. Cambridge: Cambridge University Press.

Edwards, Jeanette, and Marilyn Strathern. 2000. "Including Our Own." In *Cultures of Relatedness: New Approaches to the Study of Kinship*, edited by Janet Carsten. New York: Cambridge University Press.

Ehrenreich, Barbara. 1983. *The Hearts of Men: American Dreams and the Flight from Commitment*. Garden City, NY: Anchor Press.

Engels, Friedrich. 1977 [1883]. "Speech at the Graveside of Karl Marx." In *Karl Marx: Selected Writings*, edited by David McLellan, 681–682. Oxford: Oxford University Press.

Evans-Pritchard, E. E. 1940. *The Nuer: A Description of the Modes of Livelihood and Political Institutions of a Nilotic People*. New York: Oxford University Press.

Ferguson, James. 1999. *Expectations of Modernity: Myths and Meanings of Urban Life on the Zambian Copper Belt*. Berkeley: University of California Press.

———. 2005. "Seeing Like an Oil Company: Space, Security, and Global Capital in Neoliberal Africa." *American Anthropologist* 107 (3): 377–382.

———. 2006. "Governing Extraction: New Spatializations of Order and Disorder in Neoliberal Africa." In *Global Shadows: Essays on Africa in the Neoliberal World Order*. Durham, NC: Duke University Press.

Ferry, Elizabeth Emma. 2005. *Not Ours Alone: Patrimony, Value, and Collectivity in Contemporary Mexico*. New York: Columbia University Press.

———. 2011. "Waste and Potency: Making Men with Minerals in Guanajuato and Tucson." *Comparative Studies in Society and History* 53 (4): 914–944.

Fine, Cordelia. 2010. *Delusions of Gender: How Our Minds, Society, and Neurosexism Create Difference*. New York: W. W. Norton.

Fine, Lisa. 1993. "'Our Big Factory Family': Masculinity and Paternalism at the Reo Motor Car Company of Lansing, Michigan." *Labor History* 34 (2): 274–291.

Finkler, Kaja. 2001. "The Kin in the Gene: The Medicalization of Family and Kinship in American Society." *Current Anthropology* 42 (2): 235–263.

Finn, Janet. 1998. *Tracing the Veins: Of Copper, Culture, and Community from Butte to Chuquicamata*. Berkeley: University of California Press.

Fortson, Danny. 2007. "Global Tyre Shortage Threatens to Stop Mining Industry in Its Tracks." *Independent*, December 24.

Foster, Robert. 2008. *Coca-Globalization*. New York: Palgrave.

Franklin, Sarah, and Susan McKinnon. 2001. *Relative Values: Reconfiguring Kinship Studies*. Cambridge: Cambridge University Press.

Fricke, Tom. 2008. "Working Selves, Moral Selves: Crafting the Good Person in the Northern Plains." In *The Changing Landscape of Work and Family in the American Middle Class: Reports from the Field*, edited by Elizabeth Rudd and Lara Descartes, 17–39. New York: Lexington Books.

Gallagher, Sally K., and Christian Smith. 1999. "Symbolic Traditionalism and Pragmatic Egalitarianism: Contemporary Evangelicals, Families, and Gender." *Gender & Society* 13 (2): 211–233.

Garceau, Dee. 1997. *The Important Things of Life: Women, Work, and Family in Sweetwater County, Wyoming, 1880–1929*. Lincoln: University of Nebraska Press.

Gardner, A. Dudley. 1990. *An American Place: A Centennial Portrait of Rock Springs, Wyoming, Then & Now, 1889–1989*. Rock Springs: Western Wyoming College Pioneer Press.

Gardner, A. Dudley, and Verla R. Flores. 1989. *Forgotten Frontier: A History of Wyoming Coal Mining*. San Francisco: Westview Press.

Garey, Anita Ilta. 1999. *Weaving Work and Motherhood*. Philadelphia: Temple University Press.

Gauchat, Gordon, Maura Kelly, and Michael Wallace. 2012. "Occupational Gender Segregation, Globalization, and Gender Earnings Inequality in U.S. Metropolitan Areas." *Gender & Society* 26 (5): 718–747.

Geertz, Clifford. 1973. "Thick Description: Toward an Interpretive Theory of Culture." In *The Interpretation of Cultures: Selected Essays*, by Clifford Geertz, 3–30. New York: Basic Books.

Gibson-Graham, J. K. 2006. *The End of Capitalism (as We Knew It): A Feminist Critique of Political Economy*. Minneapolis: University of Minnesota Press.

Giesen, Carol A. 1995. *Coal Miners' Wives: Portraits of Endurance*. Lexington: University Press of Kentucky.

Gillette News Record (Gillette, Wyoming). 1971–2013.

Gillis, John. 1998. *A World of Their Own Making: Myth, Ritual, and the Quest for Family Values*. New York: Basic Books.

Goldstein, Donna. 2003. *Laughter Out of Place: Race, Class, Violence, and Sexuality in a Rio Shantytown*. Berkeley: University of California Press.

Government Accountability Office. 2012. "Air Emissions and Electricity Generation at U.S. Power Plants. GAO–12–545R. Washington, DC: GAO.

Gray, Garry C. 2006. "The Regulation of Corporate Violations: Punishment, Compliance, and the Blurring of Responsibility." *British Journal of Criminology* 46 (5): 875–892.

———. 2009. "The Responsibilization Strategy of Health and Safety: Neo-liberalism and the Reconfiguration of Individual Responsibility for Risk." *British Journal of Criminology* 49 (3): 326–342.

Grosz, Elizabeth. 1990. "Inscriptions and Body-Maps: Representation and the Corporeal." In *Feminine/Masculine/Representation*, edited by Terry Threadgold and Anne Cranny-Francis, 62–74. Sydney, Australia: Allen and Unwin.

Guiffre, Patti, and Christine Williams. 1994. "Boundary Lines: Labeling Sexual Harassment in Restaurants." *Gender and Society* 8:378–401.

Hall, Betty Jean. 1990. "Women Miners Can Dig It Too!" In *Communities in Economic Crisis: Appalachia and the South*, edited by John Gaventa, Barbara Ellen Smith, and Alex Willingham, 53–60. Philadelphia: Temple University Press.

Hall, Kira. 2003. "Exceptional Speakers: Contested and Problematized Gender Identities." In *The Handbook of Language and Gender*, edited by Janet Holmes and Miriam Meyerhoff, 353–380. Malden, MA: Blackwell.

Hall, Kira, and Mary Bucholtz. 1995. *Gender Articulated: Language and the Socially Constructed Self*. New York: Routledge.

Halle, David. 1984. *America's Working Man: Work, Home, and Politics among Blue-Collar Property Owners*. Chicago: University of Chicago Press.

Hammond, Judith A., and Constance W. Mahoney. 1983. "Reward-Cost Balancing among Women Coalminers." *Sex Roles* 9 (1): 17–29.

Han, Sallie. 2009. "Making Room for Daddy: Men's 'Belly Talk' in the Contemporary United States." In *Reconceiving the Second Sex: Men, Masculinity, and Reproduction*, edited by Marcia C. Inhorn, Tine T. Thomsen, Helene Goldberg, and Maruska La Cour Mosegaard. New York: Berghahn Books.

Handelman, Don. 1990. "Banana Time." In *Models and Mirrors: Toward an Anthropology of Public Events*, by Don Handelman. Cambridge: Cambridge University Press.

Hegewisch, Ariane, Hannah Liepmann, Jeffrey Hayes, and Heidi Hartmann. 2010. *Separate and Not Equal? Gender Segregation in the Labor Market and the Gender Wage Gap*. Report C377, 1–16. Washington, DC: Institute for Women's Policy Research.

Herickoff, Jim. 1987. "Open Letter to All TBCC Employees and the Powder River Basin Community." *News-Record*, October 28, 5.

Hilden, Patricia. 1991. "The Rhetoric and Iconography of Reform: Women Coal Miners in Belgium, 1840–1914." *Historical Journal* 34 (2): 411–436.

Hirsch, Barry, and David Macpherson. 2011. "Union Membership, Coverage, Density, and Employment by Industry, 2010." http://unionstats.com/.

Hochschild, Arlie. 1989. *The Second Shift: Working Parents and the Revolution at Home*. New York: Penguin Books.

———. 1997. *The Time Bind: When Work Becomes Home and Home Becomes Work*. New York: Metropolitan Books.

Holmes, Janet. 2000. "Politeness, Power, and Provocation: How Humor Functions in the Workplace." *Discourse Studies* 2 (2): 159–185.

———. 2006. "Sharing a Laugh: Pragmatic Aspects of Humor and Gender in the Workplace." *Journal of Pragmatics* 38:26–50.

Horkheimer, Max, and Theodor W. Adorno. 2002. *Dialectic of Enlightenment*. Edited by Gunzelin Schmid Noerr, translated by Edmund Jephcott. Stanford: Stanford University Press.

Huspek, Michael. 1986. "Linguistic Variation, Context, and Meaning: A Case of -Ing/in' Variation in North American Workers' Speech." *Language in Society* 15 (2): 149–163.

Iacuone, David. 2005. "'Real Men Are Tough Guys': Hegemonic Masculinity and Safety in the Construction Industry." *Journal of Men's Studies* 13 (2): 247–266.

Ingold, Tim. 2000. *The Perception of the Environment: Essays in Livelihood, Dwelling, and Skill*. New York: Routledge.

Jacobs-Huey, Lanita. 2002. "The Natives Are Gazing and Talking Back: Reviewing the Problematics of Positionality, Voice, and Accountability among 'Native' Anthropologists." *American Anthropologist* 104 (3): 791–804.

Jain, Sarah S. Lochlann. 2006. *Injury: The Politics of Product Design and Safety Law in the United States*. Princeton: Princeton University Press.

Jameson, Elizabeth. 1998. *All That Glitters: Class, Conflict, and Community in Cripple Creek*. Urbana: University of Illinois Press.

John, Angela V. 1980. *By the Sweat of Their Brow: Women Workers at Victorian Coal Mines*. London: Routledge & Kegan Paul.

Kalb, Don. 1997. *Expanding Class: Power and Everyday Politics in Industrial Communities, The Netherlands, 1850–1950*. Durham: Duke University Press.

Kanter, Rosabeth Moss. 1977. *Men and Women of the Corporation*. New York: Basic Books.

Keck, Jennifer, and Mary Powell. 2000. *Women into Mining Jobs at Inco: Challenging the Gender Division of Labour*. INORD Working Paper Series. Sudbury, ON: Institute for Northern Ontario Research and Development.

Kingsolver, Barbara. 1989. *Holding the Line: Women in the Great Arizona Mine Strike of 1983*. Ithaca, NY: ILR Press.

Kirsch, Stuart. 2001. "Property Effects: Social Networks and Compensation Claims in Melanesia." *Social Anthropology* 9 (2): 147–163.

———. 2006. *Reverse Anthropology: Indigenous Analysis of Social and Environmental Relations in New Guinea*. Stanford: Stanford University Press.

Lahiri-Dutt, Kuntala. 2006. "Globalization and Women's Work in the Mine Pits in East Kalimantan, Indonesia." In *Women Miners in Developing Countries: Pit Women and Others*, edited by Kuntala Lahiri-Dutt and Martha Macintyre, 349–369. Burlington, VT: Ashgate.

———. 2011a. *Gendering the Field: Towards Sustainable Livelihoods for Mining Communities*. Canberra: Australian National University Press.

———. 2011b. "The Shifting Gender of Coal: Feminist Musings on Women's Work in Indian Collieries." *South Asia: Journal of South Asian Studies* 35 (2): 456–476.

Lahiri-Dutt, Kuntala, and Martha Macintyre. 2006. "Introduction: Where Life Is in the Pits (and Elsewhere) and Gendered." In *Women Miners in Developing Countries: Pit Women and Others*, edited by Kuntala Lahiri-Dutt and Martha Macintyre. Burlington, VT: Ashgate.

Lahiri-Dutt, Kuntala, and Kathy Robinson. 2008. "'Period Problems' at the Coalface." *Feminist Review* 89 (1): 102–121.

Lambek, Michael. 2007. "The Cares of Alice Alder: Recuperating Kinship and History in Switzerland." In *Ghosts of Memory: Essays on Remembrance and Relatedness*, edited by Janet Carsten. Malden, MA: Blackwell.

Lambert, Helen. 2000. "Sentiment and Substance in North Indian Forms of Relatedness." In *Cultures of Relatedness*, edited by Janet Carsten, 73–89. Cambridge: Cambridge University Press.

Landström, Catharina. 2007. "Queering Feminist Technology Studies." *Feminist Theory* 8 (1): 7–26.

Lasch, Christopher. 1977. *Haven in a Heartless World: The Family Besieged*. Berkeley: University of California Press.

Lemon, Alaina. 2000. *Between Two Fires: Gypsy Performance and Romani Memory from Pushkin to Post-Socialism*. Durham, NC: Duke University Press.

Lewin, Ellen. 2009. *Gay Fatherhood: Narratives of Family and Citizenship in America*. Chicago: University of Chicago Press.

Lichtenstein, Neil. 2002. *State of the Union: A Century of American Labor*. Princeton: Princeton University Press.

Limerick, Patricia. 1987. *The Legacy of Conquest: The Unbroken Past of the American West*. New York: W. W. Norton.

Limón, José. 1994. *Dancing with the Devil: Society and Cultural Poetics in Mexican-American South Texas*. Madison: University of Wisconsin Press.

Long, Priscilla. 1989. *Where the Sun Never Shines: A History of America's Bloody Coal Industry*. New York: Paragon House.

Lorber, Judith. 2005. *Breaking the Bowls: Degendering and Feminist Change*. New York: W. W. Norton.

Lucas, Kristen. 2011. "Blue-Collar Discourses of Workplace Dignity: Using Outgroup Comparisons to Construct Positive Identities." *Management Communication Quarterly* 25 (2): 353–374.

Ludtke, Alf. 1985. "Organizational Order or Eigensinn? Workers' Privacy and Workers' Politics in Imperial Germany." In *Rites of Power: Symbolism, Ritual, and Politics since the Middle Ages*, edited by Sean Wilentz. Philadelphia: University of Pennsylvania Press.

Mackinnon, Catherine. 1979. *Sexual Harassment of Working Women*. New Haven: Yale University Press.

Mannheim, Bruce. 1995. "On the Margins of The Couple in the Cage.'" *Visual Anthropology Review*, 11 (1): 121–127.

Martin, Emily. 1994. *Flexible Bodies: The Role of Immunity in American Culture from the Days of Polio to the Age of AIDS*. Boston: Beacon Press.

———. 1997. "Managing Americans: Policy and Changes in the Meaning of Work and Self." In *Anthropology of Policy: Critical Perspectives on Governance and Power*, edited by Chris Shore and Susan Wright, 239–257. London: Routledge.

Marx, Karl. 1977 [1844]. "Economic and Political Manuscripts." In *Karl Marx: Selected Writings*, edited by David McLellan. Oxford: Oxford University Press.

———. 1978 [1887]. *Capital, Vol. One*. In *The Marx-Engels Reader*, edited by R. Thomas, 294–438. New York: W. W. Norton and Co.

Mastracci, Barb. 2004. *Breaking Out of the Pink-Collar Ghetto: Policy Solutions for Non-College Women*. Armonk, NY: M. E. Sharpe.

Maume, David J., Rachel A. Sebastian, and Anthony R. Bardo. 2010. "Gender, Work-Family Responsibilities, and Sleep." *Gender & Society* 24 (6): 746–768.

Mayes, Robyn, and Barbara Pini. 2010. "The 'Feminine Revolution in Mining': A Critique." *Australian Geographer* 41 (2): 233–245.

McElhinny, Bonnie. 1995. "Challenging Hegemonic Masculinities: Female and Male Police Officers Handling Domestic Violence." In *Gender Articulated: Language and the Socially Constructed Self*, edited by Kira Hall and Mary Bucholtz. New York: Routledge.

———. 1994. "An Economy of Affect: Objectivity, Masculinity, and the Gendering of Police Work." In *Dislocating Masculinity: Comparative Ethnographies*, edited by Andrea and Nancy Lindisfarne Cornwall, 159–171. New York: Routledge.

———. 2003. "Theorizing Gender in Sociolinguistics and Linguistic Anthropology." In *The Handbook of Language and Gender*, edited by Janet Holmes and Miriam Meyerhoff, 21–42. Malden, MA: Blackwell Publishing.

McGuire, Randall H., and Paul Reckner. 2002. "The Unromantic West: Labor, Capital, and Struggle." *Historical Archaeology* 36 (3): 44–58.

McKinnon, Susan. 2000. "Domestic Exceptions: Evans-Pritchard and the Creation of Nuer Patrilineality and Equality." *Cultural Anthropology* 15:35–83.

McNeil, Bryan. 2011. *Combating Mountaintop Removal: New Directions in the Fight against Big Coal*. Urbana: University of Illinois Press.

Mercier, Laurie, and Jaclyn Gier. 2006. *Mining Women: Gender in the Development of a Global Industry, 1670 to 2005*. New York: Palgrave Macmillan.

Merithew, Caroline Waldron. 2006. "'We Were Not Ladies': Gender, Class, and a Women's Auxiliary's Battle for Mining Unionism." *Journal of Women's History* 18 (2): 63–94.

Metcalfe, Andrew. 1998. *For Freedom and Dignity: Historical Agency and Class Structures in the Coalfields of NSW*. Sydney: Allen and Unwin.

Meyer, Stephen. 1981. *The Five Dollar Day: Labor, Management, and Social Control in the Ford Motor Company, 1908–1920*. Albany: SUNY Press.

Moe, Karine, and Dianna Shandy. 2010. *Glass Ceilings and 100-Hour Couples: What the Opt-Out Phenomenon Can Teach Us about Work and Family*. Athens: University of Georgia Press.

Montgomery, David. 1987. *The Fall of the House of Labor: The Workplace, the State, and American Labor Activism, 1865–1925*. New York: Cambridge University Press.

Moore, Marat. 1996. *Women in the Mines: Stories of Life and Work*. New York: Twayne Publishers.

Munn, Nancy D. 1986. *The Fame of Gawa: A Symbolic Study of Value Transformation in Massim (Papua New Guinea) Society*. Durham, NC: Duke University Press.

———. 1992. "The Cultural Anthropology of Time: A Critical Essay." *Annual Review of Anthropology* 21:93–123.

Narayan, Kirin. 1993. "How Native Is a 'Native' Anthropologist?" *American Anthropologist* 95 (3): 671–686.

Nash, June. 1993 [1979]. *We Eat the Mines and the Mines Eat Us: Dependency and Exploitation in Bolivian Tin Mines*. New York: Columbia University Press.

Ochs, Elinor. 1992. "Indexing Gender." In *Rethinking Context: Language as an Interactive Phenomenon*, edited by Alessandro Duranti and Charles Goodwin, 335–358. Cambridge: Cambridge University Press.

Ong, Aihwa. 1999. *Flexible Citizenship: The Cultural Logics of Transnationalism*. Durham, NC: Duke University Press.

Ortner, Sherry. 2003. *New Jersey Dreaming: Capital, Culture, and the Class of '58*. Durham, NC: Duke University Press.

Paap, Kris. 2006. *Working Construction: Why White Working-Class Men Put Themselves—and the Labor Movement—in Harm's Way*. Ithaca, NY: Cornell University Press.

Paechter, Carrie. 2010. "Tomboys and Girly-Girls: Embodied Femininities in Primary Schools." *Discourse: Studies in the Cultural Politics of Education* 31 (2): 221–235.

Papanikolas, Zeese. 1995. "Cowboys, Wobblies, and the Myth of the West." In *Trickster in the Land of Dreams*, by Zeese Papanikolas, 73–91. Lincoln: University of Nebraska Press.

Peirce, Charles S. 1961. *Collected Papers of Charles Sander Peirce*. Edited by Charles Hartshorne and Paul Weiss. Cambridge, MA: Harvard University Press.

Perrucci, Robert, and Shelley MacDermid. 2007. "Time and Control in a 24/7 Environment: Clock Time, Work Time, and Family Time." In *Workplace Temporalities: Research in the Sociology of Work*, edited by Beth Rubin, 343–368. Oxford: Elsevier.

Power, Michael. 1997. *The Audit Society: Rituals of Verification*. New York: Oxford University Press.

Presser, Harriet B. 2003. *Working in a 24/7 Economy: Challenges for American Families*. New York: Russell Sage Foundation.

Preston, Valerie, Damaris Rose, Glen Norcliffe, and John Holmes. 2000. "Shiftwork, Child-care, and Domestic Work: Divisions of Labour in Canadian Paper Mill Communities." *Gender, Place, and Culture* 7 (1): 5–29.

Prieto, Maggie. 1983. "Women Coal Miners Fight Sexual Harassment." *Off Our Backs* 13 (8): 17.

Puckett, Anita. 2000. *Seldom Ask, Never Tell: Labor and Discourse in Appalachia*. New York: Oxford University Press.

Rajak, Dinah. 2011. *In Good Company: An Anatomy of Corporate Social Responsibility*. Stanford: Stanford University Press.

Reichart, Karaleah. 2006. "We're to Stand Side by Side: Household Production and Women's Work in Rural Mining Communities." In *Labor in Cross-Cultural Perspective*, edited by E. Paul Durrenberger and Judith Marti, 137–154. Lanham, MD: Rowman Altamira.

Richardson, Peter. 2006. "Anthropology of the Workplace and the Family." In *The Work and Family Handbook: Multi-Disciplinary Perspectives and Approaches*, edited by Marcie Pitt-Catsouphes, Ellen Ernst Kossek, and Stephen Sweet. Mahwah, NJ: Lawrence Erlbaum Associates.

Ring, Ray. 2007. "Disposable Workers of the Oil and Gas Fields." *High Country News* 39 (6): 7–22.

Risman, Barbara J. 1998. *Gender Vertigo: American Families in Transition*. New Haven: Yale University Press.

———. 2009. "From Doing to Undoing: Gender as We Know It." *Gender & Society* 23 (1): 81–84.

Rodgers, Daniel T. 1978. *The Work Ethic in Industrial America*. Chicago: University of Chicago Press.

Rolston, Jessica Smith. 2010a. "Talk about Technology: Negotiating Gender Difference in Wyoming Coal Mines." *Signs: Journal of Women in Culture and Society* 35 (4): 893–918.

———. 2010b. "Risky Business: Neoliberalism and Workplace Safety in Wyoming Coal Mines." *Human Organization* 69 (4): 331–342.

———. 2013a. "The Politics of Pits and the Materiality of Mine Labor: Making Natural Resources in the American West." *American Anthropologist* 115 (4): 582–594.

———. 2013b. "Specters of Syndromes and the Everyday Lives of Wyoming Energy Workers." In *Cultures of Energy: Power, Practices, Technologies*, edited by Sarah Strauss, Stephanie Rupp, and Thomas Love, 214–227. Walnut Creek, CA: Left Coast Press.

Roy, Donald. 1959. "Banana Time: Job Satisfaction and Informal Interaction." *Human Organization* 18:158–168.

Rubin, Gayle. 1975. "The Traffic in Women: Notes on the 'Political Economy' of Sex." In *Toward an Anthropology of Women*, edited by Rayna Rapp, 157–210. London: Monthly Review Press.

Rudd, Elizabeth, and Larry Root. 2008. "'We Pass the Baby Off at the Factory Gates': Work and Family in the Manufacturing Midwest." In *The Changing Landscape of Work and Family in the American Middle Class: Reports from the Field*, edited by Elizabeth Rudd and Lara Descartes. New York: Lexington Books.

Ryang, Sonia. 2005. "Dilemma of a Native: On Location, Authenticity, and Reflexivity." *Asia Pacific Journal of Anthropology* 6 (2): 143–157.

Sagstetter, Beth, and Bill Sagstetter. 1998. "The Women." In *The Mining Camps Speak: A New Way to Explore the Ghost Towns of the American West*, by Beth Sagstetter and Bill Sagstetter. Denver: BenchMark Publishing of Colorado.

Sahlins, Marshall. 2011. "What Kinship Is." *Journal of the Royal Anthropological Institute*, n.s., 17: 2–19, 227–242.

Salzinger, Leslie. 1997. "From High Heels to Swathed Bodies: Gendered Meanings under Production in Mexico's Export-Processing Industry." *Feminist Studies* 23 (3): 549–574.

———. 2003. *Genders in Production: Making Workers in Mexico's Global Factories*. Berkeley: University of California Press.

Samuels, David. 2004. *Putting a Song on Top of It: Expression and Identity on the San Carlos Apache Reservation*. Tucson: University of Arizona Press.

Scharff, Virginia J. 2003. "Empire, Liberty, and Legend: Woman Suffrage in Wyoming." In *Twenty Thousand Roads: Women, Movement and the West*, edited by Virginia J. Scharff, 67–92. Berkeley: University of California Press.

Schneider, David M. 1980. *American Kinship: A Cultural Account*. Chicago: University of Chicago Press.

Scott, Rebecca. 2010. *Removing Mountains: Extracting Nature and Identity in the Appalachian Coalfields*. Minneapolis: University of Minnesota Press.

Seitz, Virginia Reinaldo. 1998. "Class, Gender, and Resistance in the Appalachian Coalfields." In *Community Activism and Feminist Politics: Organizing across Race, Class, and Gender*, edited by Nancy Naples, 213–236. New York: Routledge.

Seizer, Susan. 2005. *Stigmas of the Tamil Stage: An Ethnography of Special Drama Artists in South India*. Durham, NC: Duke University Press.

Sennett, Richard. 1988. *The Corrosion of Character: The Personal Consequences of Work in the New Capitalism*. New York: W. W. Norton.

Shever, Elana. 2008. "Neoliberal Associations: Property, Company, and Family in the Argentine Oil Fields." *American Ethnologist* 35 (4): 701–716.

Silverstein, Michael. 2003. *Talking Politics: The Substance of Style from Abe to "W."* Chicago: Prickly Paradigm Press.

Smith, Jessica. 2008. "Crafting Kinship at Home and Work: Women Miners in Wyoming." Theme issue, "Women and Work," *WorkingUSA: The Journal of Labor and Society* 11 (4): 439–458.

———. 2009. "Putting Kinship to Work: Gender and Relatedness in a Wyoming Coal Mining Community." PhD diss., University of Michigan.

———. 2010. "Workplace Egalitarianism in Nonunion Mines: Lessons from Wyoming's Powder River Basin." In *The Anthropology of Labor Unions*, edited by Paul Durrenberger and Karaleah Reichart, 103–130. Boulder: University Press of Colorado.

Smith, Jessica, and Federico Helfgott. 2010. "Corporate Social Responsibility and the Perils of Universalization." *Anthropology Today* 26 (3): 20–23.

Strathern, Marilyn. 1988. *The Gender of the Gift: Problems with Women and Problems with Society in Melanesia*. Berkeley: University of California Press.

Tallichet, Suzanne. 2006. *Daughters of the Mountain: Women Coal Miners in Central Appalachia*. University Park: Pennsylvania State University Press.

Taussig, Michael. 1980. *The Devil and Commodity Fetishism in South America*. Chapel Hill: University of North Carolina Press.

Thorne, Barrie. 1993. *Gender Play*. Milton Keynes, UK: Open University Press.

Tomori, Cecilia. 2009. "Breastfeeding as Men's 'Kin Work' in the United States." *Phoebe* 21 (2): 31–44.

Townsend, Nicholas. 2002. *The Package Deal: Marriage, Work, and Fatherhood in Men's Lives*. Philadelphia: Temple University Press.

Trouillot, Michel-Rolph. 1991. "Anthropology and the Savage Slot: The Poetics and Politics of Otherness." In *Recapturing Anthropology: Working in the Present*, edited by Richard Fox, 17–44. Santa Fe: School of American Research Press.

Valian, Virginia. 1998. *Why So Slow? The Advancement of Women*. Cambridge, MA: MIT Press.

Van Vleet, Krista. 2008. *Performing Kinship: Narrative, Gender, and the Intimacies of Power in the Andes*. Austin: University of Texas Press.

Vaught, Charles, and David Smith. 2003 [1980]. "Incorporation and Mechanical Solidarity in an Underground Coal Mine." In *The Cultural Study of Work*, edited by Douglas Harper and Helene M. Lawson. Lanham, MD: Rowman Littlefield Publishers.

Welker, Marina. 2009. "'Corporate Security Begins in the Community': Mining, the Corporate Social Responsibility Industry, and Environmental Advocacy in Indonesia." *Cultural Anthropology* 24 (1): 142–179.

———. 2012. "The Green Revolution's Ghost: Unruly Subjects of Participatory Development in Rural Indonesia." *American Ethnologist* 39 (2): 389–406.

Wentzell, Emily. 2013. *Maturing Masculinities: Aging, Chronic Illness, and Viagra in Mexico*. Durham, NC: Duke University Press.

West, Candace, and Don H. Zimmerman. 1987. "Doing Gender." *Gender and Society* 1 (2): 125–151.

———. 2009. "Accounting for Doing Gender." *Gender and Society* 23 (1): 112–122.

Weston, Kath. 1990. "Production as Means, Production as Metaphor: Women's Struggle to Enter the Trades." In *Uncertain Terms: Negotiating Gender in American Culture*, edited by Faye D. Ginsburg and Anna Tsing, 137–151. Boston: Beacon Press.

———. 1991. *Families We Choose: Lesbians, Gays, Kinship*. New York: Columbia University Press.

———. 2001. "Kinship, Controversy, and the Sharing of Substance: The Race/Class Politics of Blood Transfusion." In *Relative Values: Reconfiguring Kinship Studies*, edited by Sarah Franklin and Susan McKinnon, 147–74. Cambridge: Cambridge University Press.

———. 2002. *Gender in Real Time: Power and Transience in a Visual Age*. New York: Routledge.

Whetstone, Nancy. 1987. "Union Insults Worker, She'll Vote No." *News-Record*, October 30, 2.

White, Richard. 1991. *"It's Your Misfortune and None of My Own": A History of the American West*. Norman: University of Oklahoma Press.

Whiteside, James. 1990. *Regulating Danger: The Struggle for Mine Safety in the Rocky Mountain Coal Industry*. Lincoln: University of Nebraska Press.

Wilk, Richard. 2006. "Consumer Culture and Extractive Industry on the Margins of the World System." In *Consuming Cultures, Global Perspectives: Historical Trajectories, Transnational Exchanges*, edited by John Brewer and Frank Trentmann, 123–144. Oxford: Berg.

Williams, Cara. 2008. "Work-Life Balance of Shift Workers." *Perspectives on Labour and Income* 9 (8): 3, 5–16.

Williams, Christine. 1989. *Gender Differences at Work: Women and Men in Nontraditional Occupations*. Berkeley: University of California Press.

———. 1998. "Sexual Harassment in Organizations: A Critique of Current Research and Policy." *Sexuality & Culture* 1:19–43.

Williams, Christine, Patti Guiffre, and Kirsten Dillinger. 1999. "Sexuality in the Workplace: Organizational Control, Sexual Harassment, and the Pursuit of Pleasure." *Annual Review of Sociology* 25:73–93.

Williams, Joan. 2000. *Unbending Gender: Why Family and Work Conflict and What to Do about It*. Oxford: Oxford University Press.

———. 2010. *Reshaping the Work-Family Debate: Why Men and Class Matter*. Cambridge, MA: Harvard University Press.

Willis, Paul. 1977. *Learning to Labor: How Working Class Kids Get Working Class Jobs*. New York: Columbia University Press.

Wolff, David A. 2003. *Industrializing the Rockies: Growth, Competition, and Turmoil in the Coalfields of Colorado and Wyoming, 1868–1914*. Boulder: University Press of Colorado.

Yanagisako, Sylvia. 2002. *Producing Culture and Capital: Family Firms in Italy*. Princeton: Princeton University Press.

Yanagisako, Sylvia Junko, and Jane Fishburne Collier. 1987. "Toward a Unified Analysis of Gender and Kinship." In *Gender and Kinship: Essays toward a Unified Analysis*, edited by Sylvia Yanagisako and Jane Collier. Stanford: Stanford University Press.

Yount, Kristen. 1991." Ladies, Flirts, and Tomboys: Strategies for Managing Sexual Harassment in an Underground Coal Mine." *Journal of Contemporary Ethnography* 19 (4): 396–422.

———. 2005. "Sexualization of Work Roles among Men Miners: Structural and Gender-Based Origins of "Harazzment." In *In the Company of Men: Male Dominance and Sexual Harassment*, edited by James E. Gruber and Phoebe Morgan, 65–91. Boston: Northeastern University Press.

Index

Page numbers followed by f indicate figures; n indicates a note.

About the Author

JESSICA SMITH ROLSTON is the Hennebach Assistant Professor of Energy Policy in the Division of Liberal Arts and International Studies at the Colorado School of Mines. Her ethnographic research in the American West and Peruvian Andes traces the commodity networks that surround mined materials and implicate a wide range of actors, from miners and corporate officials to ranchers and conservation activists. Within these networks, she focuses on questions of social justice, work, gender, and corporate social responsibility. Her research appears in the journals *American Anthropologist, Signs: Journal of Women in Labor and Society, Anthropology Today*, and *WorkingUSA: The Journal of Labor and Society*. She holds a PhD in anthropology and a certificate in women's studies from the University of Michigan and completed bachelor's degrees in anthropology, international studies, and Latin American studies at Macalester College in St. Paul, Minnesota.

CPSIA information can be obtained
at www.ICGtesting.com
Printed in the USA
LVOW12s1922190917
549285LV00003B/256/P